If you are a leader in a mental health organization who is passionate about improving the efficiency — and, more importantly, the effectiveness — of everything your organization does, then *Transforming Mental Healthcare* will certainly point you in the right direction. The authors share an important combination of experiences, from clinical care and systems engineering to provide a translation of the "Lean" methodology that will help you provide continually safer, higher quality care at a lower cost and with less delay. This book goes beyond tools and methods and extends into the critically important topics of culture, leadership, and change management. *Transforming Mental Healthcare* effectively models the Lean method by first identifying problems and opportunities (gaps) before getting into causes and, finally, solutions that drive better performance. Beyond the benefits to patients, clinicians (and all staff who play various roles in the support of care) will find a more engaging, less frustrating workplace in which they can contribute to continuous improvement, if not excellence. Everybody wins!

Mark Graban
Author, Lean Hospitals, Healthcare Kaizen,
and Measures of Success

Applying the modern sciences of quality improvement to the field of behavioral healthcare may sound like a stretch; but think again. In "*Transforming Mental Healthcare,*" Sunil Khushalani and Antonio DePaolo, a psychiatrist and an engineer, show just how promising and powerful that combination can be. Every knowledgeable student of healthcare system knows today that mental health must be brought to the center of the agenda, and this timely, unique book makes improving mental healthcare practical and accessible to all.

Donald M. Berwick, MD, MPP
President Emeritus and Senior Fellow
Institute for Healthcare Improvement

Transforming Mental Healthcare is a wonderful undertaking. Ideally, we all have capability and confidence, the accumulation of life's experience, overlaid with resilience and agility, being able to perceive and process situations and then make dynamic adjustments – some fleeting others longer term – thereby improving comfort and competence. Bravo to Khushalani and DePaolo for showing how the very organizations missioned with restoring those qualities to our loved ones have the same characteristics, self-reflective in their adaptation and adjustment, constantly improving the care they deliver. Steve Spear DBA MS MS, MIT Senior Lecturer and author *The High Velocity Edge*.

Steven J. Spear DBA MS MS
Principal, See to Solve LLC
Senior Lecturer, MIT Sloan School of Management
Senior Fellow, Institute for Healthcare Improvement
Author, The High Velocity Edge

This book offers a detailed and sobering look at the current state of psychiatry in the United States. Using patient vignettes the authors explain how lean thinking could relieve suffering and help communities build sustainable mental health systems.

John Toussaint, MD
Executive Chairman at Catalysis Inc.
Author, On The Mend, Management on the Mend, *and* Becoming the Change

Transforming Mental Healthcare

Transforming Mental Healthcare

Applying Performance Improvement Methods to Mental Healthcare

Sunil Khushalani, MD
and
Antonio DePaolo, Phd

A PRODUCTIVITY PRESS BOOK

First published 2022
by Routledge
600 Broken Sound Parkway #300, Boca Raton FL, 33487
and by Routledge

2 Park Square, Milton Park, Abingdon, Oxon, OX14 4RN
Routledge is an imprint of the Taylor & Francis Group, an informa business
© 2022 Taylor & Francis

The right of SUNIL KHUSHALANI & ANTONIO DEPAOLO to be identified as author of this work has been asserted by them in accordance with sections 77 and 78 of the Copyright, Designs and Patents Act 1988.

All rights reserved. No part of this book may be reprinted or reproduced or utilised in any form or by any electronic, mechanical, or other means, now known or hereafter invented, including photocopying and recording, or in any information storage or retrieval system, without permission in writing from the publishers.

Trademark notice: Product or corporate names may be trademarks or registered trademarks, and are used only for identification and explanation without intent to infringe.
Library of Congress Cataloging-in-Publication Data
A catalog record for this title has been requested

ISBN: 9781138297463 (hbk)
ISBN: 9781032070384 (pbk)
ISBN: 9781315099224 (ebk)

DOI: 10.4324/9781315099224

Typeset in Adobe Garamond Pro
by KnowledgeWorks Global Ltd.

Contents

Forewords xi
Preface xv
Acknowledgments xvii
About the Authors xix
Introduction xxi
Contributors xxiii

1 **The Need for Performance Improvement Methods in Mental Healthcare** 1
    I.   A Focus on the Mental Health 'System' of Care... 1
    II.   A New Paradigm for the Mental Health System 4
    III. The Burden of Mental Illness 7
    IV. The Connection between Behavioral Health and Overall Health 8
    V.   Current State: Access to Care (And Its Impact on Society) 9
        A.   Boarding in the Emergency Room 12
        B.   Homelessness 13
        C.   Mental Illness in Jails 13
    VI. Current State: Safety 14
    VII. Current State: Quality 16
        A.   Underuse 17
        B.   Overuse 18
        C.   Misuse 19
    VIII. Current State: Delivery of Care (Fragmentation of Care) 20
    IX. Current State: Cost/Waste 22
    X.   Current State: Morale/Workforce Challenges 23
    XI. A Call for a Better System 27
        A.   Crossing the Quality Chasm 27
        B.   The Quadruple Aim 28
    XII. Forces of Change 28
        A.   Moving Away from the Model of a 'Cottage Industry' 28
        B.   Technology 30
        C.   The Voice of the Patient 32
    XIII. Learning from Our Context (Groundbreaking Improvement
           Efforts in Medicine) 34
    XIV. The Need to Reinvigorate and Redesign Mental Healthcare 36
    References 38

2 Value and Waste in Psychiatry 45
    I.   Value 45
        A.   Value and the Patient 46
        B.   Value and the Family 47
        C.   Value and the Organization 48
        D.   Value and the Provider 51
        E.   Value and the Payer 52
        F.   Value and the Government 52
        G.   Value and the Continuum of Care 52
        H.   Value Added, Value Enabled, and Waste 53
    II.   Waste 55
        A.   Eight Forms of Waste 55
            1.   Overproduction 55
            2.   Defects 56
            3.   Waiting 56
            4.   Transportation 57
            5.   Motion 57
            6.   Extra Processing 57
            7.   Inventory 58
            8.   Non-Utilized Talent 58
        B.   Waste Walks 59
        C.   Constraint Management 60
        D.   Waste in Psychiatry 61
        E.   Within Treatment Waste 61
        F.   Between Treatment Waste 62
        G.   The Cost of Waste 62
    References 62

3 Developing the Healthcare Workforce for Performance Improvement 65
    I.   A Newer Approach to Work 65
    II.   The Development of an Improver 70
        A.   Developing Awareness 72
        B.   Fostering an Improvement Mindset 74
        C.   Acquiring Performance Improvement Knowledge 74
            1.   Appreciation for a System 76
            2.   Knowledge about Variation 77
            3.   Theory of Knowledge 79
            4.   Psychology 81
        D.   Applying and Practicing Improvement Skills 84
        E.   Developing Performance Improvement Skills into Routine Habits 85
    III.   Preparing the Medical Professional to Learn Performance
        Improvement Skills 87
    References 89

4 Improvement Methods for Mental Health Organizations 93
    I.   Plan-Do-Check-Act Cycle 93
    II.   Standard Work 96

	III.	PDCA vs. Research		97
	IV.	A3 Thinking		97
		A. Plan		98
			1. Project Title	98
			2. Business Case	99
			3. Project Y	101
			4. Scope	102
			5. Project Management	103
			6. Measure	104
			7. Observation	105
			8. Process Map	106
			9. Sub-Process Map	108
			10. Time and Motion Study	111
			11. Spaghetti Diagrams	111
			12. Measurement for Improvement	114
			13. Measurement Tips	116
			14. Visual Representation of Data	117
			15. Goal Setting	122
			16. Root Cause Analysis	122
			17. Cause-Effect Diagram	122
			18. 5-Why's	124
		B. Do		125
			1. Brainstorming	125
			2. Try-Storming	127
			3. Pilot Study	128
			4. Change Management	128
			5. Action Plans	130
		C. Check		131
		D. Act		132
			1. Standard Work	133
			2. Monitor and Response Plan	134
			3. Cascade Plan	134
	V.	PDCA and Kata		135
	References			136
5	**Leading a New Kind of Workforce**			**137**
	I.	Leadership and Culture		138
		A. Building Trust		139
		B. Developing Strong Interpersonal Relationships		141
		C. Fostering Teamwork		145
		D. Giving Appropriate and Timely Feedback		145
	II.	High-Performing Leadership		148
		A. Toxic Cultures		148
			1. An Aggressive or Hostile Culture	148
			2. An Analysis-Paralysis Culture	148
			3. The Fire-Fighting Culture	149

  B. High-Performing Leadership: The Case of High-Reliability Organizations 149
   1. Preoccupation with Failure 150
   2. Reluctance to Simplify 150
   3. Sensitivity to Operations 150
   4. Commitment to Resilience 151
   5. Deference to Expertise 151
 III. Leadership and Motivation 152
 IV. Getting Started 154
 V. A Long-Term Investment 154
 VI. An Uphill Task 155
 References 156

Afterword 157

Index 161

Forewords

Ten years ago, Dr. Sunil Khushalani came into my office with the germ of an idea. A staff psychiatrist and Chief of an inpatient unit devoted to treating individuals with serious mental illness and substance abuse, he was frustrated. He wanted to improve his unit's efficiency and effectiveness and the care of patients throughout the hospital. As the Sheppard and Enoch Pratt Hospital CEO, I recognized the need for improvement but was initially not impressed with Sunil's ideas. I needed some convincing. He was unique among the staff psychiatrists at Sheppard Pratt in the way he combined idealism with the day-to-day practical challenges of managing patients and staff with complex demands and needs. He was also not shy to challenge the CEO to see our world differently.

My initial thought was to tell him to 'work harder.' But he persisted because, as he put it, he wanted to 'work better.' We set up another meeting and then another. He was reading about the latest innovations in improving healthcare quality and pushed these books to me. These were compelling stories about radically rethinking the quality of care from hospitals and health systems in Seattle, Pittsburgh, and Rochester, Minnesota. Sunil wanted to bring these ideas to our large psychiatric hospital with 360 beds and over 20 discrete inpatient units and our even larger outpatient behavioral healthcare system across Maryland. I was intrigued but skeptical. Sunil persisted with emails, more meetings, more examples of change. He enlisted the Medical Director of the hospital, Dr. Robert Roca, who strongly supported the idea and requested that he and Sunil go to Pittsburgh for further training. I thought no harm in letting them go. They surely would realize that what worked in general healthcare would be difficult, if not impossible, in our large psychiatric hospital and health system. They came back committed and so enthusiastic about the model(s) of quality improvement that they learned I thought they had lost all reason. But I could not deny the energy and passion with which they presented a new approach the quality improvement based on the principles of LEAN management and the Toyota Production System. They promised that they would be champions for these ideas.

Over the years, we had tried different quality improvement methods at Sheppard Pratt with some success but little staying power. How would this be different, I wondered. We could start something, but it was unlikely it would be sustained. And we lacked the technical expertise to launch such an effort based on an industrial model of improvement invented by the Toyota car company. Sunil and Bob suggested we hire an expert from the industry to help us make and sustain the changes we needed to make. So after a national search, we hired Dr. Antonio DePaolo. Antonio was a 'black belt' in quality with a resume of success in industry but no healthcare experience, much less mental health. It was risky, but hiring Antonio paid off in so many ways. A natural teacher (and learner), Antonio turned out to be the perfect person to engineer the changes along with Sunil's leadership that took place over the years as SPIRIT (Sheppard Pratt Improvement Resources Inspired by Toyota) took hold throughout Sheppard Pratt. Hundreds of staff were trained by Sunil and Antonio and they, in turn, led many hundreds of quality improvement projects based on LEAN. It transformed the culture as problems in clinical care and administration were seen as opportunities for improvement. So much of the clinical care that was subjective became objective and data-driven. So much waste was exposed and eliminated. It was the most remarkable change in my twenty-five tenure as CEO.

We presented SPIRIT at many professional meetings to ever-increasing numbers of psychiatrists and others who want to implement LEAN in their hospitals or healthcare practices. Clearly, this was a winner not only at Sheppard Pratt but throughout the field.

I suggested to Sunil a year before my retirement in 2016 that he and Antonio write a book about their ideas and experience. It was slow going as they were so busy teaching and supervising a myriad of quality improvement projects throughout the health system. I kept prodding just the way Sunil initially prodded me into launching the initiative. And this wonderful book is the result. It follows their method of combining the real world of clinical and administrative care with many anecdotes about how change can occur and be sustained. I am so proud of what they accomplished.

Steven S. Sharfstein, MD
President Emeritus
Sheppard Pratt
Clinical Professor of Psychiatry University of Maryland School of Medicine

We fear that those about whom we care will suffer from malady. We all hope that should they be in distress something will provide cure, at best, or comfort and dignity at the least.

Our own emotional equilibrations – as friends, family members, care providers, or supporters – often depend on having a tangible cause to make sense of a situation, something onto which we can assign blame and at which we imagine a treatment can be directed. Physical maladies at least (often) offer that clarity of cause and effect, even as they have their perfidious influence. That is why it is rare for the orthopedic patient to be judged for inabilities associated with an injury, nor is a neurological patient judged for the consequences of stroke.

But with mental health issues, there can be a doubling down by the affliction. Invisible in their cause though consequential in their impact, they often don't have the decency of offering outward obviousness of cause and effect, especially not at first. Instead, early inklings of difficulty – for both patients and those who care about them – are too easy to dismiss as problems of character, rectitude, discipline, maturity, and the like. So, just when there should be concern and comfort, first reactions– judgmental and dismissive– can only make matters worse.

That the wounds are often invisible as are the agents that created them makes the work of mental healthcare professionals all the more difficult and all the more important for our individual and collective well-being. They labor against something the rest of us cannot imagine, nevertheless providing the care, comfort, and cure we so desperately seek yet can never truly envision.

It's in this context that *Transforming Mental Healthcare: Applying Performance Improvement Methods to Mental Healthcare* should be welcomed and Sunil Khushalani and Antonio Depaolo should be praised. Writing with a tone sympathetic and respectful of patient and provider alike, they recognize the sheer complexity of 'systems' through which care is provided by harmonizing the contributions of many specialists toward common purpose, they explain how such complexity can express itself as obstacles and obstructions to the good intentions of those doing their very best, and the authors demonstrate how such complexity can be managed better so acts of giving care can be more collectively graceful, generating more reason for individual and shared gratitude.

In effect, they urge that the same disciplines of observation, examination, investigation, intervention, and follow-up that clinicians exercise in helping patients be applied to the systems in which those same clinicians are imbedded and through which they express their upmost professionalism and humanity.

It's in this light of description, critique, and prescription that the many poignant vignettes throughout *Transforming …* can be read as far more than alarming. The authors' promise is that such vignettes are avoidable and need not recur. Framed that way, we seem them as admonishment to do better because better is possible. Rather than infuriating, they can be read as inspiring.

It is my hope that this loving work and the loving work it addresses be information and inspiration for better experiences for all concerned.

With appreciation for those who bring light to those walking in darkness.

Respectfully,

Steven J. Spear, DBA MS MS
Principal, See to Solve LLC
Senior Lecturer, MIT Sloan School of Management
Senior Fellow, Institute for Healthcare Improvement
Author, The High Velocity Edge
Brookline MA
June 2021

Preface

We wrote this book with a focus on an individual practitioner of mental health treatment, a person supporting such work, or a manager or leader responsible for the optimum functioning of an organization that provides such treatment.

In our research, we came across quite a few books that discussed the improvement journeys of hospitals or health systems in medical or surgical settings. Other texts gave an overview of lean, six-sigma, or lean-sigma applied to healthcare. There were hardly any books that talked about the application of these methods in a mental health setting. When we started writing this book, we were regularly presenting our ideas and findings at various local, regional, and national conferences. There was a limited awareness, understanding, or even interest in our presentations. We quickly became aware that either individuals had never heard of such ideas in their mental health organizations. If they had, there was no organizational support or infrastructure to carry out such ideas.

We also believe that all improvement is not just about capturing the mind with a new method, but it is about capturing the heart of those we work with and those we serve. Our vignettes help convey a real sense of what patients and staff feel, and hence it was important for us to share this body of work with all of you.

We believe that this kind of knowledge is vital for all practitioners in any service industry, especially in the mental healthcare setting. Even after attending our workshops or presentations, there was no introductory guide with examples from such settings if someone were to take an interest. There was no easy one-stop resource with an overview and necessary steps to get started with improvement as part of daily work or explain why it made sense in that setting.

Both of us come from different vantage points. One of us (SK) is a practicing psychiatrist, and the other one (AD) is an industrial engineer. We had designed a course together at Sheppard Pratt on 'Learning to Improve,' which introduced the basics of lean methodology and guided every participant to perform their own improvement projects. This course would help them with problems they encountered – problems that affected safety, quality, delivery, cost, or morale. It was one component of a multi-pronged approach toward a culture change in the organization. The other components included short one-to-four day performance improvement events, daily improvement huddles, and the use of strategy deployment.

We thought it would be a great idea to write this book for anyone who would want to do an improvement project to solve a complex or vexing systems issue in their mental health practice setting. This approach would allow them to solve their problems and communicate their findings effectively to others. They could use the results of such a project to convince their leadership that such a systematic approach would have merit if pursued more broadly in their setting.

We ended every work week with a two-hour (or longer) conversation. We needed this brainstorming session to teach each other, and in doing so, one of us (SK) learned a lot about the field of performance improvement, and the other (AD) learned a lot about mental health. The book became a distillation of many ideas over almost four years of several such conversations.

This book is about an experiential learning approach. This approach can be undertaken by an individual or with the help of a team. A collaborative team-based set of activities can help a team examine the shortcomings of how well their care system is designed. The team would need to have humility, honesty, and a willingness to surface problems to improve their services from the perspective of the people they serve. It would require them to pay attention to *what* is being offered as care and *how* well it is being delivered in different contexts. Do patients and staff endure a significant amount of burden to get the benefits of the service? If so, this book will be an excellent place to guide practitioners to optimize their service offerings and do so with high reliability.

Practitioners and organizations that are exceptional performers are very adept at learning and learning faster than their peers. This desire to learn, improve, and keep adapting to new challenges separate them from the rest. Much of this methodology matured greatly at Toyota, the car company. It became a beacon of light to others due to their ability to be an organization to learn and adapt much faster than others. They are known to invest a great deal in fostering such a proactive, problem-solving mindset in all their workers.

We wrote this book intending to let every individual taste what it is like to develop such a mindset, look at challenges at work, and welcome these challenges as opportunities to improve from within an organization. It is as much about redesigning your work processes and settings as it is about changing yourself to thinking differently. It demonstrates how you can approach work with a different paradigm – one that will change the way you look at your work, the way you conduct yourself, and the way you lead. Once you have learned to see the problems from the perspective of the people you serve and begin to apply this way of thinking consistently, it will be hard for you to go back to business as usual.

At times, as both of us carry the baggage of our training and experiences, we use a different language to describe our respective observations and thoughts. We have gone back and forth multiple times to present our writing as a unified voice in revisions of the text. If the differences in our voices are too noticeable, and if concepts get lost in translation, it just points to the ongoing and iterative need to keep learning more from each other's perspectives. We have tried to present this as a standard approach to performance improvement in a mental health setting.

Both mental health and industrial engineering fields have many variations in how things are taught and communicated. These variations can make many such books or presentations look very different in comparison. But at the heart of all such books and presentations is a desire to improve something. Try to get a deeper understanding of the problem and the context, perform some specific experiments, learn systematically from them, and then apply such learning to the next set of issues that emerge in the course of work. Learning and practicing in this way is a continuous iterative journey.

If you keep at it, it will undoubtedly help you redesign your work, while it also enables you to reinvigorate yourself to meet today's challenges.

We wish you the very best in your endeavors and hope that we can convey our understanding and excitement to you in a clear, comprehensive, and engaging manner.

Sunil Khushalani
Antonio DePaolo

Acknowledgments

This entire book became possible due to the collaboration, coaching, mentorship, and friendship of my co-author, Antonio DePaolo. He met every big and small idea from me with genuine curiosity, interest, and an attitude of openness and possibility. Everyone should be blessed with a person like that in their lives – one who helps them learn, grow, and feel safe to share all types of suggestions and fears. He has undoubtedly made me a more thoughtful person and given my performance improvement skillset a definite boost. He has gifted me with a firm conviction about the value of these ideas.

I also feel indebted to Sheppard Pratt, its leadership, and staff, who allowed such an endeavor to occur and evolve within its context. I am incredibly thankful to Dr. Steve Sharfstein for leading the way in this regard – he also encouraged us to write about our insights and helped formulate and express our ideas better. The thoughtfulness, foresight, and courage of the rest of the executive leadership made it possible to explore this approach's possibilities. It also gave us the needed space, time, attention, and resources to make this a reality. For this, I am thankful to Dr. Robert Roca, Bonnie Katz, Ernestine Cosby, Diana Ramsay, Bryon Forbush, Dr. Harsh Trivedi, and Armando Colombo. I would also like to thank Dr. Harsh Trivedi for contributing an insightful afterword.

This book is a product of the collective improvement efforts of many Sheppard Pratt employees who took our course and applied many of these ideas to their work. Each iterative learning cycle helped us grow in our understanding of the value of these methods in healthcare. I am thankful to Janet Bryan, Susan Amrose, Gwen Bowie, Dr. John Boronow, Dr. Edward Zuzarte, Jacqueline Williams-Porter, Dr. Khizar Khan, Dr. Joshana Goga, Rick Wallace, and Shanelle Griffith, and many others. They all dedicated time to try out these ideas to improve processes at Sheppard Pratt. In addition to the medical staff, I must thank all the people who worked with the lean (or operational excellence) team to include Cary Abma, Brandon Holle, Matthew Kopp, Demetria Murphy, Maureen Mulcahy, Ryan Gruver, and Sonik Sikka.

I am grateful to the painstaking efforts of Dr. Faith Dickerson, Dr. Abhilash Desai, Emily Peterson, and Dr. Rachna Raisinghani. They took the time to read our drafts and made our book better, more precise, sharper, and more readable. They asked us a whole range of questions and made us think about the reader's point of view.

This book would not have been possible without the steadfast support of my wife, Vaishali, who is the firm foundation for all my imaginative leaps. I would like to thank my parents and elders, who have always selflessly thought about the betterment of others, have taught me to be empathic, and have held me accountable. I would also like to express my love for my two sons, Abhinav and Varun, who always keep me humble and grounded.

This book was written for individuals who serve people with mental illness and those who work on healthcare improvement. Hopefully, this book will help in efforts to create a better system of mental healthcare.

Finally, I would like to dedicate this book to my parents. My father, Dharamdas Khushalani, first introduced the idea of continuous improvement to me, and my mother, Anjanadevi Khushalani, was instrumental in teaching me to respect every individual. I will be forever indebted to them.

Sunil Khushalani, MD

I would like to thank my co-author, Dr. Sunil Khushalani, whose unrelenting passion for improving mental healthcare opened a door for me to venture into the world of mental Health. With his expertise in psychiatry and my expertise in Lean Systems, we made a formidable team in helping to improve the system of care at Sheppard Pratt. This body of work is a combination of our collective efforts.

I also want to thank all of my mentors and role models over the past 20-plus years working in the improvement space. Dr. Zahorjian, Jerry Linzey, Richard Giromini, Sensei Sugai, Joe Zachman, Dr. Steve Sharfstein, Armando Colombo, and Dr. Harsh Trivedi. I appreciate all they have done to develop and advance my career. To my mom and dad, my achievements are a result of standing on a foundation that they created.

A special thanks to all of the staff at Sheppard Pratt who came to my class to learn how to implement improvement and used that knowledge to advance the field of Mental Health. A few names, in particular, include Dr. John Boronow, Dr. Joshana Goga, Dr. Ellen Mongan, Emily Peterson, Janet Bryan, Dr. Robert Roca, and Ernestine Cosby.

Finally, I want to thank my wife, Tabitha, for her unrelenting support throughout this project. I would also like to recognize my kids Amelia, Gabriella, Antonio Jr., and Dominic. May you see this work as an example of what can happen when you pursue what you love.

I dedicate this book to all of the passionate and hard-working mental healthcare professionals across the globe. Thank you for your service toward helping the most vulnerable in our communities. You are a beacon of light to those afflicted with mental illness.

Antonio DePaolo, PhD

About the Authors

Sunil Khushalani, MD, is a psychiatrist who specializes in Addiction Psychiatry. He is passionate about learning improvement science and integrating it into the field of mental health and addictions. This book is his first on the subject of improvement science as applied to mental health. For the last decade, he worked on teaching and integrating these ideas and methods at Sheppard Pratt.

He obtained his MBBS degree from Seth Gordhandas Sunderdas Medical College/King Edward Memorial Hospital in Mumbai, India. He then completed his residency at the Department of Psychiatry at New York University Medical Center/Bellevue Hospital in 1997 and came to Sheppard Pratt in 2000. He is board-certified in Psychiatry by the American Board of Psychiatry and Neurology. He is also certified by examination by the American Board of Addiction Medicine. He was recently serving as the Medical Director of Adult Services at Sheppard Pratt and the Service Chief of the Inpatient Co-occurring Disorders Unit at the Towson Campus of Sheppard Pratt. He also served as a physician advisor for the Stanley Research Group and the Operational Excellence team at Sheppard Pratt. Now, he works as the Chief Medical Officer for Kolmac Outpatient Recovery Centers.

He is also an assistant professor at the University of Maryland School of Medicine, and he has always maintained an interest in training psychiatry residents. He helped develop a course on 'Lean Problem-Solving' at Sheppard Pratt and taught performance improvement to staff and psychiatry residents in the Sheppard Pratt System. He is a Distinguished Fellow of the American Psychiatric Association and a Fellow of the American Society of Addiction Medicine. He has been voted as a Top Doctor in Addiction Psychiatry by Castle Connolly and Baltimore Magazine.

He has conducted workshops and delivered many presentations on performance improvement in mental health at many regional, national, and international meetings.

Antonio DePaolo, PhD, is a transformation executive and a Baldrige Fellow with over 22 years of experience in improvement science. This is his first book on improvement science applied to mental health and highlights his implementation work over more than seven years at Sheppard Pratt. Before that, Antonio spent 16 years in several industries, from automotive and transportation to life science and semiconductor packaging. He most recently ventured into healthcare by joining the University of Maryland Medical System as the Vice President of Transformation and Continuous Improvement for Upper Chesapeake Health. Antonio earned his B.S. in Industrial Engineering and Masters of Industrial Engineering from the University at Buffalo. He later completed his formal education with a Doctorate of Philosophy in Management with a focus on leadership and organizational change from Walden University. Throughout his career, Antonio had several mentors, including being mentored by Japanese Sensei while leading improvement efforts at a division of The Stanley Works located in Rhode Island. His major accomplishment was the full transformation of Wabash National, a struggling trailer manufacturer in Lafayette, Indiana, where he developed the manufacturing systems and laid the groundwork for improvement. As a result of his work, the company returned to revenue growth and profitability by removing a cumulative cost burden in excess of $250M and led to the organization winning The US Senate productivity excellence award presented by Senator Richard Lugar. Antonio has volunteered his time to speak at local, national, and international settings and the American Psychiatric Association.

Introduction

This book is for any individual who is interested in learning about performance improvement within the field of mental health. Whether you are a solo practitioner of direct mental healthcare in the field or a team leader who supports, manages, or leads the delivery of mental healthcare within a large healthcare system, you will find something of interest in this book.

This book is an introductory text which assumes that the reader might be wholly unfamiliar or new to these ideas. The book begins with why there is a need to improve mental healthcare. This section is followed by an introduction to the principles behind performance improvement and then an elaboration of a basic improvement methodology. Both authors have spent a considerable amount of time implementing change, teaching improvement, and managing groups of individuals working in various mental health programs. There is a section that focuses on training the mental health workforce and a section on the leadership required to support such an undertaking.

The book is subdivided into five sections. We have included several vignettes in every section, making it easier for the reader to identify with, understand the concepts, and think about approaching improvement opportunities in one's work setting.

Section I

This section is a comprehensive introduction to the current state of the mental health system today. The section starts with a spotlight on the mental health system and highlights some of the devastating consequences of the suboptimal current state of the mental healthcare system today. It introduces a new paradigm for what an ideal mental healthcare system of the future. It also provides a guiding direction and vision for how it should be redesigned. This section also highlights the many concurrent forces of change that are making the quick adoption of these ideas necessary for the survival and viability of organizations. The mental healthcare system has a considerable degree of catch-up to do with the rest of the house of medicine. Redesigning the mental health system of care would be invigorating to the field of mental health and lead to better overall outcomes.

Section II

If you want to start your improvement efforts right away, you could start with this chapter. This section provides a good compass for any improvement journey. It dives deeper into two fundamental concepts of performance improvement – value and waste. These concepts are essentially two valuable lenses that are very useful in examining any organization from the perspective of those who would benefit from it. Value and waste are so ingrained in everything we do that it is hard to notice them in all processes at first. Once the mind truly internalizes these concepts, it becomes very hard to carry out work in the same way as before. It is very easy to ignore waste, which is right in front of our eyes, as we often confuse being busy with adding value. Everyone desires an ever-increasing degree of value from any organization and service, and continuous elimination of waste is a perfect place to start.

Section III

The real power of performance improvement comes from the continuous improvement activities of the entire workforce in the same direction. This section focuses on the potential and development of each individual to become an improver. Improvement depends on an individual's approach to their work. Problems are ubiquitous, but the response to each problem varies. A systematic and consistent improvement method can make the workplace better, the workforce feel more empowered and lead to better outcomes. The section talks about the developmental steps that someone has to go through to make involvement in improvement activities into a habit. Finally, the section talks about two specific competencies that medical professionals have to develop and how the evolution of these competencies requires further maturation and integration into daily work. If you are an educator, a manager, or a leader, this chapter will help you understand the building blocks that go into building improvement capability in everyone you manage or lead.

Section IV

This section is a practical and immediately applicable how-to set of guidance on approaching any improvement opportunity. It could serve as a stand-alone course in how to complete an improvement project. The reader is introduced to the underlying plan-do-check-act framework for improvement. The section then elaborates on a structured method of improvement based on A3 Thinking. This method is a systematic way of planning, problem-solving, communicating, and collaborating for improvement. It leads the reader through understanding the context and need to improve any process and all the required steps to meet the desired improvement goal. This section talks about the importance of metrics and the visualization of these metrics to communicate and study the impact of the improvement effort on a pilot project. It then talks about how to sustain and cascade successful pilot improvement projects. If you have time to read only one section, it would be this section.

Section V

If you are a manager or leader responsible for creating a culture and fertile environment for the widespread of such ideas in your organization, this chapter provides a useful framework. It covers aspects of both toxic and healthy improvement cultures. The section then elaborates on the elements of a high-reliability organization. Optimum leadership is the most significant determinant for creating a culture of continuous improvement.

Successful improvement projects can provide seeds of change. In the presence of the right kind of leadership and culture, such seed ideas can thrive. Otherwise, many successful individual efforts will not amount to any sustained improvement or the creation of a continuously improving mental health system. Such a long-term strategy is the necessary investment for achieving the quadruple aim — improving the experience of care, improving the health of populations, reducing per capita costs of healthcare, and improving the work-life of healthcare providers.

Sunil Khushalani
Antonio DePaolo

Contributors

Antonio DePaolo, PhD
Vice President of Transformation and Continuous Improvement
University of Maryland
Upper Chesapeake Health
Baldrige Performance Excellence Executive Fellow
Baltimore, MD

Sunil Khushalani, MD
Chief Medical Officer
Kolmac Outpatient Recovery Centers
Assistant Professor of Psychiatry
Department of Psychiatry
University of Maryland School of Medicine
Baltimore, MD

Steven S. Sharfstein, MD
President Emeritus
Sheppard Pratt
Clinical Professor of Psychiatry University of Maryland School of Medicine

Steven J. Spear DBA MS MS
Principal, See to Solve LLC
Senior Lecturer, MIT Sloan School of Management
Senior Fellow, Institute for Healthcare Improvement
Author, The High Velocity Edge
Brookline, MA

Harsh K. Trivedi, MD, MBA
President and CEO
Sheppard Pratt
Professor of Clinical Psychiatry
Department of Psychiatry
University of Maryland School of Medicine
Baltimore, MD

Section I

The Need for Performance Improvement Methods in Mental Healthcare

I. A Focus on the Mental Health 'System' of Care

Nearly one in five individuals in the United States is affected by mental illness (Ezez, 2019).[1] In 2017, according to the National Institute of Mental Health (NIMH), an estimated 18.9% of all adults aged 18 or older had any mental illness (AMI). An estimated 4.5% of all adults aged 18 or older had a serious mental illness (SMI). We all know someone who struggles with a mental illness, and more often than not, their mental illness is a chronic condition. Finding good quality, safe, and effective treatment is essential to managing these conditions. The availability of a reliable healthcare provider or system goes a long way in reducing a struggling patient's functional impairment and the stress or burden of a caretaker. As part of receiving care, a patient may have to navigate different professionals, clinics, laboratories, pharmacies, or even hospitals. Entities that offer these services can be havens of comfort, or they can be laden with obstacles in the way of receiving accessible and reliable care.

VIGNETTE 1.1

Dr. Samuel was a busy psychiatrist. He received a call from Jenny, an old acquaintance. Her boss Pete was suffering from disabling panic attacks and wanted to see a psychiatrist right away. She wondered if Dr. Samuel would see Pete soon to help him with his condition. Dr. Samuel asked her to have Pete call his office to make an appointment. When Pete called the office, he was told by the office assistant that there were no openings for an initial appointment for six weeks and offered to put his name on a waiting list. He let Jenny know who called Dr. Samuel to ask him what could be done about the long wait. Dr. Samuel then called his assistant and instructed her to 'double book' Pete for the next day so that he could be seen sometime in the morning. Dr. Samuel knew there was typically a no-show or last-minute cancellation. Pete arrived in the morning and had to wait until the lunch hour to be seen by Dr. Samuel because every other patient showed up for their scheduled appointment.

As a mental health practitioner, imagine that a loved one decided to seek services at your hospital or clinic. Think about the overall care that this person would receive at your current workplace and their complete journey from the time they enter your system to the time they leave. Ask yourself questions such as 'How quickly are they able to access services?,' 'Are questions and concerns readily addressed?,' 'How is the quality and nature of the diagnosis, treatment, and support services provided?' and 'What is the overall satisfaction and outcome for patients?' These are all great things to consider, but the real question is, 'will the current system of care be acceptable to you, or is there room for improvement?'

VIGNETTE 1.2

Colleen, a new nurse practitioner in an acute psychiatric inpatient unit, had a longer average length of stay than her peers in the same unit. Her supervising Medical Director asked her what was contributing to patients staying longer, to which she replied: 'Since their insurance covers our patients' costs, what is the advantage of reducing the length of stay?' This question surprised the Medical Director, who did not expect such a response. He began to question if new psychiatric practitioners were being trained to manage the day-to-day rather than the big picture of a patient's care. He wondered if he could shift their focus toward the total impact of patient services offered while also focusing on managing the patient cases in front of them.

Discussing cost is a thorny issue. On the one hand, medical practitioners want to provide the best care possible regardless of cost. On the other hand, such care's financial implications on both the individual and the healthcare system can cause the costs to rise for everyone. Whether the family member is financially supporting the care of a patient suffering from a chronic mental illness or a business leader is worried about choosing the best healthcare plan for all their employees, there is constant concern about the value a patient receives for the amount of money that is being spent. As costs keep rising, everyone in the healthcare system is under constant pressure to make difficult financial decisions.

VIGNETTE 1.3

Josh was admitted to a psychiatric inpatient unit for suicidal ideation. His allergy to tomatoes was listed in the medical record. For lunch, he was served a garden salad with cherry tomatoes. He let the charge nurse know who called the kitchen and informed them of the mistake. They sent a replacement tray with a pizza on it. He asked to speak to the doctor on call. He spoke out assertively about the apparent error and pointed out that the pizza was made with tomato sauce. He sarcastically said to the doctor, 'I came here for suicidal thinking, but it seems to me that someone in the hospital wants to kill me.'

Administrators routinely hear complaints about processes that don't work as desired. They often aim for a good patient experience and have to apologize to patients or family members for their bad experiences. Patient experiences are variable as they receive care. The risks associated with faulty or broken processes within a system of care are too significant. Asking employees of a health system to be careful, to try harder, or even retraining them does not easily eliminate potential errors before they affect a patient.

VIGNETTE 1.4

Sameer, a software engineer, was suffering from back pain for four years. His primary care provider treated him with oxycodone 20 mg four times a day for the last three years. After losing his job over two months ago, Sameer became depressed and started taking oxycodone six times a day. When his primary care provider found out about this, he discharged Sameer from his practice abruptly and told him to seek care elsewhere. Sameer went to the ER with worsened pain and informed the psychiatric social worker that he had been drinking 6–8 glasses of whiskey a day since he was laid off. During the assessment, he said that he was trying his best to cope. He had been feeling depressed and also felt that his pain had gotten worse. He was even tempted to use heroin when he was feeling desperate. He was out of his pain medications, and the withdrawal symptoms were excruciating. The social worker became very concerned about him, considering that the number of opioid overdose deaths had been rising astronomically.

Legislators are always concerned about how the present-day healthcare system functions so much so that it is part of every campaign today for political office. Errors, complaints, and shortcomings of the current system often make headlines in the news. Many psychiatric patients do not get the appropriate care and are falling through the cracks. Healthcare has become fragmented into specialty silos, and the providers within and between these silos often don't talk to each other leading to recurrent problems and rising expenditures.

There are several existing inefficiencies within the overall healthcare structure and processes leading to undesirable outcomes. These challenges are ubiquitous, seen all over the world, and they beg for improvements. Healthcare systems have been growing organically for decades. Looking at how our healthcare system is organized, there is a clear and imminent need for an overhaul and redesign. Practitioners need to learn to 'diagnose and treat' poorly functioning systems of care. They also need to ensure that each patient receives evidence-based care reliably.

VIGNETTE 1.5

Lashanda and Joseph were in their twenties and newly married. Joseph had been getting more and more paranoid lately and was convinced that someone was following him on his most recent drive back home. To avoid this, he drove through narrow back roads and came home late. He seemed terrified and disheveled. Lashanda was very worried about him. She called their family doctor, who advised her to take him to see a psychiatrist. After having made multiple phone calls to at least 20 different psychiatric practitioners and practices, she couldn't find a single available outpatient provider within their insurance network. One evening Joseph did not return home and called her frantically, saying he was afraid to come home. He felt that the people were following him and would find out where they lived. He did not want to put her life in danger as well.

The current health system (which also includes the mental health system) is unsatisfactory in many ways. Improving it is not only necessary, but there is an urgent need to make it accessible and sustainable. Some analysts say that rising healthcare costs make the United States less competitive in the world (Johnson, 2012) and are cannibalizing the country's other vital priorities.[2] Psychiatric providers genuinely need a new paradigm of their roles at work. They need to think about the processes that exist in their workplace. They also need to direct more focus and energy on transforming the care system to ensure that each patient receives the best care possible. The quality gaps between what is truly possible and what is currently available are large, and there is a tremendous amount of improvement work needed to close that gap. Practitioners need to learn how to engage in such imminently needed performance improvement efforts.

II. A New Paradigm for the Mental Health System

Administrators, regulators, or accrediting agencies may suggest top-down changes to the system, but they can never match the expertise, knowledge, and capacity for innovation of the healthcare workers themselves. Much like the patient experience, healthcare workers experience variation in their processes as they provide care to a patient. They are the closest to the patient (front line) and have a vantage point where meaningful understanding and change can occur in a system. Partnering with front-line staff and clinicians provides a valuable resource of ideas and inspiration for change and redesign. They know what steps are beneficial for patient care, and they also know what additional steps are superfluous.

Engaging all workers in thinking about the improvement of their workplace is not new. Several industries outside of healthcare have engaged their workforce in performance improvement for decades, which has led to the creation of very safe and highly reliable systems. When considering the progress made in the airline or automotive industry through engaging their front-line staff, the healthcare industry has not kept pace.

However, some healthcare systems are testing the waters with various improvement methodologies. These centers are learning from other industries and radically transforming the experience of care and output of their systems. They are not just improving the quality, safety, and delivery of their services but are doing it with fewer expenditures, greater engagement, and satisfaction of their employees.

Mental health practitioners are being introduced to performance improvement methods, but many in the field are still unaware and oblivious to the usefulness of these newer methods and paradigms.

In 2003, the American Psychiatric Association (APA) presented a vision for the mental health system calling for a 'genuine, responsive mental health system' (Sharfstein et al., 2003).[3] The APA task force envisioned access to treatment delivered at "the right time and place, in the right amount, and with appropriate supports such as adequate housing, rehabilitation, and case management when needed." It further stated, "Care should be based on continuous healing relationships and engagement with the whole person rather than a narrow, symptom-focused perspective. Timely access to care and continuity of care remain today as cornerstones for quality even as a continuum of services is built that encourages maximum independence and quality of life for psychiatric patients." How can the 'patchwork relic' (New Freedom Commission on Mental Health, 2003) of our current mental health system move toward this ideal future state?[4]

The healthcare system must be optimally designed to meet the current challenges of those who depend on mental health services. To accomplish this overarching goal, mental health practitioners need training and development to proactively influence the care system without succumbing to cynicism, burnout, or a feeling of learned helplessness. Clinicians can regain and maintain some sense of control and optimism by redesigning the existing mental health system. Those who design mental health systems need to draw from healthcare providers' experience of the latest science of diagnosing and treating psychiatric disorders and the vast knowledge base of improvement science.

Knowledge of improvement science can ensure that the system is optimally configured to deliver the best possible outcomes. If the system's overall performance cannot guarantee a satisfactory patient experience with reliable outcomes, having the most knowledgeable psychiatrist on staff will be insufficient.

A new holistic way about the functioning of both the individual providers and the system within which they work will enable clinicians to meet patients' needs and ensure that the resources available to them are optimally utilized.

VIGNETTE 1.6

The inpatient psychiatric unit staff noticed that families were not satisfied with the discharge process due to longer than expected wait times at the time of discharge. They also received complaints from the transportation department when discharge delays from their unit disrupted daily transport schedules. To better understand why these issues were occurring, the unit staff decided to study this process by spending five minutes every day, discussing how many of their discharged patients left at the promised time. They then discussed the barriers to achieving the goal of on-time discharge. They took the time to study each delay as a team and began noticing things such as incomplete documentation, delayed discharge orders from doctors, and insufficient time for filling prescriptions at the pharmacy. By doing so for a few months and using this information to improve their process, on-time discharges occurred more reliably. Each patient discharge provided data to the team about each patient's flow through the care process and how well their inpatient unit team was performing to meet the patient's needs.

Typically, clinicians or administrators experience or hear about problems when they have an unsatisfied patient, an error, a complaint, a complication, or a bad outcome. But usually, these are neither isolated events nor unique in their occurrence. Providers are part of a more extensive care system, and caution needs to be exercised about blaming providers for these problems because poorly designed systems will always lead to poor results. The new paradigm is to discover a pattern to these problems and work together to improve the system.

When thinking of redesigning the system, it is necessary to create a learning organization (Senge, 1990).[5] Such a system draws on data that helps providers continuously learn about the shortcomings of their system. Each time something is not performed as expected or as per a specified standard of care, well-designed learning organizations would make this variation visible to clinicians through data. Clinicians can then, in turn, pay attention and respond by studying these variants in practice. Just like the continually evolving evidence-based scientific knowledge, these variations can be utilized as opportunities to improve the system continuously.

The challenge in healthcare is the dynamic nature of the system of care where innovation, internal and external practices, and fluctuations in staff constellation are continually changing the inputs to the process. To keep the outputs of this system consistently reliable and prevent the system from gradually deteriorating over time, continuous learning from patients' experiences has to occur.

An organization is a system with multiple components. Changes in one area can have unintended consequences in other areas. A learning organization has to stay vigilant and attentive to these ongoing changes. For example, great systems function well even when a very skilled staff member no longer works there. If staff changes cause outcomes to falter, the system, per se, has not hardwired their implicit practice knowledge into its daily standard way of working.

The healthcare system is an example of a 'complex adaptive system' (CAS). A CAS is defined as a 'collection of individual agents who have the freedom to act in ways that are not always predictable and whose actions are interconnected such that one agent's actions change the context for other agents' (Committee on Quality Health Care in America, 2001).[6] As mental healthcare is delivered by people from various disciplines in a CAS, what gets delivered to the patient on a day-to-day basis is highly dependent on whether the system and the people working within it have standardized their daily work processes. It also depends on their ability as a team to adapt their system structures or processes to ensure reliable outputs, given that changes in interpersonal and social structures can impact system performance (Perla et al., 2013).[7]

In this new working paradigm, problems are not swept under the rug but surfaced actively to improve continuously. Learning is encouraged to prevent similar issues from occurring in the future. As sustained improvement is achieved, the system can then focus on growth and adaptability. Therefore, a significant part of each provider's time in this new paradigm is spent on improvement work to ensure alignment between what each patient needs and what each patient experiences in the delivery of care.

III. The Burden of Mental Illness

VIGNETTE 1.7

Suzy and Nick had been friends since their residency days in New York City. Suzy had completed a psychiatric residency, while Nick did his training in Internal Medicine. After residency, Nick moved to a rural southern town. In his first month of work in a new clinic, he was overwhelmed because many of his patients struggled with a mental illness or with an addiction. He missed his residency days when he could just refer such patients to the psychiatric or addiction clinic. There was no psychiatric clinic in his town to refer his patients to, so he had to manage all of these complex cases independently. He thought of calling Suzy. He wondered if Suzy would be willing to regularly discuss complex cases over the phone because sometimes he felt lost managing these challenging cases by himself.

Mental illnesses affect a large segment of the population. The one-year prevalence of having any mental health and substance use disorder has been reported to vary from 26.2% to 32.4% in the United States (Kessler et al., 2005; Ezez, 2007).[8,9]

According to the NIMH, neuropsychiatric disorders are the leading cause of disability in the United States. The burden of disability associated with a disease or disorder is measured in units called disability-adjusted life years (DALYs) (NIMH, 2017).[10] They represent the total number of years lost to illness, disability, or premature death within a given population. Collectively, these disorders represent 18.7% of total US DALYs. Mental and behavioral disorders comprise 13.6% of the total, while self-harm and interpersonal violence add another 3.1% to the total. Major depressive disorder leads the list of mental conditions carrying the most significant burden affecting 3.73% of US DALYs (Ezez, 2019). Anxiety and depression are the second most important cause of DALYs globally (Moreno et al., 2016).[11]

In 2005, according to a WHO report, 31.7% of all year lived-with-disability were attributed to neuropsychiatric conditions: the five main contributors to this were unipolar depression (11.8%), alcohol use disorders (3.3%), schizophrenia (2.8%), bipolar depression (2.4%), and dementia (1.6%) (Prince et al., 2007).[12]

The field of psychiatry has made considerable progress in the last few decades (Mechanic, 2007).[13] There is a greater understanding of mental health disorders; there is now a wide range of psychotherapeutic and psychopharmacological treatments available. Even though the public stigma of mental illness continues to be widespread, the American public holds positive attitudes about seeking professional help for mental health problems (Parcesepe et al., 2012).[14] A majority of mental illness care has moved from asylums and hospitals to the community. There are diagnostic manuals and evidence-based treatment guidelines for many psychiatric disorders.

Even though psychiatric disorders are common and contribute to such a significant degree of disability, many psychiatric conditions and disorders are highly treatable and manageable. Therefore, it is imperative that everyone in the mental healthcare field collectively works toward creating a better system of care, where patients can receive prompt help when they are in distress.

This system needs to be safe, effective, efficient, equitable, and patient-centered (Committee on Quality Health Care in America, 2001).[6] The current state of mental healthcare is far from this desired ideal.

IV. The Connection between Behavioral Health and Overall Health

> **VIGNETTE 1.8**
>
> Fifty-six-year-old Jose was not having a good year. In February, he had a heart attack and began to show signs of congestive heart failure. Jose developed a severe major depressive episode within a few weeks of his heart attack. He had become more forgetful, and it had been hard for him to engage in rehabilitation reliably. He was obese, had been suffering from obstructive sleep apnea, and had never followed through with his sleep specialist's recommendations with regard to using a continuous positive airway pressure (CPAP) machine. His depression was not responding to medication therapies. By July, in the same year, he had been re-hospitalized six times.

It is hard to imagine optimum physical health without good mental health. The connections between the two conditions are complex and manifold. Unfortunately, the service provider for both somatic and psychiatric disorders has been historically de-linked over time at most healthcare locations.

Mental illnesses can be a risk factor for physical conditions or a consequence of the physical condition. Mental disorders increase the risk of all diseases (communicable and non-communicable) and contribute to injuries (unintentional and intentional). The co-occurrence also impairs the individual's ability to seek help, and it adversely affects diagnosis, quality of care, treatment, and outcomes, including disability, mortality, and quality of life (Prince et al., 2007).[12] Depressive disorders can increase morbidity and mortality from medical conditions such as heart disease and diabetes (Katon, 2003).[15] Depression alone can lead to 50% greater medical costs of chronic medical illness even after factoring in a physical condition's severity. Depression can worsen lifestyle factors such as diet, smoking, exercise, and adherence to treatment recommendations. There also are adverse direct physiological effects of depression (such as reduced heart rate variability and increased platelet adhesiveness) on physical health.

The landmark Adverse Childhood Experiences (ACEs) study and follow-up reports underscored this connection as well. ACE was a significant epidemiological study that provided retrospective and prospective analysis of early traumatic experiences in over 17,000 individuals on medical and psychiatric illnesses, sexual behavior, healthcare costs, and life expectancy (Felitti et al., 1998).[16] ACEs were strongly associated with high-risk behaviors such as smoking, alcohol, substance misuse, promiscuity, and negatively impacted safety. The effects increased with the number of ACEs experienced. ACEs were also correlated with 'unintended pregnancies, sexually transmitted diseases, severe obesity, heart disease, liver disease, cancer, lung disease, and a shortened life span.' ACEs in any category increased the risk of attempted suicide from twofold to fivefold.

Patients with a history of ACEs had a greater likelihood of engaging in non-suicidal self-injurious behaviors (Felitti et al., 2010).[16]

It is well known that patients with mental illness neither access nor receive adequate physical health services (Cradock-O'Leary et al., 2002). This lack of availability may contribute to the early mortality of those suffering from severe mental illnesses.[17] According to several studies, people with severe mental conditions die 10–20 years earlier than the general population (Colton et al., 2006; Liu et al., 2017).[18,19] More recently, we have come to appreciate the ironic fact about the social determinants of health. Only about 10% of early deaths are influenced by shortcomings in healthcare systems (McGinnis et al., 2002).[20] Forty percent of premature deaths are influenced by behavioral patterns such as physical activity, smoking, and diet. Behavioral interventions have a significant potential to influence health outcomes. Yet, more resources are provided within healthcare systems, while little attention has been historically paid to these contributory behavioral determinants of health. Redesign efforts will have to pay attention to these lifestyle behaviors.

In the last decade, one signal that has shown promising results is collaborative or integrated mental healthcare for patients with depression and chronic health conditions such as diabetes, coronary heart disease, or both (Ivbijaro et al., 2014).[21] Care improved not only the outcomes of depression but also those of chronic diseases. This kind of care was also found to be cost-effective (Huang et al., 2013).[22] There have been numerous trials of collaborative care that have demonstrated it to be not just cost-effective but also clinically effective (Unützer et al., 2013).[23]

V. Current State: Access to Care (And Its Impact on Society)

VIGNETTE 1.9

Mateo had been diagnosed with bipolar disorder and alcohol use disorder. He started to drink heavily six months earlier and had become hypomanic and irritable. He was referred by his Employee Assistance Program to an addiction clinic to address his alcohol use issues. During his intake appointment, he was sarcastic, restless, and spoke rapidly. He was told that he could not be admitted to their intensive outpatient program until he was psychiatrically stable. After a considerable amount of delay, he found his way to a community mental health center walk-in clinic. When he arrived at his triage appointment, the evaluating social worker smelled alcohol on his breath. She told him that he could not be admitted to their clinic until his addiction was under control. He felt frustrated, confused, and ended up in the emergency room (ER) that night after being arrested for a DUI.

Millions of patients with mental illnesses receive psychiatric treatment every year. However, there are millions more who cannot access care when they want it. Access to care is one of the commonly occurring systemic problems encountered within the mental healthcare system (Mental Health America, 2019).[24]

Mental Health America released a report titled 'The State of the Mental Health Report in America 2019,' which ranked all US states and the District of Columbia based on several mental health and access measures. The findings reported 56.4% of Americans did not receive any treatment for their mental health condition. Even in Massachusetts, which is reportedly the state with the best access to mental healthcare, 48.6% of people with a mental illness did not receive any treatment. Rates of major depressive episodes in youth increased from 11.93% to 12.63%. According to the report, 62% of youth with a major depressive episode received insufficient or no treatment (Mental Health America, 2019).[24] A survey of more than a thousand psychiatrists in 2016 found that in the last 30 days, 30% or more reported that they could neither provide nor find a source for psychotherapy, substance abuse treatment, case management, or assertive community treatment (ACT) for their patients. ACT is an evidence-based practice known to improve outcomes for people with severe mental illness who are most vulnerable to various adverse consequences such as homelessness, hospitalizations, or incarcerations (West, 2016).[25]

Losing this crucial 'window of opportunity,' lack of access could be harmful as it might contribute to an unsafe crisis if the presenting problem was not promptly addressed. It could also have a deleterious effect on the trust of the involved person or family in the mental healthcare system. Care should be available when needed, where needed, and at the appropriate level of intensity that a person is willing to commit. There should be no 'wrong door' for a patient to access care (Whitten, 2004).[26]

A historical perspective on the contributory factors to inadequate access is informative; in 1955, there were 558,239 public (state and county) psychiatric beds available for patients with mental illness or 340 public psychiatric beds per a population of 100,000. In 2005, the number had shrunk to 52,539 public (state and county) psychiatric beds available or 17 beds per population of 100,000 (Torrey et al., 2015).[27] In a 2016 update, Torrey wrote that there were 35,000 state hospital beds or 11 per a population of 100,000. According to another report by the Substance Abuse and Mental Health Services Administration (SAMHSA), the number of 24-hour hospitals and residential treatment beds had reduced across all organizations (state, county, private, and the VA).

The de-institutionalization movement's overall idea was to treat the severely mentally ill in the least restrictive setting possible. In 1955, the Mental Health Study Act authorized the National Institute for Mental Health to establish the Joint Commission on Mental illness and Mental Health. The commission issued a report in 1961, which received attention from Congress and became the basis for the Community Mental Health Act (CMHA) of 1963. The CMHA outlined a new mental health program to reduce the number of patients under custodial care by 50% or more. Central to this new program was a vision for developing comprehensive community mental healthcare. Multiple social forces were at play here. The availability and usage of new psychiatric medications made it possible for psychiatrists to treat many patients with severe mental illnesses at lower levels of care. The development of federal social welfare programs such as Medicaid and Medicare created incentives for the care of the mentally ill to be shifted to alternative settings. These changes helped to reshape societal perceptions and views of mental illness. With growing awareness of the problems and abuses associated with ongoing institutionalized care, institutions were challenged on political, legal, and financial grounds. The net reductions in state hospital inpatient beds were much more significant than initially envisioned (Harcourt BE).[28]

The Medical Health Systems Act of 1980 expanded the idea of providing care in the least restrictive setting. This idea was based on 'the objective of maintaining the greatest degree of freedom, self-determination, autonomy, dignity, and integrity of body, mind, and spirit for the individual while he or she participates in treatment or receives services.' Unfortunately, this lofty goal has never been fully realized.

Despite this vision, there are no clear standards for how many psychiatric hospital beds are needed for those who still require more intensive levels of care. A panel of 15 experts recommended that even if there was good outpatient treatment available, along with the availability of outpatient commitment, that there would be 40–60 public psychiatric beds per 100,000 population needed for the care of the seriously mentally ill (Torrey et al., 2015).[27] Outpatient commitment or assisted outpatient treatment (AOT) is court-ordered treatment, including medication for individuals who have a history of medication noncompliance and dangerousness as a condition of their remaining in the community (Ezez, 2017).[29] Sometimes, bed capacity does not equal availability for admitting acutely ill patients because many of those beds are occupied by court-ordered forensic patients and sexual predators (Torrey, 2016).[30] According to a study in the United States where a discrete-event simulation model was built to simulate adult non-forensic patients' flow through the hospital, current bed capacity would have to be increased by 165% for the wait time for patients in the ER to be reduced from an average of 3.3 days to below 24 hours (La et al., 2016).[31]

Hospital beds may not be the only solution at a higher intensity of care. As stated earlier in this section, ACT has been very well studied over the years. The patient-to-staff ratio is low (10:1), and the patient is offered frequent visits in the community with assertive outreach and around-the-clock availability. Patients are supported through most crises without hospitalization, and care is attempted in the least restrictive environment. Patients served by ACT teams have fewer re-hospitalizations, spend less time in jails (Torrey, 2014), and less time homeless (Lehman et al., 1999).[32,33] They also increase continuity of care, patients' vocational success, and patient and family satisfaction. Despite promising evidence, these services are not readily available.

Similarly, involuntary treatments in the form of AOT or conditional release are very useful in maintaining seriously mentally ill individuals on medication. This treatment is designed and intended to prevent further deterioration and to avoid self-harm or harm to others. Conditional release is a method of release from involuntary hospitalization as part of an aftercare plan and reduces the duration of a hospital stay. It requires the patient to participate in outpatient care instead of an extended hospital stay. These interventions can considerably reduce re-hospitalizations, homelessness, victimization, violent behavior, and incarcerations. Forty-six states and the District of Columbia allow AOT, yet the current laws have historically been underutilized and underfunded (Ezez, 2019).[34]

Another cited shortage is that of psychiatrists in the United States. An article from 2010 had the following headline '45,000 More Psychiatrists, Anyone?' (Carlat, 2010).[35] According to this article, the estimated need in the United States is about 25.9 psychiatrists per 100,000 population. At the time of the study, there were roughly 10 per 100,000 practicing full-time psychiatrists in the United States. A healthier ratio is about 15 additional psychiatrists per 100,000 individuals to make up the difference in the number of psychiatrists needed to take care of a population of around 300 million individuals (Konrad et al., 2009).[36] These assumptions were based on patients needing outpatient psychiatry with an average of 20 minutes dedicated to 'psychopharmacology-oriented' visits per month. The assumptions also excluded patients with schizophrenia, addiction, ADHD, oppositional defiant disorder, conduct disorder, and dysthymia, among others in the study.

Moreover, the study did not consider the need for higher intensity services, which provides a highly conservative projection given our current care models. If one were to consider the need for sub-specialists like geriatric, pediatric, or addiction psychiatrists, the shortage is also quite significant (Kirwin et al., 2013; Manderscheid et al., 2007).[37,38] However, it is unclear if the system has created artificial bottlenecks on clinicians providing care, thus exacerbating the access problem.

Another concerning statistic is that 55% of psychiatrists are 55 or older, and recently only approximately 4% of US medical school graduates have been applying for residency training in psychiatry (Weil, 2015).[39] If psychiatrists are not replaced at the rate at which older psychiatrists retire, this will further compound the access problem.

Several systemic problems arise due to inadequate access to care, including ER boarding, homelessness, and incarceration.

A. Boarding in the Emergency Room

> ### VIGNETTE 1.10
> Eighteen-year-old Jordan suffered from severe autism spectrum disorder and was currently residing in a group home. His mother Keysha was getting calls from the staff about him, stating that he had become unstable and violent at his group home. Jordan would disrobe himself at times or try to grab female staff during other times. He had not been sleeping at night and kept pacing. The clinical team decided that he should be sent to the ER. After reaching the ER, he boarded there for more than five days because his family was told that there were no appropriate inpatient psychiatric beds available for him.
>
> This ER experienced a massive influx of patients who suffered from severe mental illnesses. The ER was often at capacity but couldn't find appropriate inpatient placements for these unstable patients. Many family members became frustrated and complained. The ER was placed on bypass status multiple times in the last year, which turned away patients in crisis and asked ambulances to take patients to other ERs. The ER staff also didn't feel adequately prepared to deal with psychiatric issues, especially physical aggression.

An unintended consequence of access problems is the phenomenon of *boarding* in the ER. Boarding is the practice of keeping admitted patients on stretchers in hospital ERs for more than a few hours because there are no inpatient beds available. Nine of ten ERs report this problem lamenting that they are operating at or above capacity (McHugh et al., 2011).[40] As patients wait in the ER for an appropriate psychiatric bed, they have to contend with sub-optimal care where the focus is just on crisis stabilization rather than adequately addressing deeper issues that maintain the patient's high-risk status. They become trapped in this bottleneck, which causes overcrowding problems in the ER leading to delays in care, patient neglect, increased errors, risk of aggression, recidivism, and less optimal outcomes. ERs can be busy, noisy, and cramped, making it even more challenging for already agitated patients and distressed caregivers. Reports indicate there is a greater likelihood of deaths related to ER overcrowding (Sun, 2010).[41] This kind of boarding may also make it hard for non-psychiatric patients to access emergency care as ERs may have a limit to the total number of patients they can accommodate. According to a 2011 report by the Agency for Healthcare Research and Quality (AHRQ), 500,000 ambulances are diverted each year from the closest hospital because they are at capacity (McHugh et al., 2011).[40]

ER boarding becomes even more pronounced when one considers patients who require specialized care. It is more challenging to find appropriate care for populations with complex needs such as patients in the pediatric and geriatric age groups, patients with intellectual disabilities, trauma, aggressive behaviors, eating disorders, or addiction. Many patients have disorders that are hard to treat with quick medication checks alone. Such disorders need intensive psychotherapy, and there is a considerable evidence base in support of these psychotherapeutic services. There are sound economic arguments for these treatments. Still, evidence-based specialized psychotherapeutic services such as cognitive behavior therapy (CBT) and comprehensive dialectical behavior therapy (DBT) are hard to find and access. Even if one finds the correct therapy, limits within a patient's insurance coverage might restrict access to these practitioners. Practitioners usually take whatever modalities they know about and try to apply them to existing cases, whether or not the therapy is the right fit or whether the offering optimally utilizes existing resources. The larger issue is the supply of practitioners does not match the unique demands of persons in the population.

The problem of boarding in the ER has been described as 'a canary in the coal mine.' It is an obvious symptom of a system that is neither fully capable of identifying nor consistently resolving mental health problems at a lower intensity of care. It is also an overstretched system for those needing a higher intensity of care. The system cannot accommodate all their needs for such patients once they have become sicker or destabilized (Swartz, 2016).[42] However, some patients will remain chronically in need of higher levels of care, and if adequate hospital beds are not available, then the ERs will remain bottlenecks.

B. Homelessness

VIGNETTE 1.11

On his daily walk to work, Vincenzo saw a few homeless individuals lying on the sidewalks and under a nearby bridge. He wondered how they could manage to find food, stay warm and safe during the winter conditions. One day he saw a homeless woman who was talking to herself loudly. She was communicating in unintelligible phrases and yelling at cars that were passing by. She was often seen carrying all her belongings in a little cart and had also been seen collecting leftover food from trash cans.

Over the last six decades, as psychiatric hospital bed availability and access have decreased, homelessness has increased, and so have crimes and arrests associated with homelessness (Markovitz, 2006).[43] It has been estimated that about one-third of the homeless population has a SMI, 74–87% of homeless people are prone to be victimized (Treatment Advocacy Center, 2016), and 63–90% of homeless individuals have a lifetime risk of being arrested (Roy, 2014).[44,45] Previously, hospitalized individuals with mental illness are almost three times as likely to eat out of a garbage can and much more likely to treat the garbage can as their primary source of food (Gelberg, 1988).[46]

C. Mental Illness in Jails

VIGNETTE 1.12

The police picked up Brenda on theft charges, and she was currently locked up in the detention center. On day one, security guards had to intervene in a fight between her and other inmates. She felt that her cellmates were trying to harm her. She reported that her cellmates were trying to control her mind by moving their hands, and she even felt 'pressure in her organs' every time they came close to her. She also thought they were sending signals to her brain, which was giving her bad headaches. On day two, she was lying on the floor, curled up in distress due to severe abdominal cramps and diarrhea. She was feeling very uncomfortable and had thoughts of killing herself. It was ultimately found out that the patient had an opioid use disorder and was going through methadone withdrawal.

Another related consequence of the access issue is the number of mentally ill individuals who become incarcerated. According to a report by the Treatment Advocacy Center, there are more than three times more seriously mentally ill persons in jails and prisons than in hospitals. In some states like Arizona and Nevada, the rate is nearly ten times more. About 16% of those individuals in jails and prisons are thought to have a SMI. The number of mentally ill inmates has been rising over the last few decades to nearly equal the number of individuals with mental illness who were similarly incarcerated in the mid-nineteenth century. This phenomenon had moved Dorothea Dix, an advocate for the mentally ill, to call for the reform of the treatment of the mentally ill and to render more humane treatment (Torrey et al., 2010).[47] Even though incarceration's exact impact on mental health in the population is uncertain, there is considerable evidence of low rates of identification and treatment of psychiatric conditions in the incarcerated population. Incarcerated individuals are also at high risk of victimization, violence, self-harm, suicide, and all-cause mortality (Fazel et al., 2016).[48] A British psychiatrist and mathematician, Lionel Penrose, postulated an inverse relationship between the number of mentally ill individuals in hospitals and those in prisons (Penrose, 1938).[49] In recent decades, solutions such as reforming the treatment laws, creating better incentives for ongoing treatment rather than incarceration, improving payment models, and structural changes such as mental health courts have been suggested.

When following a patient's path in need of mental healthcare, if mental health appointments can't be easily accessed, bottlenecks are created, resulting in overcrowded ERs, homelessness, and incarcerations. There is a need to rethink the adequacy and allocation of resources, how our system is designed, and empathize with patients and families who require help. The imperative is to innovate, increase availability to care, and ensure the added stress patients and families feel during difficult times does not reinforce adverse health outcomes.

VI. Current State: Safety

VIGNETTE 1.13

Cassandra was admitted to an inpatient unit for the treatment of alcohol withdrawal. She had a history of severe withdrawal and delirium during her last detoxification attempt. She informed the admitting nurse that she was also on methadone for opioid use disorder, and she took 90 mg of methadone. The nurse saw the dose in the paperwork that came with the patient from the ER. Cassandra's physician prescribed 90 mg of methadone and 50 mg of chlordiazepoxide four times a day for alcohol withdrawal symptoms. During rounds at 4 AM, Cassandra was experiencing slow breathing and appeared cyanotic. She was immediately sent to the ER and had a full recovery. When investigating the root cause, it was discovered that the methadone dose was not confirmed with the methadone clinic. She had been put on a fast taper of methadone by the clinic because she was seen using illicit drugs outside the clinic. She was on 90 mg before the methadone taper was initiated. The last dose administered to her at the clinic was 30 mg. She received three times as much methadone as compared to what she was supposed to receive. She did not disclose this to the ER or the admitting nurse.

The Institute of Medicine (IOM, 2000) published its report 'To Err is Human: Building a Safer Health System.'[50] The report articulated that an alarming number of deaths (as many as 98,000) attributable to preventable medical errors were occurring in hospitals every year. Subsequent studies have indicated that even this may be a gross underestimation (Leape, 2005).[51]

A recent analysis in 2016 indicated that medical error might be the third leading cause of death in the United States (Makary et al., 2016).[52] In a study conducted in a state psychiatric hospital, a review of 31 patient records for prescription, transcription, and administration errors for 1,448 patient-days discovered a total of 2,194 medication errors. Nineteen percent of the errors were judged to carry a low risk, 23% were considered to have a moderate risk, and 58% were regarded as high risk (Grasso et al., 2003).[53] Preventable errors might be leading to 210,000–400,000 deaths a year (James, 2013).[54]

One of the proposed reasons for the gap between the ideal and the current state of safety is the mental health system's complexity. There is a great deal of ambiguity in how providers should perform their work and how many providers' work should be synchronized systematically. When providers are faced with ambiguities or challenges, they tend to work around these challenges rather than resolving the cause of these issues. Increased use of workarounds leads to treatment ambiguities, which can deteriorate the care system and cause a greater number of vulnerabilities. Occasionally, these vulnerabilities coalesce and lead to disastrous consequences (Spear, 2005).[55] The 'Swiss cheese' model of system failure illustrates this concept visually. Each process goes through many steps. Each step or layer is like a slice of cheese, and the holes are the vulnerabilities in each layer. An organization has multiple defensive layers or redundancies which prevent errors from reaching the patient, even if errors pass through a hole or two. Holes or vulnerabilities can appear anew, or existing holes can often change in size or change their place, leading the holes to align. Sometimes, when the holes in each of the defensive layers align, accidents or harm to the patient can occur. At other times, there could be near misses when the defensive layers have stopped the error from reaching the patient. Studying and eliminating these holes alerted by near-misses can strengthen an organization over time.(Reason, 2000).[56] See an illustration of this in Figure 1.1.

Another safety concern in psychiatric settings is aggression. Scarce inpatient hospital beds, shortened lengths of stay, and Emergency Medical Treatment and Labor Act (EMTALA) obligations (according to which inpatient psychiatric units cannot deny care to aggressive patients if they have the capacity or capability to treat such patients) are leading to admissions of a significant number of high-risk patients. These patients can be very aggressive or destructive when they are unstable psychiatrically. There are reports of property destruction and violence toward mental health professionals leading to lower staff morale and injuries, which can become as extreme as a homicide. Reducing and minimizing the prevalence and impact of such aggression is imperative. Both mechanical and chemical restraints have been used to deal with very aggressive patients. When used judiciously, these interventions can prevent harm. But there are also efforts to reduce seclusion and restraint interventions because they carry the potential of physical and psychological

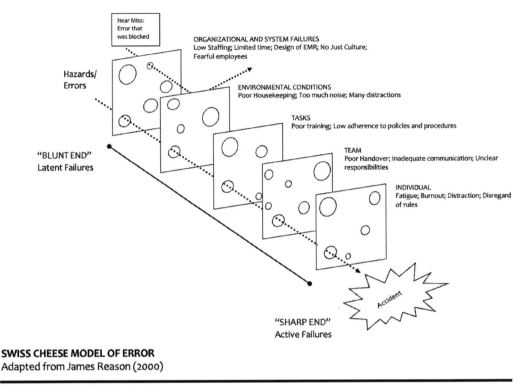

Figure 1.1 The Swiss cheese model of error. (Adapted from Reason, 2000.)

harm to both patients and staff. Seclusion and restraint practices provide little therapeutic benefit to the patients; some commentators even describe them as evidence of treatment failure.

In addition to injuries from aggressive patients toward other patients and staff, there are several other safety problems in psychiatric hospital settings. Falls, delirium, complications from medications (Neuroleptic Malignant Syndrome, Serotonin Syndrome, and severe dystonia), inpatient suicides, and elopement are safety concerns in need of attention.

On a positive note, the spotlight on patient safety has acted as a catalyst to mobilize a broad conversation around not just errors or defects but patient safety as an essential attribute of providing care in a system. The conversation has rightly begun to move from blaming deficient individuals to understanding and improving flawed systems. The system needs to be designed to make it easier to do the right thing and more challenging to do the wrong thing (IOM, 2000).[50] Additionally, experts recommend applying safety science or improvement science methods to achieve a reliable healthcare delivery system. Systems are ultimately responsible for minimizing the incidence and impact of and maximizing recovery from adverse events (Emanuel L et al., 2008).[57] Patients must not be harmed while receiving care.

VII. Current State: Quality

Since the 1990s, evidence has accumulated that the overall American healthcare system is flawed and has significant quality problems. The RAND Corporation found that Americans, irrespective of race, ethnicity, or socioeconomic status, were getting the right care only half the time (Kenney, 2010).[58]

In 1998, the Institute of Medicine of the National Academies convened a committee on the Quality of Health Care in America. The committee intended to produce a series of reports that would identify strategies for improving the quality of America's healthcare system. This committee defined quality as a threefold problem: underuse, overuse, and misuse.

A. Underuse

VIGNETTE 1.14

Forty-two-year-old Adam started having problems with alcohol use in his twenties. He had been seeking treatment for alcohol-related problems in his thirties. Adam had attempted detoxification five times and completed stays at three inpatient rehabilitation centers. His routine was to attend AA groups regularly at a nearby church where he had a sponsor. He had always been shy as a child and avoided social situations as a teenager. As an adult, it was hard for him to talk to others, especially women, as he would get anxious around them. Socializing became more manageable after he had a couple of beers. His wife had left him, and recently when he was let go of his job, he became suicidal and was hospitalized at a nearby community hospital. For the first time, he was diagnosed with a social anxiety disorder and offered medication for this condition. A psychiatric resident-in-training informed Adam about the FDA (Food and Drug Administration) approved medications for the treatment of Alcohol Use Disorder – Disulfiram, Naltrexone, and Acamprosate. The resident added that these could reduce the risk of relapses, and some could even help him with his constant cravings. After visiting several different treatment settings over 20 years, he wondered why no professional had ever mentioned these medication treatments before.

It has been reported that mental health clinicians use less evidence-based practices as compared to non-evidence-based practices. In a landmark study published in 2003, analyzing 439 quality indicators for 30 acute and chronic conditions, it was discovered that only 57.7% of patients suffering from depression received the recommended care, whereas, for the group of patients struggling with alcohol dependence, only 10.5% of patients received the recommended care (McGlynn et al., 2003).[59] According to a paper published in 2009, fewer than half of the patients with schizophrenia received treatment that adhered to the guidelines. The adherence to guidelines was worse in the outpatient sector than in the inpatient sector and for psychosocial treatments compared to psychopharmacological treatments (Mojtabai et al., 2009).[60] Another study that looked at conformance to guidelines for pharmacological treatment of schizophrenia and monitoring of antipsychotic side effects found that community mental health center treatment practices were largely conformant to pharmacological treatment guideline recommendations but not as conformant to monitoring for antipsychotic side effects. The exception to the rule was clozapine for residual positive symptoms, which in this study was found to be used only 31% of the time (Keller et al., 2014).[61] A study examining the use of clozapine reported that of the 30% of patients with treatment-resistant schizophrenia, only 5% were prescribed clozapine. This lower usage is despite the superior efficacy of clozapine and the fact that all treatment guidelines recommend clozapine after inadequate response to at least two antipsychotics. The monitoring of side effects occurred in the range of 11–53%, depending on the side effect being monitored. In another study, only 19% of those with SMI and a substance use disorder were treated for both conditions (New Freedom Commission on Mental Health, 2003).[4]

B. Overuse

VIGNETTE 1.15

Nin worked as a clinical pharmacist in a specialized geriatric setting and monitored patients' medication regimens in a skilled nursing facility. She observed that at least a third of the patients are admitted on more than nine different medications (The US Center of Medicare and Medicaid Services had defined a quality measure that targeted patients on more than nine medications). Most patients were often on more than four medications for psychiatric indications. She was also concerned about the patients being started on antipsychotics for the management of non-specific agitation. She found that the antipsychotics ordered for agitation during inpatient stay were often continued as discharge prescriptions. She was worried about the potential negative consequences of the long-term use of antipsychotics on these already vulnerable patients. She worked with the treatment team to help them de-prescribe medications that were unnecessary or even harmful.

Overuse is defined as a healthcare service provided under circumstances in which its potential for harm exceeds the possible benefit. An example of overuse is prescribing an antibiotic for a viral infection like a cold, for which antibiotics are ineffective. Another example of overuse is the excessive use of antipsychotics in nursing home patients. Antipsychotics are often used to treat behavioral and psychological symptoms in dementia (BPSD). No antipsychotic is approved by the FDA for this purpose. There is approximately a 1.5 times greater risk of mortality with their use in dementia. This category of medications carries a black box safety warning about this risk from the FDA. Patients who take newer antipsychotics are two to three times more likely to suffer cardiovascular events. The American Geriatric Society recommends avoiding this group of medications until non-pharmacological options have failed and the patient is a safety risk to themselves or others.

In some nursing homes, nearly 50% of the residents were prescribed antipsychotics. In 1987, Congress called for greater oversight of antipsychotic use in nursing homes bypassing regulations to address such overuse of the Omnibus Budget Reconciliation Act of 1987 (OBRA-87). It put forth approved indications for the use of antipsychotics in this population. Following the passage of this regulation, the use of typical antipsychotics declined. With the introduction of atypical antipsychotics, the use in this population went up. In 2011, the Inspector General for the Department of Health and Human Services asserted that nursing homes should be held accountable because many residents were receiving antipsychotics in violation of federal standards. By 2016, the national prevalence of antipsychotic use in long-stay nursing home residents without psychosis had declined from 24% to 16% in this population (Introcaso, 2018).[62]

More recently, there has been an increased off-label use of ketamine to treat depression in ERs and private clinics much ahead of the presented or published evidence. Experts have recommended a more 'rational and guarded' response given the level of evidence and limited knowledge about long-term efficacy and risk (Schatzberg, 2014).[63]

Looking at the use of Electroconvulsive therapy (ECT), a study in 1995 reviewed variation in ECT use. There was evidence of both underuse and overuse. This study looked at variation in ECT use in 317 metropolitans' statistical areas in the United States (Hermann et al., 1995).[64] The report showed no use reported in 115 metropolitan statistical areas, whereas, in the remaining 202 areas, annual ECT use varied from 0.4 to 81.2 patients per 10,000 population. The variation was considered higher than for most medical and surgical procedures. It was unclear whether this represented underuse in some areas or overuse in some areas. The extent of variation suggested a lack of consensus regarding the use of ECT. An essential variable in the availability of ECT was whether the psychiatrist had a favorable attitude about ECT (Latey & Fahy, 1988).[65]

C. Misuse

VIGNETTE 1.16

Colleen worked as an administrator and was recently promoted to oversee compliance. On reviewing reports for physician billing, she noticed that a few physicians had been chronically out of compliance with their percentage of correct billing codes. The institution had set a standard over the last year of more than 90% coding accuracy for physicians. Five physicians had struggled to meet this standard, and two had chronically been under 60% accuracy rate for the last two years. She also heard from her coding compliance auditor that one physician, in particular, was rude to her when an auditor pointed such deficiencies to him. She called for an urgent meeting with this particular physician and the medical director because she was concerned that this was an area of vulnerability for the hospital. She also set up an in-service meeting for all the psychiatrists to re-orient them on the importance of following proper coding guidelines.

In 2012, it was believed that $272 billion was being lost to fraud (The Economist, 2014).[66] These occurrences increased the burdens of documentation, auditing, and reporting for everyone in the system. There was a high degree of fraud in some parts of the mental health system (Kusserow, 2014).[67] Falsifying records, false billing, improper coding, and providing unnecessary services are examples of such nefarious practices. In 1998, the Health Care Financing Administration (HCFA) terminated 80 Community Mental Health Centers (CMHCs) from the Medicare Partial Hospitalization program to curtail fraud, error, and abuse. In 2011, four CMHC's owners in Miami-Dade County, Florida, were convicted for fraudulently billing Medicare about $200 million for medically unnecessary Partial Hospitalization Services. The Recovery Audit Contractor (RAC) program was started under the Medicare Modernization Act of 2003 (MMA). At the end of a RAC demonstration project in a few states, the program had recovered close to $700 million on behalf of Centers for Medicare and Medicaid Services (CMS).

Another example of misuse is ordering unnecessary tests. According to the Department of Justice, a laboratory in San Diego agreed to pay the federal government $256 million to resolve claims of unnecessary urine drug and genetic testing (Morse, 2015).[68]

Such misguided activities lead to an increased emphasis on catching bad actors – an increased investment in compliance and audit divisions in organizations to catch nefarious practices. This added emphasis on compliance can lead to increased attention paid to optimizing and providing the correct amount of documentation as a conscientious practitioner does not want to be accused of fraud or abuse. Doctors and compliance staff are now focused on discussions about up-coding and down-coding (inaccurate assignment of billing codes that increase or decrease reimbursement). While these practices are important for accuracy and integrity, they also impact the amount of time, energy, attention, and resources that go into patient care or other aspects of quality improvement. Unfortunately, a considerable proportion of efforts to improve quality are focused on reduced fraud and misuse (Chassin, 1998).[69] It would serve the public better to focus efforts on reducing overuse and underuse. Doing so will increase the availability of resources and access to care.

Most consumers would not accept the low quality of food in a restaurant, a dirty room in a hotel, or substandard services from a bank or a retailer. How can patients accept low quality from the mental healthcare system? Healthcare providers have the responsibility of ensuring that the quality of our services matches our treatment ideals.

VIII. Current State: Delivery of Care (Fragmentation of Care)

VIGNETTE 1.17

Bonita suffered from Bipolar disorder and Fibromyalgia. She went to a walk-in clinic because she was seeking admission to a partial hospitalization program. She reported that she felt unstable because she had been fighting with her spouse. The psychiatrist diagnosed her as being in an unstable, manic state. When asked if she saw any outpatient providers, she said that she saw multiple providers regularly. She was under the care of a primary care provider and an OB-GYN physician whom she had seen for a couple of years. During the prior year, when she was admitted to the partial hospitalization program, she was referred to a community mental health clinic. At this clinic, she had to see a therapist first before she could see a psychiatrist. Her primary care doctor had also referred her to a pain clinic where she saw a nurse practitioner and a physical therapist. When asked if having so many providers ever caused a problem, she said they were all in different locations. Their electronic medical record (EMR) systems did not communicate with each other. She had to ensure that all her doctors had an updated medication list. Bonita was afraid that she might be prescribed a medication by a provider that might interact with another medication that she was already receiving if she did not give them an updated list. Once in the past, she was prescribed carbamazepine by her psychiatrist, which made her oral contraceptive less effective. She ended up becoming pregnant. Her psychiatrist had not asked her about her contraceptive practices then and did not know that she was on hormonal contraceptive pills.

It is not uncommon for a patient to see more than one provider to care for their complex comorbid conditions. Patients are often referred to a psychiatrist and also a non-physician therapist. The psychiatrist completes an initial assessment, develops an initial treatment plan, and typically manages the patient's medications. The therapist frequently completes their initial evaluation and adds to the treatment plan based on their expertise. The therapist also typically provides psychotherapy, teaches coping skills, and makes referrals to community resources. This range of providers quickly grows in size if a patient also suffers from addictions, a complex set of chronic medical conditions, or a severe psychiatric illness course with relapses and remissions. These exacerbations may then take them to other settings or a higher level of care within the continuum of care. They could be referred to the ER, an inpatient program, partial hospitalization program, or a psychosocial rehabilitation program where they may see yet another set of providers. The potential for variation and error increases proportionately depending on the number of handoffs between providers and care settings. In a complex system of care, which spans over long periods and where there are multiple providers, the system has to ensure that care is delivered with higher reliability and quality at every stage of treatment. The errors and variations at every stage can adversely impact the net outcomes for patients.

Often, information is not relayed from one setting to another. Providers in different locations do not communicate with each other about the care of the patient, or the care plan in the acute setting changes sometimes without eliciting the knowledge of a provider who may know the patient well (what has worked well, what hasn't, the patient's values and preferences). The EMR of one setting may differ from another, which makes coordination or communication harder and creates an additional burden of redundancy in collecting patient vital information and history.

Even if they were linked together, there is no guarantee that a new provider will read the patient's entire history before beginning treatment. The existing payment model does not adequately reimburse clinician time when there is a need to work collaboratively on complex patient cases across the care continuum.

Sometimes outpatient providers, to their consternation, find out serendipitously that a patient they had been taking care of for months or years had been hospitalized. During this hospitalization, the patient's diagnosis, care plan, and medications may have changed entirely without any of their knowledge or input. At times, they learn something new about the patient, but they are sometimes disappointed when their patient is misdiagnosed based on incomplete information.

The growth of specialists and the narrowing of scope for certain practitioners have made this problem worse. For instance, it is not that psychiatrists cannot manage both medications and provide psychotherapy (only a few psychiatric practitioners still do this). The reimbursement or payment model discourages this and encourages fragmentation of care. Sometimes, many psychiatrists choose not to deal with addiction or the effects of severe trauma. When this happens, there could be an increase in the number of practitioners a patient has to see.

The journey through this discontiguous maze is often disorienting, stressful, and unsafe for the patients. The arduous task of coordinating care and understanding medical information and care planning complexities is left to cognitively or emotionally challenged patients. Sometimes, information or treatments offered in different settings are in disagreement or adversely interact with each other.

Three types of continuity would be beneficial and desirable in all treatment settings: (a) informational – knowledge about the patient's condition as well as the patients' preferences and values, which should follow the patient as they go from one provider to another, (b) management – if a patient sees multiple providers over a long period, services should be offered in a timely and complementary manner and the care delivered should provide predictability, consistency, security, and flexibility to patients, and (c) relational – a consistent core of staff provides the patient a sense of what to expect and overall coherence to their care (Haggerty et al., 2003).[70]

Failures in care coordination can lead to hospital readmissions, complications, declines in functioning, and poorer outcomes, including homelessness, suicide, or the possibility of violence, especially for the chronically mentally ill.

Readmissions for those with chronic psychiatric illness and those who have already had two or more prior hospitalizations can occur in 40–50% of patients within 12 months (Gaynes et al., 2015).[71] Mood disorders, schizophrenia, other psychotic disorders, and alcohol and substance use disorders were four of the top 10 conditions associated with these readmissions. The one-year cost to Medicaid alone in 2011 totaled $832 million (Pincus, 2014).[72] Twenty percent of US Medicare beneficiaries were re-hospitalized within 30 days of discharge, which had an annual cost of $17.4 billion (Jencks, 2009).[73] Psychiatric disorders accounted for the highest number of all-cause, 30-day readmissions for Medicaid patients 18–64 years of age in those discharged from hospital-based psychiatric units (Hines et al., 2014).[74]

The transition from inpatient to community settings is a particularly vulnerable period for psychiatric patients. Due to the fragmentation and resulting complexity of the current system, care is carried out by multiple providers, involves numerous steps, and requires coordination between multiple siloed organizations. A patient is left to navigate this complex maze on their own. This complexity makes the process too overwhelming for the psychiatric patient to coordinate without assistance. Further, it makes them vulnerable and highly dependent on care coordination for optimal post-discharge outcomes.

There are other kinds of issues related to the delivery of care. It is believed that the lack of adopting known best care processes is a significant contributor to waste in the US healthcare system, and it is estimated that this led to between $102 and $154 billion in wasteful spending in 2011 (Berwick & Hackbarth, 2012).[75]

IX. Current State: Cost/Waste

VIGNETTE 1.18

Carter had been taking an antidepressant for the last ten years. His wife's insurance plan covered him. Her company changed the insurance options during the open enrollment period, where his antidepressant was not a preferred medication on his new insurance policy and required prior authorization. He called his psychiatrist's office, who had to call his insurance company. After 30 minutes on the phone, the psychiatrist was still unsuccessful in obtaining authorization for the antidepressant. Carter was informed that the request would be sent to the 'exceptions department.' The patient called the psychiatrist three days later and had still not heard anything about his prescription. When the psychiatrist called the insurance company representative again, they informed him that they had no record of his last call and offered to fax a form to him. He was also told that the processing of this form could take up to three business days. Carter, in the meantime, ran out of his antidepressant and experienced withdrawal symptoms. He was given the option by the pharmacy of paying cash for the medication until the authorization process could be sorted out.

Currently, the US healthcare system is the most expensive globally (Squires et al., 2015) and yet underperforms compared to other developed nations on many dimensions of performance, such as access, efficiency, and equity (Davis et al., 2014).[76,77] A study published in 2010 claimed that more than half the healthcare spending was wasteful (Fred, 2016).[78] In December 2016, it was reported that the United States spent $3.2 trillion on healthcare or an average of $10,000 per person (Pear, 2016).[79] In 2011, US healthcare costs were 18% of the gross domestic product. Our healthcare costs are exceedingly steep compared to every other developed nation and are making our country uncompetitive in the global marketplace. Excess cost in healthcare leads to reduced benefits and reduced resources available for other worthy programs. The United States spends 50% more than the next highest nation (France) and almost twice what the United Kingdom spends (Squires et al., 2015).[76] We would conservatively save approximately $558 billion a year in the United States. if we were to rein in costs from six large categories of waste (overtreatment, failures of care coordination, failures in the execution of care processes, administrative complexity, pricing failures, and fraud and abuse). This amount is slightly more than 20% of the total healthcare expenditures (Berwick & Hackbarth, 2012).[75] To achieve this goal, it would require a systematic, wide-reaching, and cooperative effort from many stakeholders. Rather than making drastic cuts to benefits and services offered to vulnerable individuals or even placing more bureaucratic hurdles on an already stretched workforce, improvement science could help meet this challenge.

A paper by the RAND Corporation proposed a conceptual framework that delineates three types of waste – administrative, operational, and clinical. Administrative waste is partly due to the administrative overhead, which is a net result of the US insurance and payer systems' complexity. Dealing with multiple payers is an administrative nightmare – they all have different forms, procedures, and expectations for similar tasks. There is no apparent reason for these differences among payers, and it takes up valuable time and resources to understand and then deal with these varied processes. Operational waste is due to shortcomings in the efficiency of healthcare processes, which can add to costs and signal quality problems. Clinical waste occurs due to treatments or interventions offered that are of questionable benefit (Bentley et al., 2008).[80]

Given that our overall healthcare costs are already very high, requests for more resources have not been met with the enthusiastic provision of more resources to free up these bottlenecks. As resources have been cut, the healthcare system has also been burdened with tasks, activities, and interventions of questionable or little value (Erickson et al., 2017).[81] Evidence-based or imminently needed interventions cannot be paid for as there is a perceived shortage of financial resources. Also, it could be that the allocation or deployment of resources does not match or is not proportional to the needs of the situation.

X. Current State: Morale/Workforce Challenges

VIGNETTE 1.19

Susanne had worked hard to get through medical school and into a psychiatric residency training program. As a first-year resident-in-training, she worked long hours, went home feeling tired, and was always hard on herself. She kept up on all the assigned readings but felt overwhelmed by all the information she had to assimilate. Overnight calls were very stressful for her, and she felt underprepared to deal with all the complex and unpredictable scenarios.

> Sometimes Susanne was the only psychiatrist on the scene, and often she was asked all sorts of thorny questions. At other times, she felt she was just an underpaid worker and was not satisfied with the amount and quality of supervision she received. She was drinking a couple of beers each night to relax and to go to sleep. Last week, when she was tired and feeling sleep-deprived, she made an error in dosing a patient. The patient had an adverse reaction that needed an intervention. She followed standard protocols and wrote up an incident report. For this, the senior chief resident criticized her, and since then, she had felt very remorseful. She couldn't stop thinking that she had made a mistake and should have never chosen medicine as her career. Over the next few days, she isolated herself and kept ruminating. She felt like quitting her training program. She also worried that she would have a hard time paying off all her medical student loans if she left at that time. For the first time in her life, she started having passive thoughts of death. She also felt she couldn't talk to anyone about it. If anyone were to find out that she felt this way, she believed it would adversely affect her future career prospects.

If one can call it a system at all, our overall system of care is poorly designed, overstretched, inadequate, of low quality, and expensive. It is not reliably safe and not meeting the individual's needs it is supposed to serve well. It is also not well designed for those working in it.

It is not because our professionals are not smart, hard-working, or don't care. Instead, many professionals working in a healthcare system feel overworked and overwhelmed. Many physicians and nurses also feel burnt out.

A survey of physicians conducted in 2014 found that 54.4% of all physicians exhibited at least one symptom of burnout (Shanafelt et al., 2015).[82] The World Health Organization (WHO) defines burnout as a syndrome resulting from chronic workplace stress that has not been successfully managed. It results in feelings of energy depletion or exhaustion, increased mental distance from one's job, and reduced professional efficacy (Ezez, 2019).[83]

Some of the key drivers of physician burnout are excessive workloads and job demands, inefficient work environments, loss of meaning in work, misalignment of individual and organizational values, problems with work-life integration and balance, inadequate work support and resources, loss of autonomy, flexibility, and control over one's work, and a lack of social support and feeling of community at work (Shanafelt et al., 2017).[84]

Doing something meaningful and in keeping with one's values can energize physicians and keep them engaged. Physicians resist doing tasks imposed by regulations (or interpretation of regulations) that do not add much value. For instance, psychiatrists find generating frequent treatment plan documents and revisions, in addition to their initial assessments and progress notes, wasteful. Many believe that treatment plans neither support treatment nor help to document progress. They also seem unnecessarily duplicative when the thought process has already been conveyed within progress notes.

Another significant factor leading to increased job demands is documentation in the EMR. Many physicians say that they are spending considerably more time completing documentation for the same patient workload. This burden reduces the time for face-to-face patient care. Many physicians are completing documentation from home (euphemistically termed 'pajama time') and taking time away from personal self-care or family engagement. EMRs provide some advantages over paper charts. Benefits include increased legibility, the ability to interface them with laboratories and pharmacies, interaction and allergy checks when entering orders, and improved ability to ensure coding compliance. However, EMRs are taxing the energy and time of an already overwhelmed workforce.

The situation for nurses is equally grim and concerning. The level of burnout in 40% of hospital nurses exceeds the norms for other healthcare workers. Job dissatisfaction among hospital nurses is four times greater than the average of all US workers, and one-fifth of all nurses report wanting to leave their present jobs within a year (Aiken et al., 2002).[85] Burnout can increase patient safety risk, and it will have to be addressed if we are to address patient safety (Hall et al., 2016).[86] Psychiatric nurses are at a greater risk for burnout than nurses in other specialties (Pompili et al., 2006).[87]

Some environmental characteristics that contribute to burnout in nurses include injuries related to the work environment, patient aggression, shift work, and the quality of the work environment (Madathil et al., 2014).[88] Another important factor is the level of autonomy perceived in the workplace. The number of work hours, caseloads, control over one's schedule, mandated shifts, and being pulled to areas or duties other than one's regular primary duties can all adversely affect nurses' perceptions of their work.

The skill level and leadership characteristics of nursing managers also significantly affect the degree of nursing burnout. Inpatient units have experienced decreased patient lengths of stay and high staff turnover. Psychiatric units are constantly faced with the challenge of increasing complexity and constraints on resources. A nurse manager is a crucial determinant of training, supervision, and resource allocation to the nursing and support staff on the unit. The manager also sets the tone of a unit with respect to physician-nurse relationships and serves as a liaison to upper-level management. An investment in leadership and manager training can pay off by contributing to reductions in occupational stress. As psychiatric inpatients' medical complexity has increased, the skill level needed to manage these complicated patients has also increased. The monitoring of both physical and psychological problems has become necessary. More robust nurse-physician communication and relationships lead to lower burnout (Hanrahan et al., 2010).[89]

VIGNETTE 1.20

Shirin was a hard-working nurse. Over the last 25 years, she had always followed all the rules wherever she had worked. She never cut corners and always received high praise for her care from her patients and families, and she was both responsive and compassionate. She had been feeling quite frustrated in the last few years following an accreditation survey or regulatory audit. When problems were detected, more non-clinical work was added to her plate. According to her, most of this additional work was not helping to improve the quality of care. Over her career, she felt she was spending more time with the EMR and less time with patients. It was not that she did not want to document. Still, she sincerely cared about patients, and all the information that the hospital expected her to collect and document pulled her away from face-to-face interactions with them. During her interactions with patients, she made her feel alive, motivated, and fully tapped into her talent as a caregiver.

She had recently experienced some problems with her nurse manager, who criticized her care plan documentation quality. The care plans were

> under scrutiny due to an upcoming audit, and she was concerned about her manager's reaction. The nurse manager and the medical director also had an adversarial relationship, and she also feared a further strain on the nurse manager-medical director relationship. She often found herself thinking about quitting nursing and doing something else. Meanwhile, she had also been checking postings for new jobs at other hospitals.

In a survey of US hospital clinical pharmacy practitioners, 61.2% of pharmacists reported burnout. Emotional exhaustion largely contributed to burnout. Predictors of burnout included inadequate time for teaching and administrative tasks, the uncertainty of healthcare reform, an excess of non-clinical duties, difficult pharmacist colleagues, and the overall feeling that their contributions were underappreciated (Jones, 2017).[90]

Medical students have also reported a high degree of burnout. Almost 50% experience burnout, and 10% have experienced suicidal ideation during medical school. Recovery from burnout leads to less suicidal ideation (Dyrbye et al., 2008).[91]

Typically, the push for quality is promulgated in organizations in the form of an increased collection of measures, which does not always lead to an increase in quality but instead traps even more time in work that does not add value. The current use of many measures often focuses on aiding accountability rather than improving patient care. Several government-mandated measures add to the cost of care and do not add any value (Berwick, 2016).[92] Using time on gathering information for reports that are not very helpful to the overall improvement of systems contributes to the waste in the system and the degree of burnout. Many of these proximal process measures do not impact distal downstream outcomes; they could be reduced or eliminated without affecting the quality of care and prevent healthcare providers from developing a distaste toward quality improvement.

Some institutions are dealing with the problem of burnout proactively not only by embarking on interventions for individuals but also by engaging them in organizational interventions. A primary care clinic attempted to improve physician well-being by engaging in a continuous improvement process and longitudinal monitoring of physician well-being (Dunn et al., 2007).[93] The interventions were designed to enhance the physician's sense of control over the work environment, the order in the clinical setting, and meaning in the clinical work. An earlier study had discovered that the amount of time spent by physicians on activities they considered meaningful was inversely related to the degree of burnout (Shanafelt et al., 2009).[94] Successful systems are configuring their practices to have professionals work at the top of their license. This reconfiguration means that the professionals utilize the full extent of their education, training, and experience and not spending time doing activities that could be carried out by those with much less education or training (Cheney, 2018).[95] Instead of administrative tasks, there is a greater focus on education, research, and improvement activities.

Medical professionals play a significant role in redesigning systems that maximize value for their patients because their daily work provides an organization real-time patient feedback. Not only are these skills vital for the betterment of psychiatric systems, but they also keep the workforce engaged, empowered, and provide a sense of control. This sense of control had been eroded over the years by third-party payors, ongoing regulatory changes, and increased documentation burden. Improvement and redesign work helps to revitalize the workforce through active engagement of critical medical resources by first focusing on easing the intense workload.

XI. A Call for a Better System

VIGNETTE 1.21

Twenty-four-year-old Luiz's parents were confused. In the last three years, Luiz was hospitalized five times. He had received different diagnoses each time he left the hospital. Three of his hospitalizations had been in the same hospital, but he was under different psychiatrists' care each time. The diagnoses he received over the last few years included bipolar disorder, intermittent explosive disorder, disruptive mood dysregulation disorder, and substance-induced mood disorder. One day, the current psychiatrist informed them that Luiz had a borderline personality disorder in a family meeting. Luiz's father, who was skeptical of psychiatric professionals, to begin with, got upset in the family meeting. He said, 'my son is crazy, but all of you are even crazier. I don't think anyone here knows what they are talking about,' and stormed out of the family meeting.

A. Crossing the Quality Chasm

In 2001, after 'To Err is Human' brought much-needed attention to fundamental systemic problems, a second report was released titled, 'Crossing the Quality Chasm: A New Health System for the 21st Century' (Committee on Quality Health Care in America, 2001).[6] They provided principles and guidance for redesigning the healthcare system to meet the American people's needs. It emphatically stated, "…we are also confident that this higher level of quality cannot be achieved by further stressing current systems of care. The current care systems cannot do the job. Trying harder will not work. Changing systems of care will." However, there is still a struggle with focusing on the right changes that will lead to improved patient flow and eliminate waste in a medical professional's workday.

The report set forth six aims for improvement to address key dimensions of the healthcare system; it stated that a system should be 'safe, effective, patient-centered, timely, efficient, and equitable.' It acknowledged the imagination and valuable pluralism at the local level and asserted that the local efforts could benefit from adopting a simple set of rules to guide redesign efforts. It imagined the provision of safe, evidence-based care to all who could benefit; individualized care that was respectful of an individual patient's preferences, needs, and values and provide care with minimal waste (Committee on Quality Health Care in America, 2001).[6]

The report anticipated that such an undertaking would face challenges. One of the challenges is the need to redesign care processes for the *chronically ill* so that settings and providers could deliver coordinated, seamless care over time. It rightfully recognized that healthcare had lagged in adopting tools to organize and provide care. According to the Quality Chasm report, there were quality and safety problems because the healthcare system relied on 'outmoded systems of work.' It went on the say that despite all their efforts, the healthcare workforce was not entirely successful because providers were working in poorly designed work systems. Among their recommendations, the report spelled out ten rules of a redesign, some of which included providing care based on continuous healing relationships, customization based on patient needs and values, and striving for a continuous decrease in waste.

Continuous healing relationships are not available to most of those with mental illnesses (Sharfstein et al.).[3] A paper published in 2005 reported that 133 million individuals in the United States, or at least half of the people in the United States, suffered from at least one chronic condition (Bodenheimer et al., 2009).[96] Indeed, most of the conditions that the mental health system treats, such as depression, schizophrenia, addiction, autism, dementia, anxiety disorders, are all chronic conditions and deserve the benefits of continuous healing relationships. Making such healing relationships possible requires healthcare professionals to shift their thinking. There is a need to go beyond merely managing the inpatient stay and focus improvement efforts on the communication and coordination between different levels of care. Looking at care from the patient's lens through the greater health system will provide the insight needed to make meaningful changes in work practices toward improving the efficient and effective use of our skilled healthcare providers.

B. The Quadruple Aim

The US healthcare system would have to balance improving the experience of care, improving the health of populations, and reducing per capita costs of healthcare – which has come to be known as 'The Triple Aim' (Berwick et al., 2008).[97] More recently, a fourth aim was added: to 'improve the work-life of healthcare providers,' making it 'The Quadruple Aim' (Bodenheimer and Sinsky, 2014).[98] Organizations will have to accept the charge of improving all four aims to prevent optimizing one aspect of care at another's expense. For example, when adding healthcare professionals' tasks to enhance care experience, there must also be a review and reduction of their existing workload. In many cases, this does not happen and causes an excessive burden on caregivers to complete an ever-expanding list of tasks.

XII. Forces of Change

A. Moving Away from the Model of a 'Cottage Industry'

VIGNETTE 1.22

Bertha, a retired social worker, had struggled with recurrent major depression. She had four hospitalizations over the last five decades. She remembered the earliest admission to a private psychiatric hospital, where she could sit with an individual psychiatrist a few times a week for hour-long therapy sessions. This admission was before the era when antidepressant medications were available. She believed both she and the psychiatrist came to understand her life story and her values and feelings. Last month when she was admitted to the psychiatric service in the same hospital 50 years later, she was troubled that, in 24 hours, five professionals asked her the same questions. When she met the psychiatrist for the first time, he asked her many questions to complete his assessment and focused much of his time talking about medications.

> After a seven-day stay in the hospital, she was disappointed that the psychiatrist never once asked her opinion about the care she was currently receiving. Moreover, he did not ask her any questions about her past career as a social worker.

Over the last few decades, the nature of psychiatric work has changed. Compared to past practices, fewer clinicians are working as solo practitioners (Ranz et al., 2006). A more significant number have moved toward working in a group, clinic, hospital, or health system.[99] From predominantly individual encounters with a psychoanalytically oriented psychiatrist in years past to being cared for by a team in a hospital or a clinic, the nature of the work has changed. So have the providers' expectations.

Most practitioners who work in hospitals are accustomed to the need to follow a complex set of regulations that affect their practice, such as CMS or Joint Commission regulations. Adherence to these regulations affects the accreditation of the systems where they work and could impact these systems' reputation and viability. How the individual hospital or clinic interprets these regulations can also affect how the work is structured. For example, how a master treatment plan needs to be completed, who all need to complete the plan, or how often it needs to be updated is left to interpretation.

Medicine is trying to move away from the model of a 'cottage industry' to the mode of 'post-industrial care' (Swensen et al., 2010).[100] In a cottage industry, services are rendered by artisans who are dedicated to their customers and provide customized products and services. The artisans usually function as individual experts and prize their autonomy, but each artisan's output is variable, and performance is largely unmeasured. There is limited standardization, oversight, or coordination. What a customer receives depends on who serves them. On the other hand, in post-industrial care, there is an expectation of standardized processes and reliability (the care one gets should not depend on whom one sees or on the day or time someone arrives in the hospital). Also, measurement of performance and outcomes over time is expected and expectations of quality, transparency, and accountability.

In many areas of medicine, operating in a cottage industry mode has come with its costs. It has led to significant variability and a very uneven delivery of care where many do not receive evidence-based care or receive harmful care. To transform medicine toward post-industrial care, one sees a proliferating number of published guidelines based on scientific evidence, an expectation to work in teams, improve handoffs to others who care for the patient, and a push toward pay-for-performance and value over time, not just volume. The general trend is to move away from fee-for-service models of payment. There is a desire to increase the overall coordination between different levels of care and increase care's value. Many changes proposed via the Affordable Care Act (ACA), the Medicare Access and CHIP Reauthorization Act (MACRA), or the Merit-based Incentive Payment System (MIPS) signal the end of a business-as-usual way of caring for our patients (Emanuel, 2017).[101] It is hard to imagine the transformation expected by these legislative changes where all providers worked in their idiosyncratic ways, without attention being paid to how well they function as a system. They will require awareness of how their patients are doing and broader attention to their overall system's value of services.

Are psychiatric providers ready for these kinds of system-wide changes that will enable them to achieve 'high-reliability' or pursue the 'quadruple aim' or changes where their reimbursement will be linked to certain populations' pre-specified outcomes? Many psychiatric providers are not trained in the right kind of skillset and the mindset required to practice effectively in this kind of system or healthcare environment. Such training will require a significant adjustment in the providers themselves and the training programs and organizations that employ them (Bennett, 2000).[102]

B. Technology

VIGNETTE 1.23

In a customer satisfaction survey, a patient described her time with hospital professionals. 'Both my psychiatrist and my social worker kept looking at the computer screen every time they met me. It did not matter much to them that I was crying or I was often feeling miserable. It seemed more important to them to type that piece of information rather than comfort me. Only when I got angry or expressed suicidal urges that they seemed to look engaged. It felt so mechanical. Sometimes there was so much typing going on in the room that I could not even hear my voice.'

There is a gradual and often painful transition to the EMR in inpatient and outpatient settings across the country. It is clear from many reports and commentaries that it has changed the nature of the encounter with the patient and is changing psychiatry's nature.

The computer screen has become an important entity, a powerful force to reckon with in the clinician's office. Often, however, it competes with the patient for time and attention during a session. A common observation is that clinicians are not even looking at the patient for a significant proportion of time but are looking at the computer screen instead. The conversation or narrative flow is awkwardly being decided by what screen is showing on the clinician's template. The field of mental health is heavily dependent on interpersonal interaction and requires providers to have difficult conversations in times of stress, and requires them to listen and pay attention to facial cues and body language. The EMR adds pressure to clinicians who are typing or clicking radio buttons while listening and moving their gaze away from the patient while they are speaking. The clinician risks losing not only valuable clinical information but also risks rupturing their alliance with the patient. A recent research study on primary care doctors showed that they spend a third of their time with patients looking at computer screens (Montague, 2014).[103] If practitioners are trying to finish most of their notes in mental health with the patient in the room, they are probably spending more than 30% of their time typing. On the other hand, if they are fully paying attention to the patient, they might have to move a significant amount of documentation time to later in their workday.

Ironically, while the EMR has made physician's writing more legible, it allows multiple team members to access the record simultaneously and provides easy access to records, the clinician's burdens have substantially increased. Clinicians are spending more time entering information into an EMR than the time it took to enter the information into a paper chart. This lost time reduces the clinician's flexibility, the time to reflect in a day, and overwhelms the cognitive bandwidth of already busy clinicians. Further, the clinician sacrifices the time to learn, communicate with families and other providers, consulting with colleagues, taking a break to be fully present with family when one is at home, and so forth. Laptops at home and virtual private network (VPN) access have made it tempting to 'finish work' from home, but in effect, have extended the workday.

Psychiatry is a very descriptive specialty. There is little reliance on objective measures or biological tests and a greater emphasis on the patient's narrative and self-report of history. The task of entering a comprehensive history into the EMR can be daunting. The provider sometimes has to describe events that lead a patient to get admitted into the hospital. The complex multi-faceted history of present illness in an admission note; the biopsychosocial formulation's richness; the thought-process to justify either medical necessity or revisions in treatment plans and the uniquely idiosyncratic occurrences in a daily progress note. Entering each of these elements can be quite labor-intensive. What are the contents of a good and thorough document?

A good and thorough document could include detailed biographical information; developmental history and milestones; a description of a person's social context, family composition and dynamics, personal, legal, and military history; an account of significant events and traumas in the course of their life. It could also include details of medical conditions that may or may not have relevance to the patient's presenting problem; the range of medications, supplements, and illicit substances consumed; responses to various treatments, medication, and otherwise; a level of insight and motivation for further treatment. Incredibly, providers manage to gather and type this information in 45–90 minutes. Patients can describe thoughts, feelings, fears, hopes, and dreams. How does one capture this interaction's richness in a typed document, and how much documentation is necessary? The documentation can mention specific objective observations, subjective statements, and quotes, enumerate test results to describe the infinite possibilities of occurrences accurately. Moreover, large sections of these notes are not easily standardized in a template format. A lot of documentation is added to either reduce liability (which requires more documentation, more 'quotes' are recommended by risk managers) or justify coding for billing purposes. Sometimes when a clinician sees a chronic patient daily in a hospital, very little changes in the patient's condition, but a clinician still has to document a full mental status in a progress note. A clinician documents a complete note to justify a billing code as clinicians are paid per service. Sometimes, it takes practitioners more time to write a note than to see a patient. It is almost as if the clinician is serving the EMR instead of the EMR supporting the clinician to provide the best patient care (Verghese, 2008).[104]

As healthcare services' payment is tied to performance or value, additional documentation demands are being placed on clinicians. Documentation of additional process measures is being mandated, which often does not increase quality but instead traps even more time in work that seems unnecessary or wasteful. One more thing that slows the work down is the addition of mandatory fields or hard stops, which are added into the workflow to ensure complete documentation. These required fields are added to satisfy a regulatory requirement or collect information on a metric that the system is trying to improve.

The presumption used to be that if you did not document an activity, you did not do it. We have also seen providers documenting activities that they may or may not have been doing. Examples include pre-programmed smart phrases or sentences that type up with ease, based on entering a few keystrokes, making this kind of falsification very easy. There is a sense that clinical documentation has been degraded even though more time is being spent documenting (Friedberg et al., 2014).[105]

Some clinicians are very sparse in their notes, making it hard to get a sense of the evolving narrative. Some, on the other hand, are very detailed, and it takes a significant amount of time to sift through their notes to get clarity and separate 'signal from the noise.' It is a pleasure to find a very well-organized record but very time-consuming if the visible descriptive free text is poorly organized.

EMRs from various hospitals do not communicate with each other. Paper printouts of records from EMRs of ERs or other hospitals can run several pages long. Clinicians have to flip through numerous pages to get the pertinent nuggets of information relevant to the patient's care that day. Even printouts to patients need to be thoughtfully designed, or else they add to the confusion and stress for patients, family members, or the next-level provider. The additional amount of time required for this task could be due to the clinician typing speed or the unavailability of an integrated dictation system incorporated into the EMR, or a scribe's availability (uncommon is psychiatry as yet). It could also be because the structured template is poorly designed so that it leads to a lot of scrolling or screen transitions, which takes up more time than checking boxes on a piece of paper.

The most significant element that is vital to the patient-provider relationship is the therapeutic alliance. Creating an alliance has been and will always be a crucial therapeutic tool in psychiatry. It is also, at times, very subtle and fragile. The strength of the alliance can significantly affect patient outcomes. This alliance is very much at risk under the weight of the documentation burdens in today's EMR. Technology must help make the clinician's workload easier while enabling improved care processes. Most of the current EMR products today are clunky and create a new set of unintended consequences. It will take a significant effort, taking ideas from various specialists from different fields, to solve this wicked problem at the human-technology interface.

C. The Voice of the Patient

VIGNETTE 1.24

Tracy has been bringing her seventeen-year-old grandson, Richie, to the psychiatrist regularly ever since he was 12. When Richie's parents died in an accident, Tracy became his legal guardian. Richie had a tough childhood. Developmentally Richie was affected by Fetal Alcohol Syndrome and his school years were stormy. A local psychiatrist worked diligently over the years to truly understand his diagnosis and shape his treatment.

In addition to features of Bipolar disorder, Richie also suffered from Obsessive-Compulsive Disorder and Tourette's syndrome. He tended to use curse words impulsively, which led to many parent-teacher conferences and even a few school suspensions. It took years to get his psychiatric treatment optimized. Even though Tracy had a very limited income from her pension, her consistency and diligence provided a stabilizing force to her grandson's care. She had a very calm temperament and was a perfect counterpoint to his affective storms. She was kind, supportive, encouraging, but quite firm. Richie knew that he could not get away with tantrums easily and came to learn that his grandmother would hold him accountable for his actions.

She brought him to his appointments without fail, and she kept meticulous records, including daily mood and behavior charts. Also, she read about his conditions regularly and asked questions respectfully. She had read about anticonvulsants' use in children with mood instability and suggested it to the psychiatrist before he even thought of it. Her involvement and diligence in Richie's care led to a marked improvement in his case, and his school performance began to improve.

Over the past 50 years, the consumer movement has evolved to become an essential and impactful voice on the practice of mental healthcare. This is a social movement where consumers unite together to protect their interests.

The power dynamics between the providers and patients are shifting due to the Internet, social media, and the easy availability of the latest information. Direct-to-consumer advertising has shaken the traditional role of the expert. There is an expectation for less paternalism (authority figures making decisions for patients) and more collaboration.

A guiding principle in care today is that the patient, family, or the 'consumer' needs to be listened to, empowered, activated, and involved in shared decision-making. The field of mental health and the consumer movement share common goals and acknowledge the 'virtues of self-determination, patient choice, and recovery' (Sharfstein et al., 2006).[106]

The consumer perspective has emerged due to the restructuring of the mental health system over several decades (Tomes, 2006).[107] Patients and families have fought hard to have a say in a domain where the voices of the medical profession, the insurance industry, the pharmaceutical and medical device industry, and the service industry (hospitals, community mental health centers, nursing homes, etc.) are strong. Consumer and family organizations are influencing legislation, policy, research, reimbursement, and psychiatry practice. They ensure that the outcomes they consider essential, such as living independently or holding a job, are included (Campbell, 1997).[108]

Today, it is common for a patient to expect a notice of their rights upon admission, to have informed consent decisions with their providers about treatments, to fill out advance directives. Also, patients rate their experience in a patient satisfaction survey or ask to speak to patient advocates if they are displeased with a particular encounter in a healthcare setting.

In their document, the WHO, 'Improving Health Systems and Services for Mental Health,' proposes an organizational pyramid for an optimal mix of mental health services. At the base of the pyramid is the emphasis on self-care. There is an explosion of self-help resources in the form of books, websites, and organizations that support a patient's journey and help them better manage their conditions and improve their functioning (WHO). It is not uncommon for a patient to ask a provider about the latest medication or therapy that has come to their attention.

Ed Wagner from the MacColl Institute for Healthcare Innovation has advocated for the chronic care model. He has asserted that the prevalent system, which is better designed to deal with acute conditions, does not meet the needs of patients with chronic conditions or the providers who take care of such patients. By 2030, an estimated 171 million individuals are estimated to require chronic disease management. The majority of patients with mental illnesses that seek treatment have chronic conditions. Self-management support is an essential element of this model. It asserts that the outcomes depend significantly on the effectiveness of self-management (Wagner, 2001).[109]

Psychopharmacological treatments help but are incomplete solutions. In addition to helping patients, they often lead to significant side effects. Clinicians will have to be continually listening to their patients' voices and perspectives to keep improving their treatment modalities and the mental healthcare delivery system. Although psychiatric treatments have become more humane, the field of mental health has a long way to go and will need to partner with patients and their caregivers. Ultimately, the patient or the family member can truly judge the value of what is provided to them and what adds to their burdens.

XIII. Learning from Our Context (Groundbreaking Improvement Efforts in Medicine)

Quality improvement is not a new thing in medicine. One can read about systematic quality improvement efforts in medicine as far back as 1854, with the highly skilled and methodical work of Florence Nightingale. She was instrumental in reducing the mortality of British troops who fought in Crimea (from 42.7% to 2.2%) by careful examination of care processes and outcomes. Historical records show how she kept detailed notes and gathered and interpreted data, making her a forerunner of modern-day statistical quality improvement. Her 'Coxcombs' were a great example of how well she collected, tabulated, and graphically displayed data (Sheingold and Hahn, 2014).[110] See an example in Figure 1.2.

She diligently worked in this way for decades, and in addition to her role as a nurse, she was also a skilled writer, statistician, advocate, hospital planner, and social reformer (Neuhauser, 2003).[111] She embodied the prototypical improver who did her work and worked to improve the system in which she did her work.

Until recently, most healthcare providers have been focusing on what is being provided. They have not focused as much on the processes or the structures within which care is provided.

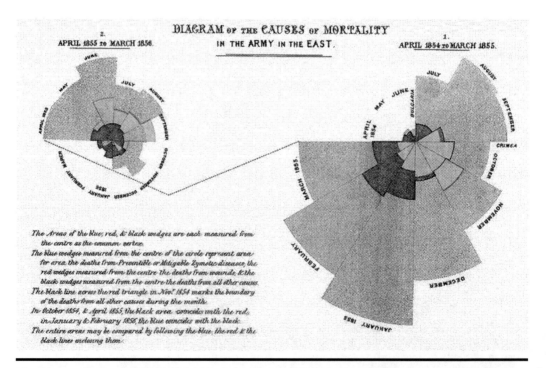

Figure 1.2 Florence Nightingale's 'Coxcombs' Which Illustrate Causes of Death in the Army.

More recent is the recognition that healthcare is provided within the context of a system that can function well or poorly and is amenable to optimization, improvement, and redesign. What is becoming more visible and widespread now is a proactive and deliberate approach to improving systems. Healthcare systems are witnessing a lesser reliance on individuals' heroism and a greater reliance on the power of well-functioning teams creating sustainable processes.

For the last two to three decades, followers of prominent quality experts W. Edwards Deming and Joseph M. Juran are using performance improvement models such as the Model for Improvement, TQM, Lean, and Six Sigma in medicine. Institutions are trying to pursue the Leapfrog award, the Shingo Prize, and the Baldrige Award, which stimulates organizations to improve their system's performance. The number of practitioners, the amount of published literature on this topic, and the number of healthcare organizations using systematic performance improvement methodologies are growing exponentially.

Joseph M. Juran remarked, "as the health industry undertakes ... change, it is well advised to take into account the experience of other industries to understand what worked and what has not ... [I]n the minds of many, the health industry is different. This is certainly true with regards to the health industry's history, technology, and culture. However, the decisive factors in what works and what does not are the managerial processes that are alike for all industries" (Manos et al., 2006).[112]

Hospitals are trying to preserve their values and mission while systematically utilizing some of these robust improvement methods. The search for solutions has extended into other thriving industries as health systems have struggled with financial pressures. In other instances, healthcare institutions have embarked on this journey due to poor performance from a quality and safety perspective. Some healthcare institutions have also embraced these methodologies to innovate and gain a competitive advantage.

Even though there may be differences between the healthcare industries and the manufacturing sector, the requirements for successful change are similar. There needs to be demonstrated commitment from the senior management, the involvement of the practitioners themselves, and the recognition that local front-line expertise can be vital in the identification of possible solutions. These methods also require long-term thinking, perseverance, and patience. Some differences need to be considered. Healthcare has, in most cases, been impacted by geography. Most people want to access care close to where they live. Telemedicine is challenging this paradigm. Also, the variability of patients is immense, and specialists wield a significant degree of influence. Within a highly specialized service sector, the socio-technical aspects of bringing about change or implementing projects in healthcare assume much greater importance (Sloan et al., 2014).[113]

Many hospitals and health systems have now published accounts of applying improvement methodologies in their local contexts (Kenney, 2012; Toussaint and Gerard, 2010; Merlino et al., 2014), and the results are awe-inspiring.[114–116] They can demonstrate substantial improvements in safety, quality, delivery, cost, and morale. There is an emphasis on reducing waste and creating value in 'patient-centered' environments. There are success stories of improvements in access, waiting times, flow, productivity, management of supply chains, and information technology implementation. These organizations are changing from the inside (Spear, 2005), improving their work systems while improving patient's health and their fiscal health. Many successful organizations are learning that it is not just improving processes or structures but investing in the development of people working within the organizations that bring about sustainable change.[55]

Health systems are working on creating just cultures and making reporting adverse events psychologically safer, necessary for improving patient safety (Boysen, 2013).[117] Clinicians recognize that they cannot only depend on idealized standards of perfect performance by individual providers: they need to create high-reliability systems that predict and compensate for mistakes that individuals can potentially make (Chassin & Loeb, 2013).[118]

Even though using improvement methods can lead to rapid improvements in quality, safety, access, and cost, it takes much more to sustain these improvements and change organizations' culture and management styles. Some of these exemplary organizations now serve as beacons of light, leading the way for the rest to emulate new ways of systematically reframing the work of healthcare.

While pockets of excellence or 'spot repair' haven't led to widespread awareness or spread of these problem-solving or improvement efforts, there has not been a fundamental shift in how healthcare is delivered (Elster et al., 2012).[119] These ideas and methodologies have not penetrated the psychiatric healthcare system in any significant or meaningful way. When one scans the psychiatric literature or the agenda of the major psychiatric conferences, presentations on such topics are still relatively uncommon or very sparsely attended. Knowledge about the groundbreaking work by organizations in improving quality such as the 'Institute of Healthcare Improvement (IHI)' and the National Patient Safety Foundation (NPSF) that recently merged with IHI are relatively unknown to mental health practitioners in our conversations with them.

Most healthcare providers still do not work within an implicit paradigm that a part of their job is to improve the system in which they work. The process of doing their daily work has not been meaningfully linked with learning to do it better (Spear, 2005).[55] The system of care is not steadily improving while care is being delivered. Most improvement efforts are still being carried out in a reactive, piecemeal manner. They are being driven either by enthusiastic early adopters, forward-thinking leaders, or in response to pressures by internal auditors or external regulatory bodies.

XIV. The Need to Reinvigorate and Redesign Mental Healthcare

VIGNETTE 1.25

Dr. Alvarez was a community psychiatrist who had started practicing in a rural area. She was asked to assess a new patient, Peter, who was in his seventies. His sister brought in this patient because he had stopped eating and communicating in the past month. When he did speak in a feeble impoverished voice, he kept saying that he did not want to live anymore. He had stopped going to church or interacting with his friends. He regularly met his friends for a weekly poker game, which he had stopped doing months ago. His sister brought him to the clinic and expected the psychiatrist to develop a diagnosis for her brother at their first session. In her seventies, she was struggling with poor health and lived alone in a retirement community. Peter was having difficulties with thinking and communicating, and due to his limited recall and insight, the challenge of making a quick diagnosis became apparent.

Peter had a history of being anxious and had learning difficulties as a child. He had suffered multiple traumas in his adolescent years and had brief periods of manic behaviors that his sister had not witnessed. Peter also had a history of exposure to a tick bite and multiple head injuries while playing football in college. He had been quietly gambling away his retirement money and was using cocaine and cannabis intermittently after his retirement. His sister did not know about much of his recent history as she did not see him often. Any one of these factors could have been contributing to his presenting symptoms.

The pressure to understand and do something soon for an individual with multiple interweaving layers of problems with just this minimal window into his life is never easy. There was very little objective data available in that first hour informing Dr. Alvarez on how to proceed. Past medical records were not available right away to help clarify details of his past.

The need for psychiatric services is greater than ever. Today, the field of psychiatry is thriving as it has undergone greater sub-specialization. This sub-specialization underscores its far-reaching influence, its need for so many different populations in so many varied treatment settings. Mental health practitioners take care of very ill patients – those suffering from psychosis, dementia, suicidal tendencies, addictions, personality disorders that other specialties have preferred not to treat (Sharfstein, 2010).[120]

Competent mental health practitioners can demonstrate a comprehensive knowledge of psychopathology, an ability to deploy a diverse set of skills, a willingness to communicate and interact with affected individuals who suffer from a complex set of challenging problems (Katschnig, 2010).[121] It is not always easy to define the boundaries of psychiatric disorders as they look and feel similar to a whole host of normal human behaviors. They also intersect with a host of social issues. Mental health practitioners have not had the advantage of having laboratory tests or imaging studies to help diagnose psychiatric conditions, like their peers utilize in internal medicine, pediatrics, or neurology.

Arriving at a reliable diagnosis requires skilled observation abilities; the ability to listen and be patient; clinicians need to gather biological, psychological, social, cultural, and even spiritual bits of information across the life span, and at times, from more than just one person. All this information has to be then assimilated carefully to develop a formulation, which can then tell the affected individual and the practitioner what exactly is causing concerns at the present moment. To add to the complexity, sometimes these longitudinal patterns, such as the depressive and manic phases of bipolar disorder, only become evident over prolonged periods, spanning over the years. In contrast, the individuals are assessed subjectively during very limited cross sections of time.

Good psychiatric care involves utilizing biomedical and psychotherapeutic approaches and paying attention to non-technical dimensions such as relationships, meanings, and values. For instance, a common factor in successful outcomes across various forms of psychotherapies has been the therapist's ability to establish a therapeutic alliance and utilize its leverage to help a patient overcome their challenges. Competent practitioners pay attention to the personal narrative and the sociocultural contexts in which these narratives play out.

The field has strived to promote dignity and the value of all individuals and has worked toward restoring hope, self-efficacy, empowerment, and social inclusion of severely disadvantaged individuals affected by mental illness (Bracken et al., 2012).[122] Patients and practitioners have had to deal with patient-specific challenges and decades of misconceptions, stigma, prejudices, and discrimination by various members of society. These barriers have affected not just how psychiatric patients have been treated over centuries but have also determined the number of resources that have been made available to deal with these commonly seen difficulties.

There have been critical junctures in the history of psychiatry. Changes occurred when treatments such as psychoanalysis or antidepressant or antipsychotic medications were introduced. Progress also occurred with brain imaging at a structural or functional level or the exploration of genetics. At other times, it has been a social change that has brought about a difference in the mode of practice, such as creating humane asylums due to the advocacy efforts of Dorothea Dix, de-institutionalization, or the introduction of managed care. With every social change, the field of mental healthcare has had to modify itself and respond to the current challenge while preserving its core tenets and its focus on the needs of patients.

Mental healthcare is at a crossroads again where the nature of medicine in general, and that of mental healthcare, in particular, is being influenced dramatically by a significant number of pressures. There is a need to care for an increasing number of individuals, and more effective treatments encourage patients to come forward for help. The cost of healthcare in the United States is the highest of all developed nations and is forcing society to confront this issue. There is a growing push for highly reliable care; increased safety, quality, efficiency, accountability, and transparency are becoming routine expectations. To add to the complexity, newer kinds of neuro-modulation services, technologies like the EMR, mobile apps, and other ways of interacting such as telemedicine, simulation software, or virtual reality, make inroads into psychiatric environments. These new technologies are bringing about changes at a very rapid pace. The restructuring of the healthcare system has led to reduced physician autonomy, increased time pressures, and new challenges. These changes have the potential to increase the levels of burnout, which has already reached epidemic proportions.

The provider community will have to take a hard look to understand the collective needs of our patients. They will have to figure out smarter ways of redesigning systems to meet these current challenges while preserving its most valued elements. The need has never been greater nor more urgent. Mental health practitioners must draw from all the domains of their knowledge, experience, strengths, and vision to redesign the infrastructure, processes and demonstrate desired outcomes. The identity, credibility, reliability, effectiveness, and future of mental healthcare will depend on how well these various domains are utilized and integrated by the provider community.

We have presented a broad overview of the problems facing the field of mental healthcare thus far. To get to the desired future state in the mental health field will require a paradigm change. We invite each of you to take a fresh look at how you approach your work. We suggest that you not just be a passive witness to the performance improvement ideas put forth in the subsequent sections, but we are hopeful that you will become an active agent of change. Awareness and improvement will mainly come through the act of 'doing' and engaging in experiential learning.

The power of these ideas and methods is seen not just when individuals change but when teams, organizations, and communities collectively adopt and employ them. These methods have transformed various organizations and industries. Why should the field of mental health stay behind? We all deserve better.

References

1. Ezez. 2019. "Mental Illness". *Nimh.nih.gov.* https://www.nimh.nih.gov/health/statistics/mental-illness.shtml. Accessed June 22, 2019.
2. Johnson, Toni. 2012. "Healthcare Costs and U.S. Competitiveness". *Council on Foreign Relations.* https://www.cfr.org/backgrounder/healthcare-costs-and-us-competitiveness. Accessed July 9, 2019.
3. Sharfstein, Steven; Clemens, Norman & Everett, Anita, et al. 2003. "APA Task Force on A Vision for a Mental Health System". *Michigan.gov.* https://www.michigan.gov/documents/visionreport040303_1_83176_7.pdf. Accessed June 12, 2019.

4. New Freedom Commission on Mental Health. 2003. *Achieving the Promise: Transforming Mental Health Care in America*. US Department of Health and Human Services.
5. Senge, Peter. 1990. "The Fifth Discipline". *The Art & Practice of Learning Organization*. Doubleday Currency, New York, NY.
6. Committee on Quality Health Care in America, Institute of Medicine. 2001. *Crossing the Quality Chasm: A New Health System for the 21st Century*. National Academy Press, Washington, DC.
7. Perla, Rocco J.; Provost, Lloyd P. & Parry, Gareth J. 2013. "Seven Propositions of the Science of Improvement". *Quality Management in Health Care* 22 (3): 170–186. Ovid Technologies (Wolters Kluwer Health). doi:10.1097/qmh.0b013e31829a6a15.
8. Kessler, Ronald; Chiu, Wai Tat & Demler, Olga, et al. 2005. "Prevalence, Severity, and Comorbidity of 12-Month DSM-IV Disorders in the National Comorbidity Survey Replication". *Archives of General Psychiatry* 62 (6): 617. American Medical Association (AMA). doi:10.1001/archpsyc.62.6.617.
9. Ezez. 2007. "NCS-R Twelve-month Prevalence Estimates". *Hcp.med.harvard.edu*. https://www.hcp.med.harvard.edu/ncs/ftpdir/NCS-R_12-month_Prevalence_Estimates.pdf.
10. Ezez. 2019. "NIMH U.S. DALYs Contributed by Mental and Behavioral Disorders". *Nimh.nih.gov*. https://www.nimh.nih.gov/health/statistics/disability/us-dalys-contributed-by-mental-and-behavioral-disorders.shtml. Accessed June 12, 2019.
11. Moreno, Eliana María & Moriana, Juan Antonio. 2016. "Clinical Guideline Implementation Strategies for Common Mental Health Disorders". *Revista de Psiquiatría y Salud Mental (English Edition)* 9 (1): 51–62. Elsevier BV. doi:10.1016/j.rpsmen.2016.01.007.
12. Prince, Martin; Patel, Vikram & Saxena, Shekar, et al. 2007. "No Health without Mental Health". *The Lancet* 370 (9590): 859–877. Elsevier BV. doi:10.1016/s0140-6736(07)61238-0.
13. Mechanic, David. 2007. "Mental Health Services Then and Now". *Health Affairs* 26 (6): 1548–1550. Health Affairs (Project Hope). doi:10.1377/hlthaff.26.6.1548.
14. Parcesepe, Angela M. & Cabassa, Leopoldo J. 2012. "Public Stigma of Mental Illness in the United States: A Systematic Literature Review". *Administration and Policy in Mental Health and Mental Health Services Research* 40 (5): 384–399. Springer Science and Business Media LLC. doi:10.1007/s10488-012-0430-z.
15. Katon, Wayne J. 2003. "Clinical and Health Services Relationships between Major Depression, Depressive Symptoms, and General Medical Illness". *Biological Psychiatry* 54 (3): 216–226. Elsevier BV. doi:10.1016/s0006-3223(03)00273-7.
16. Felitti, Vincent J. & Anda, Robert F. 2010. "The Relationship of Adverse Childhood Experiences to Adult Medical Disease, Psychiatric Disorders and Sexual Behavior: Implications for Healthcare". Chapter in Lanius, Ruth A., et al. (arg.). *The Impact of Early Life Trauma on Health and Disease: The Hidden Epidemic*, pp. 77–87. Cambridge University Press, Cambridge. doi:10.1017/CBO9780511777042.010.
17. Cradock-O'Leary, Julie, et al. 2002. "Use of General Medical Services by VA Patients With Psychiatric Disorders". *Psychiatric Services* 53 (7): 874–878. American Psychiatric Association Publishing. doi:10.1176/appi.ps.53.7.874.
18. Colton, Craig & Manderscheid, Ronald. 2006. "Congruencies in Increased Mortality Rates, Years of Potential Life Lost, and Causes of Death Among Public Mental Health Clients in Eight States". *Preventing Chronic Disease* [serial online]. http://www.cdc.gov/pcd/issues/2006/apr/05_0180.htm. Accessed June 8, 2019.
19. Liu, Nancy; Daumit, Gail & Dua, Tarun, et al. 2017. "Excess Mortality in Persons with Severe Mental Disorders: A Multilevel Intervention Framework and Priorities for Clinical Practice, Policy and Research Agendas". *World Psychiatry* 16 (1): 30–40. Wiley. doi:10.1002/wps.20384.
20. McGinnis, J. Michael; Williams-Russo, Pamela & Knickman, James R. 2002. "The Case For More Active Policy Attention To Health Promotion". *Health Affairs* 21 (2): 78–93. Health Affairs (Project Hope). doi:10.1377/hlthaff.21.2.78.
21. Ivbijaro, Gabriel O; Enum, Yaccub & Khan, Anwar, et al. 2014. "Collaborative Care: Models for Treatment of Patients with Complex Medical-Psychiatric Conditions". *Current Psychiatry Reports* 16 (11). Springer Nature. doi:10.1007/s11920-014-0506-4.

22. Huang, Yafang; Wei, Xioming & Wu, Tao, et al. 2013. "Collaborative Care for Patients with Depression and Diabetes Mellitus: A Systematic Review and Meta-analysis". *BMC Psychiatry* 13 (1). Springer Nature. doi:10.1186/1471-244x-13-260.
23. Unützer, Jürgen; Harbin, Henry & Schoenbaum, Michael, et al. 2013. "The Collaborative Care Model: An Approach for Integrating Physical and Mental Health Care in Medicaid Health Homes". *HEALTH HOME, Information Resource Center*: 1–13.
24. Mental Health America. 2019. *The State of Mental Health in America*. https://www.mhanational.org/sites/default/files/2019-09/2019%20MH%20in%20America%20Final.pdf. Accessed June 8, 2019.
25. West, Joyce; Clarke, Diana & Duffy, Farifteh, et al. 2016. "Availability of Mental Health Services Prior to Health Care Reform Insurance Expansions". *Psychiatric Services* 67 (9): 983–989. American Psychiatric Association Publishing. doi:10.1176/appi.ps.201500423.
26. Whitten, Lori. 2004. "'No Wrong Door' for People with Co-occurring Disorders". *NIDA Notes* 19 (4).
27. Torrey, E. Fuller; Entsminger, Kurt & Geller, Jeffrey, et al. 2015. "The Shortage of Public Hospital Beds for Mentally Ill Persons". *The Treatment Advocacy Center*. Arlington, VA. http://www.treatmentadvocacycenter.org/storage/documents/the_shortage_of_publichospital_beds.pdf. Accessed February 19, 2017.
28. Harcourt, Bernard E. 2011. "Reducing Mass Incarceration: Lessons from the Deinstitutionalization of Mental Hospitals in the 1960s". *SSRN Electronic Journal*. Elsevier BV. doi:10.2139/ssrn.1748796.
29. Ezez. 2017. "Assisted Outpatient Treatment Laws – Treatment Advocacy Center". *Treatmentadvocacycenter.org*. https://www.treatmentadvocacycenter.org/component/content/article/39. Accessed February 19, 2017.
30. Torrey, E. Fuller. 2016. "A Dearth of Psychiatric Beds". *Psychiatric Times*, *33*(2).
31. La, Elizabeth; Lich, Kristen & Wells, Rebecca, et al. 2016. "Increasing Access to State Psychiatric Hospital Beds: Exploring Supply-Side Solutions". *Psychiatric Services*, 67(5): 523–528.
32. Torrey, E. Fuller. 2014. *American Psychosis*. Oxford University Press, New York, NY.
33. Lehman, Anthony; Dixon, Lisa & Hoch, Jeffrey, et al. 1999. "Cost-effectiveness of Assertive Community Treatment for Homeless Persons with Severe Mental Illness". *British Journal of Psychiatry* 174 (4): 346–352. Royal College of Psychiatrists. doi:10.1192/bjp.174.4.346.
34. Ezez. 2019. "AOT Can Help Some with Mental Illness Survive and Thrive – Treatment Advocacy Center". *Treatmentadvocacycenter.org*. https://www.treatmentadvocacycenter.org/fixing-the-system/features-and-news/3765-aot-can-help-some-with-mental-illness-survive-and-thrive-.
35. Carlat, Daniel. 2010. "45,000 more Psychiatrists, Anyone?" *Psychiatric Times*, *27*(8), 1–1.
36. Konrad, Thomas; Ellis, Alan & Thomas, Kathleen, et al. 2009. "County-Level Estimates of Need for Mental Health Professionals in the United States". *Psychiatric Services* 60 (10). American Psychiatric Association Publishing. doi:10.1176/appi.ps.60.10.1307.
37. Kirwin, Paul; Blazer, Dan & Bartels, Stephen, et al. 2013. "The Institute of Medicine (IOM) Report, the Mental Health and Substance Use Workforce for Older Adults: In Whose Hands? A Road Map for the Future of Our Field". *The American Journal of Geriatric Psychiatry* 21 (3): S35–S36. Elsevier BV. doi:10.1016/j.jagp.2012.12.073.
38. Manderscheid, Ronald & Randolph, Frances. 2007. "An Action Plan for Behavioral Health Workforce Development". http://annapoliscoalition.org/wp-content/uploads/2013/11/action-plan-full-report.pdf. Accessed June 8, 2019.
39. Weil, Thomas P. 2015. "Insufficient Dollars and Qualified Personnel to Meet United States Mental Health Needs". *The Journal of Nervous and Mental Disease* 203 (4): 233–240. Ovid Technologies (Wolters Kluwer Health). doi:10.1097/nmd.0000000000000271.
40. McHugh, Megan; VanDyke, Kevin & McClelland, Mark, et al. 2011. "Improving Patient Flow and Reducing Emergency Department Crowding: A Guide for Hospitals". Agency for Healthcare Research and Quality, Rockville, MD. https://hsrc.himmelfarb.gwu.edu/cgi/viewcontent.cgi?referer=http://scholar.google.com/&httpsredir=1&article=1041&context=sphhs_policy_facpubs. Accessed June 8, 2019.
41. Sun, B. 2010. "EMF-5: Emergency Department Crowding: Community Determinants and Patient Outcomes". *Annals of Emergency Medicine* 56 (3): S109. Elsevier BV. doi:10.1016/j.annemergmed.2010.06.388.

42. Swartz, Marvin S. 2016. "Emergency Department Boarding: Nowhere Else to Go". *Psychiatric Services* 67 (11): 1163–1163. American Psychiatric Association Publishing. doi:10.1176/appi.ps.671102.
43. Markovitz, Fred E. 2006. "Psychiatric Hospital Capacity, Homelessness, and Crime and Arrest Rates*". *Criminology* 44 (1): 45–72. Wiley. doi:10.1111/j.1745-9125.2006.00042.x.
44. The Treatment Advocacy Center. 2016. "A Background Paper on Serious Mental Illness and Homelessness". Office of Research and Public Affairs, Arlington, VA. https://www.treatmentadvocacycenter.org/storage/documents/backgrounders/smi-and-homelessness.pdf. Accessed June 8, 2019.
45. Roy, Laurence; Crocker, Anne & Nicholls, Tonia, et al. 2014. "Criminal Behavior and Victimization among Homeless Individuals with Severe Mental Illness: A Systematic Review". *Psychiatric Services* 65 (6): 739–750. American Psychiatric Association Publishing. doi:10.1176/appi.ps.201200515.
46. Gelberg, Lillian & Linn, Lawrence. (1988). "Social and Physical Health of Homeless Adults Previously Treated for Mental Health Problems". *Psychiatric Services* 39 (5): 510–516.
47. Torrey, E. Fuller; Kennard, Aaron & Eslinger, Don, et al. 2010. "More Mentally Ill Persons Are in Jails and Prisons Than Hospitals: A Survey of the States". *The Treatment Advocacy Center*, Arlington, VA. http://www.treatmentadvocacycenter.org/storage/documents/final_jails_v_hospitals_study.pdf. Accessed June 10, 2017.
48. Fazel, Seena; Hayes, Adrian & Bartellas, Katrina, et al. 2016. "Mental Health of Prisoners: Prevalence, Adverse Outcomes, and Interventions". *The Lancet Psychiatry* 3 (9): 871–881.
49. Penrose, Lionel. 1938. "Mental Disease and Crime: Outline of a Comparative Study of European Statistics". *British Journal of Psychiatry* 18 (1), 1–15.
50. Institute of Medicine (IOM). 2000. *To Err Is Human: Building a Safer Health System*. National Academy Press, Washington, DC.
51. Leape, Lucian L. & Berwick, Donald M. 2005. "Five Years After To Err Is Human". *JAMA* 293 (19): 2384. American Medical Association (AMA). doi:10.1001/jama.293.19.2384.
52. Makary, Martin A & Daniel, Michael. 2016. "Medical Error—The Third Leading Cause of Death in the US". *BMJ*: i2139. doi:10.1136/bmj.i2139.
53. Grasso, Benjamin C; Genest, Robert & Jordan, Constance, et al. 2003. "Use of Chart and Record Reviews to Detect Medication Errors in a State Psychiatric Hospital". *Psychiatric Services* 54 (5): 677–681. American Psychiatric Association Publishing. doi:10.1176/appi.ps.54.5.677.
54. James, John T. 2013. "A New, Evidence-based Estimate of Patient Harms Associated with Hospital Care". *Journal of Patient Safety* 9 (3): 122–128. Ovid Technologies (Wolters Kluwer Health). doi:10.1097/pts.0b013e3182948a69.
55. Spear, Steven J. 2005. "Fixing Health Care from the Inside, Today". *Harvard Business Review* 83 (9): 78.
56. Reason, James. 2000. "Human Error: Models and Management". *BMJ* 320 (7237): 768–770. doi:10.1136/bmj.320.7237.768.
57. Emanuel, Linda; Berwick, Donald & Conway, James, et al. 2008. "What Exactly Is Patient Safety?" In: Henriksen, Kerm, Battles, James & Keyes Margaret, et al. (Eds.). *Advances in Patient Safety: New Directions and Alternative Approaches (Vol. 1: Assessment)*. Agency for Healthcare Research and Quality, Rockville, MD.
58. Kenney, Charles. 2010. *The Best Practice*. Public Affairs, New York.
59. McGlynn, Elizabeth; Asch, Steven & Adams, John, et al. 2003. "The Quality of Health Care Delivered to Adults in the United States". *New England Journal of Medicine* 348 (26): 2635–2645. Massachusetts Medical Society. doi:10.1056/nejmsa022615.
60. Mojtabai, Ramin; Fochtmann, Laura & Chang, Su-Wei, et al. 2009. "Unmet Need for Mental Health Care in Schizophrenia: An Overview of Literature and New Data From a First-Admission Study". *Schizophrenia Bulletin* 35 (4): 679–695. Oxford University Press (OUP). doi:10.1093/schbul/sbp045.
61. Keller, William; Fischer, Bernard & McMahon, Robert, et al. 2014. "Community Adherence to Schizophrenia Treatment and Safety Monitoring Guidelines". *The Journal of Nervous and Mental Disease* 202 (1): 6–12. Ovid Technologies (Wolters Kluwer Health). doi:10.1097/nmd.0000000000000093.
62. Introcaso, David. 2018. "The Never-Ending Misuse of Antipsychotics in Nursing Homes". Blog. HEALTH AFFAIRS BLOG. https://www.healthaffairs.org/do/10.1377/hblog20180424.962541/full/. Accessed June 10, 2017.

63. Schatzberg, Alan F. 2014. "A Word to the Wise About Ketamine". *American Journal of Psychiatry* 171 (3): 262–264. American Psychiatric Association Publishing. doi:10.1176/appi.ajp.2014.13101434.
64. Hermann, Richard; Dorwart, Robert & Hoover, Claudia, et al. 1995. "Variation in ECT Use in the United States". *American Journal of Psychiatry* 152 (6): 869–875. American Psychiatric Association Publishing. doi:10.1176/ajp.152.6.869.
65. Latey, R. H. & Fahy, T. J. 1988. "Some Influences on Regional Variation in Frequency of Prescription of Electroconvulsive Therapy". *British Journal of Psychiatry* 152 (2): 196–200. Royal College of Psychiatrists. doi:10.1192/bjp.152.2.196.
66. The $272 billion swindle. 2014. *The Economist*. 26–27.
67. Kusserow, Richard. 2014. "Kusserow's Corner: Mental Health Ranks High on Fraud Scale". http://health.wolterskluwerlb.com/2014/09/23/. Accessed June 12, 2019.
68. Morse, Susan. 2015. Millennium Health to pay $256 Million Over Charges that It Billed for Unnecessary Urine, Genetic Tests. *Healthcare Finance*. http://www.healthcarefinancenews.com/news/millennium-health-pay-256-million-over-charges-it-billed-unnecessary-urine-genetic-tests. Accessed June 29, 2017.
69. Chassin, Mark R. 1998. "Is Health Care Ready for Six Sigma Quality?" *The Milbank Quarterly* 76 (4): 565–591. Wiley. doi:10.1111/1468-0009.00106.
70. Haggerty, Jeannie; Reid, Robert & Freeman, George, et al. 2003. "Continuity of Care: A Multidisciplinary Review". *BMJ* 327 (7425): 1219–1221. doi:10.1136/bmj.327.7425.1219.
71. Gaynes, Bradley; Brown, Carrie & Lux, Linda, et al. 2015. "Management Strategies To Reduce Psychiatric Readmissions". Technical Brief No. 21. AHRQ Publication No.15-EHC018-EF. *Agency for Healthcare Research and Quality*. Rockville, MD. https://www.ncbi.nlm.nih.gov/books/NBK294451/. Accessed June 12, 2019.
72. Pincus Harold. 2014. "Care Transition Interventions to Reduce Psychiatric Re-Hospitalizations". National Association of State Mental Health Program Directors, Alexandria, VA. https://www.nasmhpd.org/sites/default/files/Assessment%20%233_Care%20Transitions%20Interventions%20toReduce%20Psychiatric%20Rehospitalization.pdf. Accessed June 12, 2019.
73. Jencks, Stephen; Williams, Mark & Coleman, Eric. 2009. "Rehospitalizations among Patients in the Medicare Fee-for-Service Program". *Journal of Vascular Surgery* 50 (1): 234. Elsevier BV. doi:10.1016/j.jvs.2009.05.045.
74. Hines, Anika; Barrett, Marguerite & Jiang, Joanna, et al. 2014. "Conditions With the Largest Number of Adult Hospital Readmissions by Payer, 2011. HCUP Statistical Brief #172". *Agency for Healthcare Research and Quality*, Rockville, MD. https://europepmc.org/abstract/med/24901179. Accessed June 12, 2019.
75. Berwick, Donald & Hackbarth, Andrew. 2012. "Eliminating Waste in US Health Care". *JAMA*, 307(14), 1513–1516.
76. Squires, David & Anderson, Chloe. 2015. "US Health Care from a Global Perspective: Spending, Use of Services, Prices, and Health in 13 Countries". *Issue Brief (Commonwealth Fund)* 15: 1–15.
77. Davis, Karen; Stremikis, Kristof & Squires, David, et al. 2014. "Mirror, Mirror on the Wall". How the Performance of the US Health Care System Compares Internationally. Commonwealth Fund, New York. http://www.resbr.net.br/wp-content/uploads/historico/Espelhoespelhomeu.pdf. Accessed June 12, 2019.
78. Fred, Herbert L. 2016. "Cutting the Cost of Health Care: The Physician's Role". *Texas Heart Institute Journal* 43 (1): 4–6. doi:10.14503/thij-15-5646.
79. Pear, Robert. 2016. "U.S. Health Spending in 2015 Averaged Nearly $10,000 Per Person", *New York Times*.
80. Bentley, Tanya GK; Effros, Rachel & Palar, Kartika, et al. 2008. "Waste in the US Health Care System: A Conceptual Framework". *The Milbank Quarterly* 86 (4): 629–659.
81. Erickson, Shari; Rockwern, Brooke & Koltov, Michelle, et al. 2017. "Putting Patients First by Reducing Administrative Tasks in Health Care: A Position Paper of the American College of Physicians". *Annals of Internal Medicine* 166 (9): 659. American College of Physicians. doi:10.7326/m16-2697.
82. Shanafelt, Tait; Hasan, Omar & Dyrbye, Lotte, et al. 2015. "Changes in Burnout and Satisfaction With Work-Life Balance in Physicians and the General US Working Population Between 2011 and 2014". *Mayo Clinic Proceedings* 90 (12): 1600–1613. Elsevier BV. doi:10.1016/j.mayocp.2015.08.023.

83. Ezez. 2019. "Burn-out An 'Occupational Phenomenon': International Classification of Diseases". *World Health Organization.* https://www.who.int/news/item/28-05-2019-burn-out-an-occupational-phenomenon-international-classification-of-diseases. Accessed December 11, 2020.
84. Shanafelt, Tait D. & Noseworthy, John H. 2017. "Executive Leadership and Physician Well-being". *Mayo Clinic Proceedings* 92 (1): 129–146. Elsevier BV. doi:10.1016/j.mayocp.2016.10.004.
85. Aiken, Linda; Clarke, Sean & Sloane, Douglas, et al. 2002. "Hospital Nurse Staffing and Patient Mortality, Nurse Burnout, and Job Dissatisfaction". *JAMA* 288 (16): 1987. American Medical Association (AMA). doi:10.1001/jama.288.16.1987.
86. Hall, Louise; Johnson, Judith & Watt, Ian, et al. 2016. "Healthcare Staff Wellbeing, Burnout, and Patient Safety: A Systematic Review". *PLOS One* 11 (7): e0159015. Public Library of Science (PLOS). doi:10.1371/journal.pone.0159015.
87. Pompili, Maurizio; Rinaldi, Gaetano & Lester, David, et al. 2006. "Hopelessness and Suicide Risk Emerge in Psychiatric Nurses Suffering From Burnout and Using Specific Defense Mechanisms". *Archives of Psychiatric Nursing* 20 (3): 135–143. Elsevier BV. doi:10.1016/j.apnu.2005.12.002.
88. Madathil, Renee; Heck, Nicholas & Schuldberg, David. 2014. "Burnout in Psychiatric Nursing: Examining the Interplay of Autonomy, Leadership Style, and Depressive Symptoms". *Archives of Psychiatric Nursing* 28 (3): 160–166.
89. Hanrahan, Nancy; Aiken, Linda & McClaine, Lakeetra, et al. 2010. "Relationship Between Psychiatric Nurse Work Environments and Nurse Burnout in Acute Care General Hospitals". *Issues in Mental Health Nursing* 31 (3): 198–207.
90. Jones, G. Morgan; Roe Neil & Louden Les, et al. 2017. "Factors Associated With Burnout Among US Hospital Clinical Pharmacy Practitioners: Results of a Nationwide Pilot Survey". *Hospital Pharmacy* 52 (11): 742–751. SAGE Publications. doi:10.1177/0018578717732339.
91. Dyrbye, Liselotte; Thomas Matthew & Massie F. Stanford, et al. 2008. "Burnout and Suicidal Ideation among U.S. Medical Students". *Annals of Internal Medicine* 149 (5): 334. American College of Physicians. doi:10.7326/0003-4819-149-5-200809020-00008.
92. Berwick, Donald M. 2016. "Era 3 for Medicine and Health Care". *JAMA* 315 (13): 1329. American Medical Association (AMA). doi:10.1001/jama.2016.1509.
93. Dunn, Patrick; Arnetz Bengt & Christensen, John, et al. 2007. "Meeting the Imperative to Improve Physician Well-being: Assessment of an Innovative Program". *Journal of General Internal Medicine* 22 (11): 1544–1552. Springer Science and Business Media LLC. doi:10.1007/s11606-007-0363-5.
94. Shanafelt, Tait; West, Colin & Sloan Jeff, et al. 2009. "Career Fit and Burnout Among Academic Faculty". *Archives of Internal Medicine* 169 (10): 990. American Medical Association (AMA). doi:10.1001/archinternmed.2009.70.
95. Cheney, Christopher. 2018. "How Workflow Optimization Addresses Physician Burnout | Health Leaders Media". *Healthleadersmedia.com.* https://www.healthleadersmedia.com/clinical-care/how-workflow-optimization-addresses-physician-burnout. Accessed June 12, 2019.
96. Bodenheimer, Thomas; Chen, Ellen & Bennett, Heather. 2009. "Confronting the Growing Burden of Chronic Disease: Can the U.S. Health Care Workforce Do the Job?" *Health Affairs* 28 (1): 64–74. Health Affairs (Project Hope). doi:10.1377/hlthaff.28.1.64.
97. Berwick, Donald M; Nolan, Thomas and Whittington, John. 2008. "The Triple Aim: Care, Health, and Cost". *Health Affairs* 27 (3): 759–769.
98. Bodenheimer, Thomas & Sinsky, Christine. 2014. "From Triple to Quadruple Aim: Care of the Patient Requires Care of the Provider". *The Annals of Family Medicine* 12 (6): 573–576.
99. Ranz, Jules M; Vergare, Michael & Wilk, Joshua, et al. 2006. "The Tipping Point From Private Practice to Publicly Funded Settings for Early- and Mid-Career Psychiatrists". *Psychiatric Services* 57 (11): 1640–1643. American Psychiatric Association Publishing. doi:10.1176/ps.2006.57.11.1640.
100. Swensen, Stephen J; Meyer, Gregg & Nelson, Eugene, et al. 2010. "Cottage Industry to Postindustrial Care—The Revolution in Health Care Delivery". *New England Journal of Medicine* 362 (5): e12. Massachusetts Medical Society. doi:10.1056/nejmp0911199.
101. Emanuel, Ezekiel J. 2017. *Prescription for the Future: The Twelve Transformational Practices of Highly Effective Medical Organizations.* Public Affairs.

102. Bennett, Michael J. 2000. "Retraining the Practicing Psychiatrist". *Psychiatric Services* 51 (7): 932–934. American Psychiatric Association Publishing. doi:10.1176/appi.ps.51.7.932.
103. Montague, Enid & Asan, Onur. 2014. "Dynamic Modeling of Patient and Physician Eye Gaze to Understand the Effects of Electronic Health Records on Doctor-Patient Communication and Attention". *International Journal of Medical Informatics* 83 (3): 225–234. Elsevier BV. doi:10.1016/j.ijmedinf.2013.11.003.
104. Verghese, Abraham. 2008. "Culture Shock—Patient as Icon, Icon as Patient". *New England Journal of Medicine* 359 (26): 2748–2751. Massachusetts Medical Society. doi:10.1056/nejmp0807461.
105. Friedberg, Mark; Chen, Peggy & Van Busum, Kristin, et al. 2014. "Factors Affecting Physician Professional Satisfaction and their Implications for Patient Care, Health Systems, and Health Policy". *Rand Health Quarterly* 3 (4).
106. Sharfstein, Steven S. & Dickerson, Faith B. 2006. "Psychiatry and the Consumer Movement". *Health Affairs* 25 (3): 734–736. Health Affairs (Project Hope). doi:10.1377/hlthaff.25.3.734.
107. Tomes, Nancy. 2006. ""The Patient as a Policy Factor: A Historical Case Study of the onsumer/Survivor Movement in Mental Health". *Health Affairs* 25 (3): 720–729. Health Affairs (Project Hope). doi:10.1377/hlthaff.25.3.720.
108. Campbell, Jean. 1997. "How Consumers/Survivors Are Evaluating the Quality of Psychiatric Care". *Evaluation Review* 21 (3): 357–363. SAGE Publications. doi:10.1177/0193841x9702100310.
109. Wagner, Edward; Austin, Brian & Davis, Connie, et al. 2001. "Improving Chronic Illness Care: Translating Evidence Into Action". *Health Affairs* 20 (6): 64–78. Health Affairs (Project Hope). doi:10.1377/hlthaff.20.6.64.
110. Sheingold, Brenda H & Hahn, Joyce. 2014. "The History of Healthcare Quality: The First 100 Years 1860–1960". *International Journal of Africa Nursing Sciences* 1: 18–22.
111. Neuhauser, D. 2003. "Florence Nightingale Gets No Respect: As a Statistician That Is". *BMJ Quality & Safety* 12 (4): 317–317.
112. Manos, Anthony; Sattler, Mark & Alukal, George. 2006. "Make Healthcare Lean". *Quality Progress* 39(7): 24.
113. Sloan, Terry; Fitzgerald, Anneke & Hayes, Kathryn, et al. 2014. "Lean in Healthcare–History and Recent Developments". *Journal of Health Organization and Management* 28 (2). Emerald. doi:10.1108/jhom-04-2014-0064.
114. Kenney, Charles. 2012. *Transforming Health Care: Virginia Mason Medical Center's Pursuit of the Perfect Patient Experience*. CRC Press.
115. Toussaint, John, & Gerard, Roger. 2010. *On the Mend: Revolutionizing Healthcare to Save Lives and Transform the Industry*. Lean Enterprise Institute.
116. Merlino, Joseph P; Omi, Joanna & Bowen, Jill (Eds.). 2014. *Lean Behavioral Health: The Kings County Hospital Story*. Oxford University Press.
117. Boysen, Philip G. 2013. "Just Culture: A Foundation for Balanced Accountability and Patient Safety". *Ochsner Journal* 13 (3): 400–406.
118. Chassin, Mark & Loeb, Jerod. 2013 "High-Reliability Health Care: Getting There from Here". *The Milbank Quarterly* 91 (3): 459–490.
119. Elster, S.; Feinstein, K. W., & Vrbin, C. M. (Eds.). (2012). *Moving Beyond Repair: Perfecting Health Care*. Pittsburgh Regional Health Initiative.
120. Sharfstein, Steven S. 2010. "Psychiatry is Alive and Well". *World Psychiatry* 9 (1): 33–34. Wiley. doi:10.1002/j.2051-5545.2010.tb00262.x.
121. Katschnig, Heinz. 2010. "Are Psychiatrists an Endangered Species? Observations on Internal and External Challenges to the Profession". *World Psychiatry* 9 (1): 21–28. Wiley. doi:10.1002/j.2051-5545.2010.tb00257.x.
122. Bracken, Pat; Thomas, Philip & Timimi, Sami, et al. 2012. "Psychiatry Beyond the Current Paradigm". *British Journal of Psychiatry* 201 (6): 430–434. Royal College of Psychiatrists. doi:10.1192/bjp.bp.112.109447.

Section II

Value and Waste in Psychiatry

In Section I, we introduced the reader to the current state of mental healthcare. We examined mental health as a 'system' of care. We provided actual scenarios and perspectives that address the need for change. Also, we highlighted gaps in the continuum of care that can lead to failure during care delivery. To improve the current state of mental healthcare, there is a need to understand the value and waste in a system and measure the value provided. This chapter will define value and review value from the patient's perspective, the family, the provider, the payer, and the system. Additionally, this chapter concludes with the definition of waste and how to identify waste within a system of care.

I. Value

The definition of value in healthcare is health outcomes per dollar spent over time (Porter, 2010).[1] Porter's definition is not a novel concept as societies have reasoned what a fair price would be for goods and services over the past several millennia. However, providers and systems need to know what the numerator, 'health outcomes,' truly represents. From a mental health perspective, value has been described as whether or not a given disorder or disease gets better or worse over time. Value includes symptom relief, restored or improved functioning from a physical and mental health perspective, and sustained recovery for a better quality of life (Roca, 2015).[2] It also includes a subjective sense of normalcy and wellbeing and a restoration of hope. However, patients typically view value more broadly as benefits received for burdens endured (Toussaint & Berry, 2013).[3] The benefit of a healthcare service received must be equal to or outweigh the time, cost, and stress burden endured by the patient.

The value definition implies that healthcare organizations can maintain value by proportionately reducing both the benefits and burdens endured (Roca, 2015).[2] This thinking can place healthcare organizations in an uncomfortable situation of monetizing healthcare outcomes while keeping costs in line with payer expectations. Maintaining value has to be accomplished while maintaining financial stability. However, when compromising both ends of the equation, organizations fail to match or exceed patient expectations yielding buyer's remorse and reputational damage. Healthcare organizations must protect against eliminating the vital benefits of their services because it leaves patients feeling cheated, deprived, or offended. It also has adverse effects on the patient's health, which defeats a healthcare organization's purpose. Therefore, real improvement suggests a slant toward ever-increasing value rather than merely maintaining the current level of services.

A. Value and the Patient

The patient is the primary customer of a healthcare system because they directly receive the benefits from the services rendered. In a mental healthcare setting, patients often feel vulnerable and defenseless, complicating and compromising care delivery. Therefore, when considering making improvements to the system, an organization must do so with the patient in mind.

Womack and Jones (2015) suggested that patients want a healthcare provider to:

i. Solve their health problem completely,
ii. Tailor a treatment plan that provides precisely what they want,
iii. Provide treatment where they want it,
iv. Provide treatment when they want it,
v. Reduce the number of decisions they must make, and
vi. Reduce the time it takes to solve their problems.[4]

This list of benefits received suggests that quality and service delivery are important factors in the value equation. Quality is a measure of excellence that is free of defects, deficiencies, or variation. Delivery is a measure of excellence that is free of delay for information or tasks. Thus, the value equation becomes:

$$\frac{\text{Health Outcomes} \times \text{Quality} \times \text{Delivery}}{\text{Cost}}$$

Some organizations may not fully buy into these concepts because the cost to fulfill them can become exponentially burdensome to the system as a whole. However, this forces organizations and providers to rethink the current system of care and design new processes to improve health outcomes, quality, and delivery without significantly increasing cost and time. Organizations that take the time to innovate new systems of care and add more value to the patient will flourish. Those organizations that do not innovate nor improve the value equation will be out of favor with patients and providers alike, thus offering less differentiation from current competitors and potentially driving new competitors into the market. A patient portal is a simple example of how healthcare organizations are differentiating themselves from one another. When a patient can access prior visit information, review treatment plans, manage medication refills, and schedule appointments through an online portal, there is a clear improvement in value provided without the burden of calling a provider and requesting services.

Technology provides plenty of benefits as well as some new burdens to patients. Continuing the example illustrated in Section I is the widespread adoption of the modern-day electronic medical record (EMR). During a routine visit, the EMR becomes the primary object of a providers' attention rather than the patient, thus moving psychiatry further away from the therapeutic value that a mental health professional provides. To this day, there is little understanding of how to build an EMR that supports mental healthcare needs. An EMR also offers several benefits to the patient. A few benefits include having legible documentation, transferring prescriptions to a pharmacy with a few clicks, and flagging medication interactions to prevent injuring patients.

The one unique aspect of the value discussion in mental healthcare is the patient's motivation. It is the relative readiness of a patient to accept treatment. Consider the stages of change depicted in Figure 2.1.

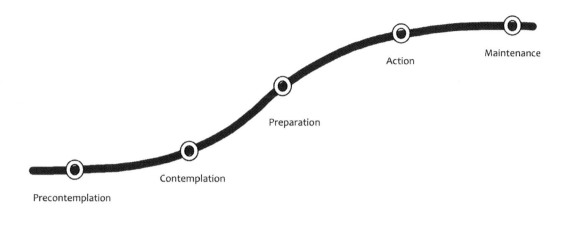

Figure 2.1 Stages of change. (Gold, 2018, adapted from DiClemente & Prochaska.)[5]

The relative readiness of a patient to accept treatment determines the pace at which providers can add value. Some patients are 'prepared' to change or take action in agreement with the provider's instructions on an inpatient psychiatric unit. However, some of the remaining patients might be in 'pre-contemplation' or 'contemplation' stages of change. They may require additional time to understand their own needs and may need more time to achieve optimum health. The time it takes to move patients along the stages of change continuum will significantly alter the value equation.

B. Value and the Family

VIGNETTE 2.1

Joey suffered from severe Tourette's disorder and tended to curse significantly. His parents had to continually protect and advocate for him in healthcare and school settings. He had recently suffered a severe ankle injury while skateboarding in the park. He was in excruciating pain as his parents took him to the ER. Any increase in his level of stress or anxiety tended to increase his motor tics, vocal tics (he would make loud grunting sounds), and his tendency to curse. His severe pain had pushed him over the edge. His mother was sure that he would settle down once treated with the proper orthopedic care and pain management. She warned the triage nurse about his condition and tendencies, but the triage nurse had a minimal understanding of Tourette's disorder. Both of the nurses who came to check on Joey were met with offensive expletives. Even though his mother kept insisting that Joey's cursing was not the problem that brought him into the ER, the nurses requested a psychiatric consultation because they were offended and shocked at Joey's 'poor manners.' They also had doubts about his mother's parenting skills. The wait for the x-ray and care by an orthopedic provider took five hours. The provider applied a cast, gave him a mild sedative and analgesic, and soon Joey was fast asleep.

Joey's mom waited an additional three hours for the psychiatric social worker to arrive. She saw Joey sleeping. She gently aroused Joey and asked him if he wanted some juice and wanted to go home. Joey asked for a soda. The social worker finished her assessment in 20 minutes and apologized to Joey's mother for the misunderstanding in the ER. Despite Joey's adequate care for his ankle injury, the family left unsatisfied.

The family of a patient who benefits from the service can both be a primary and a secondary customer. When families provide guardianship and act as the legal authority to make choices on behalf of a patient, they assume a primary customer role. Within this context, the guardian must become part of the treatment team to ensure successful health outcomes and good quality and delivery of care.

Families or caretakers are secondary customers of the system and often provide stability and support during an inpatient stay and when a discharged patient returns home. Families and caretakers must be willing partners in the recovery of a mental health patient and work to understand the social and environmental dynamics surrounding that patient. Therefore, providers and mental healthcare systems often deliver training to families and caregivers to reduce transition issues from inpatient environments to home environments.

Sometimes, the parent or caregiver may also require therapy. This need complicates the care model and requires clinicians who have a good grasp of family dynamics to ensure a stable discharging location once a patient is well enough to leave an inpatient setting. Also, if there is a family dynamic that requires family counseling sessions, inpatient mental healthcare systems have to complete these tasks without additional reimbursement, thus burdening the system of care. Suppose a family dynamic or safety concern prevents a patient from returning home. In that case, the provider will seek alternative discharge locations to residential or group home environments where the patient has the best chance of staying safe and stable.

Further, a family may relinquish their rights and responsibilities as a care provider. For example, when a patient depletes all covered mental health days in an insurance plan, the family may choose to make a patient the ward of the state to allow for continued healthcare services without assuming the responsibility of costly medical bills. Unfortunately, adult patients may end up in state hospitals, prisons, in a shelter, at an unlicensed group home, or become homeless. Therefore, there is a great need to look at how the larger social support system can support families through difficult times when mental health conditions prevent patients from returning home.

C. Value and the Organization

VIGNETTE 2.2

Rita was exhausted. Her mother took her to the ER because she was feeling suicidal. After waiting in the ER for eight hours, the hospitalist finally admitted her to the psychiatric inpatient unit. During the first 24 hours, five different practitioners evaluated her and asked her many similar questions. First, an admitting nurse began the process. Next, the on-call resident wrote an admission-holding note. Then a physician's assistant completed the medical history and physical. The next morning, the admitting psychiatrist interviewed her, followed by the social worker. By the fifth time, she was so upset that she screamed at the social worker and stormed out of the office. She yelled, "Don't you all talk to each other?"

Many healthcare organizations measure health outcomes, quality, delivery, and cost. However, when developing a family of measures, they must also consider how organized their team is around a common mission. Factors of an organization that contributes to the value equation include key operational needs such as staff safety, engagement, and morale. Also, healthcare organizations strive to research and advance value in healthcare practices and innovate new modalities for patients to access care. Moreover, psychiatric organizations focus attention on increasing access to care through introducing new technologies and utilizing philanthropic means.

Each additional factor adds a level of complexity to the organization. Organizations that have a good value proposition for their patients tend to grow rapidly. However, rapid growth often increases system complexity experienced by the patient and family within the system and can cause a loss of focus on the value equation. To protect against this, organizations must ensure continued focus on increasing benefits without adding more burden. Consider the diagram in Figure 2.2 that illustrates the segmentation of organizational value in the form of a house.

While there are several different versions of this house in the literature, the basic structure is the same. Employee engagement is a foundational factor for any organization to build a successful

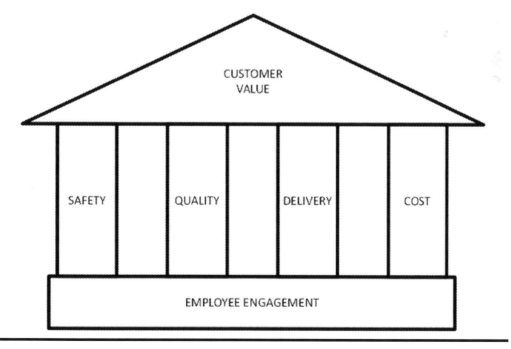

Figure 2.2　House of value.

model of care. Disengaged employees weaken the ability to provide the right level of care at the right time and cannot focus on improvement to the existing system of care.

There is an ongoing debate on how much time organizations should spend providing value versus improving the value offered due to limited resources. However, there is universal agreement that both are important for long-term organizational viability. At first glance, it might seem impossible to consider such an engagement model in healthcare. However, every year healthcare organizations participate in employee engagement surveys. Outside of improved pay and benefits, the top four universal improvements needed by staff are trust, communication, recognition, and collaboration. Addressing these four gaps is as simple as engaging in a focused reduction of inefficiency in the workplace. The employees benefit by feeling more connected to the organization, and the organization benefits through the reduction or elimination of waste.

From a foundation of engagement, the pillars of safety, quality, delivery, and cost support the value provided. Organizations depict safety as a separate pillar because there are several factors to consider. First, staff safety is vital in a healthcare environment due to bloodborne pathogens, exposure to infectious diseases, sharp objects, heavy lifting, patient aggression, and so forth. Second, patient safety is vital in a healthcare environment due to medication administration, the need to prevent patient harm, patient falls, etc. Third, the setting of care where staff work and patients heal should ensure cleanliness, be free from hazards, and so forth. Thus, a strong safety culture enhances organizations' ability to achieve value in the eyes of the patient.

When considering the quality and delivery pillars, clinics or hospitals must consider what happens to a patient before, during, and after rendering a service. Satisfaction surveys provide a static look at an organization and do not enable healthcare providers to consider improvement as a significant part of daily work. Also, due to their retrospective nature, surveys prompt healthcare organizations to be reactive rather than proactive. The house of value focuses on organizations proactively achieving the vision and mission.

Improving value has to be a continuous process without which quality and delivery can erode over time. For example, the wait time for a local clinic is four weeks long. Some may wait, while others may try to find an alternative provider, and as soon as an option opens up that takes same-day appointments, the patient's value proposition changes. Therefore, the improvement of services and the continuous improvement of value are necessary for an organization to stay relevant to patients' and families' needs.

In healthcare, given that patients require individualized care based on their unique set of circumstances, one patient's expectations may not precisely match the expectations of another. For example, some patients may require psychotherapy. In contrast, others need socioeconomic help, and yet others need medications to help cope with acute behavioral exacerbations, chronic conditions, or side effects of other medications. The concept of value gets complicated quickly when patients require a combination of psychotherapeutic, socioeconomic, and biomedical treatments.

An alternate way to look at the diagram in Figure 2.2 is to consider the concept of 'True North' metrics (Rother, 2009).[6] Imagine the house is nothing more than a dial on a compass pointing the way to achieve the organizational mission. When embarking on a journey in the wilderness, an explorer would not do so without a compass or some navigational tool as a guide. A compass helps to provide the direction as a team heads out for exploration. Likewise, when embarking on improvement in a healthcare system, the organization must determine where 'True North' is. Organizations only have a finite set of resources, and they must channel this resource base to focus on the drivers of value that ultimately achieve improvements in care. This reference point in space and time is what organizations need to align and focus on to maintain vigilance and focus on the patient.

To achieve 'True North' and ultimately a focus on value, the organization must focus on the point of engagement with a patient. The point of engagement is the moment in time when a healthcare organization interacts with a patient, whether informally providing information about a program, admitting a patient for a service, rendering a service, receiving payment after a service rendered, or referring a patient to an additional service of care. Each activity (when a patient encounters an organization) is a point of engagement. Thus, the total patient experience is the cumulative beneficial effect of all points of engagement for an entire interaction. In service organizations, the longer the tenure of the service, the more points of engagement exist, and the more difficult it is to achieve a perfect patient experience. Therefore, utilizing improvement methods becomes necessary to sustain and improve the value provided.

Providing a safe experience of care at the right time for the right cost is the best way, to sum up each section within the house of value. This new definition allows an organization to segment the equation of value into its most basic components; Employee Engagement (providing), Safety (a safe), Quality (better care, better health, and at the customer's expected level of experience of care), Delivery (at the right time), and Efficiency (for the right cost). By doing so, the organization can learn to measure the value they provide, thus leading to better questioning, improved solutions, and achieve positive change.

As we discussed in the context of the 'quadruple aim,' employee engagement will also be enhanced by improving the work-life of healthcare providers. Reducing burnout and improving the wellness of employees will lead to better patient quality and safety outcomes.

D. Value and the Provider

VIGNETTE 2.3

Sigourney has had five admissions to the psychiatric unit this year. She has seen three different psychiatrists and a psychotherapist during this time. One psychiatrist in an inpatient setting diagnosed her as having Major Depressive Disorder with complex post-traumatic stress disorder (PTSD). The provider was focusing a lot of her time teaching the patient 'safety,' 'grounding,' and 'healthy boundaries.' Another psychiatrist in the partial hospitalization setting thought she was 'bipolar' and started her on a mood stabilizer to deal with her 'ultra-rapid mood swings' and 'impulsivity.' Her outpatient psychotherapist thought that the patient had a borderline personality disorder and wondered when to work on 'projective identification' and how to introduce 'mentalization' and 'distress tolerance' into her care. Her outpatient psychiatrist wondered about the role of attachment in her developmental history. However, none of these four practitioners shared their respective formulations with the patient or each other. Meanwhile, the patient could not stop cutting herself, cycled in and out of many relationships, and kept running into difficulties because of her anger, rage, and destructive tendencies.

A tertiary customer within the value equation is the provider. A provider is well versed in methods and procedures, keeps up with the latest technological trends, advancements in medication regimens, and evidence-based practices. Thus, a provider will often know what is best for patients in their care. This is where healthcare can deviate from Womack's definition of a patient getting what they want because what they want does not always equate to what they need. A patient addicted to painkillers may want medication but what they need is a more tightly monitored or discontinuation of opioids, mental health consultation, and optimum treatment of their pain and psychiatric condition.

The provider must also make a judgment call for every patient at the point of admission to the appropriate level of care and determine the point of discharge. For instance, a provider must decide if the inpatient setting services will help a patient stay safe, feel better, and function better. Also, while an organization may be compensated for extra time spent in the inpatient setting, the provider must ensure adequate progress in health and the patient is stable and functioning well enough to be discharged. Moreover, when considering the social determinants of health that include housing, transportation, money, etc., a provider must work with their support team to determine if a patient can be discharged safely. Thus, the provider adds a component of patient safety and stability to the value equation. When moving from one level of care to the next, it becomes crucial for providers to discuss their decisions with one another to ensure smooth patient transitions.

E. Value and the Payer

Complicating matters further are the payers who act as a tertiary customer working on behalf of the patient and the collective group to lower the burden and cost of services. Payers also represent the patient to ensure healthcare organizations are providing the right care. Payers become valuable advocates for patients, but they can also interfere with care delivery. Therefore, payers and healthcare organizations must work collaboratively to ensure reimbursement rates compensate organizations for the care provided. When the cost of services outpaces reimbursement rates, a severe shortage of services can affect the viability of mental health in community settings. Additional burdens can also change the value equation considerably for the patients.

Also, the payer's procedures to control costs can increase the cost to the healthcare system. For example, requiring providers to obtain prior authorization or reauthorization for many medications that a patient may need impacts the number of patients a doctor can see on a given day, thus increasing the overall health system's cost.

F. Value and the Government

Federal and State governments employ several regulatory bodies that monitor compliance. There are privacy and safety regulations, third-party surveyors providing certification for participation in Medicare or Medicaid programs, and a host of agencies providing grants for mental healthcare initiatives and research. Each of these can add value to community mental health. Each grant can also help organizations research new services, thus benefiting more people who need psychiatric care. Therefore, organizations consider these governmental agencies as tertiary customers. While some contend the government provides more burden than value, they are the largest paying customer in the healthcare system. Thus, maintaining compliance with their demands is imperative to stay operational.

G. Value and the Continuum of Care

A majority of patients seeking acute inpatient care will continue to need services post-discharge. While an acute inpatient care setting works to provide enough stability and functioning to the patient so the patient can return home, there is usually a long road to recovery. Those that continue treatment outside the acute care setting, either in a day program, an intensive residential program, or an outpatient treatment program, will continue to improve symptom relief and functioning. However, when disparate organizations provide different levels of care, it becomes difficult to assess how much value a patient receives over the series of patient encounters. Every healthcare organization is focused on its silo rather than looking at the overall impact of care on the patient. While population health initiatives are fostering the inclusion of mental health into general healthcare settings, there is an ongoing challenge due to the cost component of the value equation.

Additional adverse socioeconomic challenges often plague patients who seek mental health services. Even with the best-laid plans to provide symptom relief and improved functioning, if a patient returns to a homeless environment without the necessary resources to procure medications, most of what was accomplished in an acute inpatient care setting will be lost. Thus, an improved cross-organizational focus on the continuum of care and supportive social infrastructure is necessary to improve patient value for the mentally ill.

Also, patients admitted with challenging psychiatric disorders (i.e., aggression) can be hard to place back into the community once discharged from inpatient settings. Organizations that operate outside healthcare, such as nursing homes or group homes, can refuse to accept discharged patients with mental or behavioral issues. When this happens, patients become stuck in the most expensive level of care, which wastes public dollars and prevents access to other patients in need. The disjointedness of the total system results in inefficient or ineffective healthcare.

H. Value Added, Value Enabled, and Waste

A process step is value-added if the process step improves the symptom level or functioning of the patient, is completed the first time correctly, and the patient is willing to pay for it. If any of these three elements are missing, then the activity or process step is not value-added. Process improvers use these elements to challenge every step within a process and every process within a system to determine how much time staff spend on value-added activity versus non-value-added activity.

VIGNETTE 2.4

Carl was a busy professional and disliked waiting in the provider's offices. He found it to be an affront to his sense of professionalism. He was even more appalled when the provider did not apologize and carried on as if it was business as usual. Carl made it a point to change physicians if they made him wait for more than 30 minutes without a valid reason.

Learning to separate 'activity' from 'value' is a fundamental concept in performance improvement. The improvement approach is to increase the ratio of time spent on value-added work. To accomplish this, an organization must work toward eliminating inefficiency by removing non-value-added activities. Consider the diagram in Figure 2.3.

Work that is not value-added but necessary to ensure a seamless transition between activities is 'value-enabling' work. For example, the time it takes to calibrate a glucometer is value-enabling work. A patient may not see the value directly related to them at the moment, but it assures

54 ■ *Transforming Mental Healthcare*

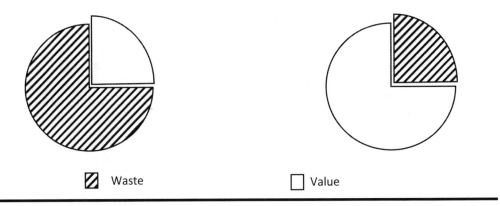

Figure 2.3 Improving the ratio of value-added time in processes.

accurate glucose readings so that providers are administering the proper care. The value-enabled steps create indirect value by preventing delays or errors in care.

The diagram in Figure 2.4 depicts a process as an abstract strip of time with interspersed value-added steps, value-enabled steps, and non-value added waste steps.

Organizations need to maximize the value-added time, reduce the value-enabled time, and work to eliminate the wasted time. Consider the same abstract strip after a series of improvements to a process in Figure 2.5.

At a conceptual level, working to reduce and eliminate the non-value-added steps creates a win-win scenario for the patient, the family, the payer, the provider, the organization, and the government. Lower costs, less waste affecting the delivery of quality care, and improved outcomes all lead to improving the value equation. The upfront investment in time to improve becomes well worth it as organizations can react to changing demand patterns more readily.

Modern ambulatory clinics offer an example of improved value. They removed waiting areas in the front of the clinic (Chang, 2019) and focused on flowing patients through the clinic without the need for a patient to stop, sit, and wait for services.[7] In years past, clinicians used waiting

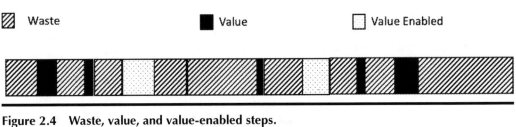

Figure 2.4 Waste, value, and value-enabled steps.

Figure 2.5 Waste, value, and value-enabled steps after improvement.

rooms as a way to slow down the work. However, by eliminating waiting rooms and focusing on flowing patients through exam rooms at the pace of varying patient demand, the clinician focuses on completing the care process for patients when needed.

II. Waste

An activity or task is non-value added when at least one of the three value-added equation elements is not satisfied. Another term for non-value added is waste. Many professionals argue that describing every step of the process as either value-added or waste is shortsighted because there are plenty of activities that do not fit the strict definition of value but help the patient. They may be right. However, this thinking breeds complacency with the status quo causing organizations to rationalize a lack of focus on innovation and improvement. Also, as populations grow, there is a continual and unsustainable cost increase to healthcare annually. The imperative for healthcare organizations is to strive for ways to provide the lowest waste and highest value model that consistently delivers good patient-centered care.

One of the more notable observers of waste in a system was Taiichi Ohno, a systems engineer at Toyota. He broke down waste into seven basic categories. The categories are Overproduction, Defects, Inventory, Transportation, Motion, Waiting, and Processing. The eighth form of waste, non-utilized talent, was added several years later (Ohno, 1988).[8]

A. Eight Forms of Waste

1. Overproduction

The waste of overproduction is defined as processing either too soon or too much. Systems tend to overproduce because the various process steps within the system are not operating at the same rate, or there are inherent quality issues. In some cases, the process steps become overburdened with demand, or there is an uneven workload from one process step to the next. A system must produce only what is required, how it is required, and when it is required to achieve perfect flow.

A great example of overproduction waste in mental healthcare is how clinicians document care during an inpatient stay. For example, a typical acute psychiatric inpatient unit day might start with breakfast, medication administration, vital sign monitoring, and a goals group. In a group that focuses on 'Goals of the Day,' each patient fills out a self-assessment form. The group leader then leads a discussion on what each patient wants to work on during the day to improve their stability and functioning. At the same time, an attending provider is working independently from the unit activity, calling outpatients one at a time to monitor how they are doing and asking them what they will work on during the day. Both the group leader and the attending provider enter the same patient progress information into the EMR. This duplication of efforts is a classic case where two resources accomplish the same task of daily goals. They are overproducing more information than needed for the care of the patient.

During the rest of the day, the nurse, social worker, and mental health workers enter patient progress notes into the EMR. However, the provider does not review all progress notes because it is too time-consuming. Also, most of this information does not pass along to the next level of care because the outpatient providers only want an abbreviated summary. However, acute care health systems continue to overproduce their documentation because the culture has moved to a "if it's not documented, then it wasn't done" mentality. A better approach for highly skilled staff might be to document by exception only rather than documenting for the sake of documenting.

2. Defects

> ### VIGNETTE 2.5
> Laurie admitted herself to an inpatient psychiatric unit. Her doctor diagnosed her with major depressive disorder and started a medication regimen. She participated in groups on the unit regularly and met with her treatment team and psychiatrist every day. She gradually increased her sleep to eight hours a day, and her appetite her eating habits went from skipping meals to eating each meal completely. After two weeks, her health improved with respect to safety and stability, and she was communicating effectively with others. After establishing the aftercare plan, her treatment team discharged her from the hospital. Laurie came back to the inpatient unit two weeks later, and the treatment team diagnosed her with bipolar disorder, as she was in a full-blown manic state. In looking through her previous inpatient record, the provider noticed that the provider did not elicit a family history of bipolar disorder in the last inpatient stay, and neither did he elicit Laurie's history of two prior severe postpartum depressive episodes.

Waste of defects occurs when making errors in the process that causes mistakes or rework. Examples of defects include diagnostic errors, medication errors, incorrect or missing documentation, and so forth. Each defect can lead to an unsatisfied patient experience or adversely affect the patient's care when receiving a service.

An example of defects occurs when a clinician improperly diagnoses a patient. The experts suggest misdiagnosis can happen as much as 40% of the time. These numbers are startling, considering that for every 1 million patients, four hundred thousand will not receive the proper diagnosis on the first visit to a mental healthcare system. The three main reasons for diagnostic disagreement are inconstancy of the patient (5%), the inconstancy of the clinician (32.5%), and inadequacy of the nomenclature (62.5%) (Aboraya et al., 2006).[9] By not diagnosing the patient correctly the first time, the entire first stay is a waste. Albeit there may have been some improvement in the patient's insight, understanding, and functioning during the first stay, the more considerable need to sustain patient stable functioning once discharged is unmet, rendering the service wasteful.

3. Waiting

The waste of waiting occurs when there is idle time within a process, causing a patient to wait. Idle time can occur within a process step when two team members are waiting on each other or between process steps when placing patients to a lower level of care. Waiting in one area of a process usually means there is an overburden in another area. Therefore, anytime there is waiting in a process, there is a need to look upstream to address unevenness in flow. A good example of waiting waste is during the blood draw and testing process. The time a provider waits from blood draw to results can often lengthen the length of stay.

4. Transportation

The waste of transportation is the combined movement within a system. This movement could be the movement of supplies from a warehouse to the point of use or patients' movement between process steps. A more practical example of the waste of transportation from a patient perspective is the number of patient trips to the outpatient clinic. In many cases where patients need a prescription refill or do not require intense therapy, telemedicine services or internet-based services provide value by reducing wasted transportation.

5. Motion

VIGNETTE 2.6

Dr. Ali was frustrated. When changing an observation level before the EMR, he picked the patient chart, flipped to the orders page, and wrote the observation level. Today, when Dr. Ali changes an observation level, he signs into a network terminal, signs into his EMR, picks the patient from a patient list, and clicks the order button. After that, he picks an order set with multiple dropdown menus to select a new observation level and explains why he is changing the observation level. Even though electronic records are more legible, he longs for the simplicity and ease of paper charts.

The waste of motion is associated with movement within a single process step. For example, the number of keystrokes for an office worker to gain access to a form or the time spent to get a pen from a supply cabinet. Nurse flow can be problematic when they do not have what they need at their fingertips. The waste of motion is also a great way to consider how friendly a process step is from an ergonomics perspective. When a patient is undergoing withdrawal management in their first 24 hours on a unit, the nurse needs the right equipment such as clothing, gloves, and supplies to help the patient in need. In many cases, a simple withdrawal management kit provides all of the items needed in a single case to minimize the number of steps to complete the task, thus reducing the waste of motion.

6. Extra Processing

VIGNETTE 2.7

George, a hospital administrator, was amazed at how much staff talk in healthcare. He feels healthcare is a very verbose culture and was surprised at how much of his time was spent in meetings.

After a few months, he realized that many important safety discussions take place in multiple meetings. Many conversations went round and round, and topics were often repeated. He found there was no structured problem-solving approach in place. He also noticed there were many good ideas discussed, but there was no tracking for them. Also, he found that accountability and project management skills were lacking.

The waste of extra processing occurs when there are extra steps within a process that do not add value. For example, auditing the charts for compliance or relying on inspection processes to ensure quality work. Another example is asking the same history multiple times during one admission and again when a patient goes to a different level of care, such as partial hospitalization or outpatient. The whole cycle repeats itself when a person readmits to a hospital. This back and forth could go on for years if a patient has several re-hospitalizations. Only a very small percentage of information on new admission notes come from prior admission notes. Much of a new admission note has to be re-entered by a clinician.

7. Inventory

VIGNETTE 2.8

Samantha was in charge of the pharmacy budget for the hospital. She had to stay within her allocated limit. Unfortunately, the newly released antipsychotics and injectable medications were expensive. Most of them were not on the formulary. Providers often requested these costly medications for their patients to prevent the discontinuation of their standing medications, which they had been prescribed on the outside. However, many of these medications stocked in the pharmacy went unused and often expired.

She prepared a presentation on the usage patterns of non-formulary medications. When the providers saw the data, they remarked that although this has been going on for years but no one had brought it to their attention. Many providers did not understand the financial implications of their decisions on the pharmacy budget.

The waste of inventory is when organizations hold more inventory than needed. Too much supply can clutter a work area and require more storage locations than necessary. Often, oversupply occurs when there is unevenness in response to patient needs. A good way to determine where there is a need for improvement is to look for the buildup of inventory in the system. Every time there is a buildup of inventory, the system does not flow optimally. Examples of inventory waste include the batching of billing data for entry at the end of a week or waiting until the end of the day to complete documentation for a set of patients.

8. Non-Utilized Talent

VIGNETTE 2.9

Luiz was a mental technician on an inpatient unit. He had a calm demeanor, was very cordial with patients, perceptive, and could sense what a patient, nurse, or doctor wanted. He had sharp observation skills and believed that if he had a good rapport with the patients, it would become easy whenever there is a conflict or a moment of high stress. Luiz had excellent de-escalation skills and was amazed at all the policies and practice recommendations for seclusion and restraint use. He wished someone would ask him for his thoughts because he felt that using seclusion and restraint was not therapeutic. He had seen many of his peers injure themselves when going hands-on a patient. Also, he felt that he was more successful when he could calm a patient or even prevent a patient from getting aggressive with just his words and his interactional style.

The waste of non-utilized talent occurs when organizations do not utilize and engage their existing human capital.

Several organizations employ staff to manage the waste in the system. Whether there are flow issues, auditing quality, controlling inventory, processing too much work, investigating safety concerns, and so forth, organizations limit themselves from focusing on innovation and achieving their full potential.

Additionally, when clinicians are not working at the top of their license because they are working around a set of wasteful practices, the patient does not benefit from the waste built into the system. Workarounds in healthcare systems add to the cost of care.

Bill Lareau (2003) expanded the thoughts on non-utilized talent waste to include various types of waste.[10]

i. *Goal alignment waste* or when competing priorities end up causing a system to become slow or stuck in neutral when trying to improve.
ii. *Task waste* or spending time on wasteful activities.
iii. *Control waste* or when managers are staying busy asking about how processes are going rather than working to improve anything.
iv. *Workaround waste* or the waste associated with employees having to find different methods to capture information because the source is closely guarded.
v. *Information waste* or the waste associated with missing, inaccurate, or collecting irrelevant data.

It is possible to re-categorize some of these human wastes as the waste of defects, the waste of processing, or even the waste of motion. More importantly, organizations can start to review and improve processes based on the patient value they provide. If an activity does not provide value, an organization must figure out a way to reduce or eliminate wasteful activity. In some cases, a focused team can root out the waste. In other cases, there may be a need to innovate a new way to complete a process to achieve a breakthrough in performance.

B. Waste Walks

VIGNETTE 2.10

When a mental health hospital was having difficulties with numerous transfers to the Emergency Department (ED) that were non-emergent, they tasked an Industrial Engineer to review the process. To experience the waste firsthand, he requested that the unit manager call him the next time the hospital transferred a patient to the ED. The next day, there was a need to move an elderly patient to the ED with declining health throughout the day. The engineer rode with the patient in the ambulance and to the hospital ED. The ED nurse found a 44-page document accompanying the patient. She could not understand where to look for the needed information, threw the paperwork aside, and directly asked the engineer why the patient was sent to the ED. After a series of tests and about 4 hours, the ED physician diagnosed the patient with dehydration, ordered fluids, and required the patient to stay overnight before returning to the mental health hospital. The lessons learned from this observation was the ED staff need clear and concise information because they feel the burden of time where seconds count. They also require different pathways developed for non-emergent patients to prevent them from utilizing valuable ED resources. After much discussion, the medical hospital worked with the ED to develop procedures for curbside consults when needed, x-rays on-demand, and medical screenings on site before sending a patient with non-emergent needs to the ED. The mental health hospital also worked to streamline their documentation between admissions and social work departments to better coordinate the care between the two hospitals. These actions reduced unnecessary transfers by 20% and improved the quality of documentation that aligned with the ED needs.

The best way to understand waste is to experience it through a waste walk. Direct waste observations are critical to successful improvement. Examples like vignette 2.10 are pervasive and happen everywhere. The more an organization takes the time to review the points of interaction with patients to understand the experienced waste, the more an organization will provide improved value.

C. Constraint Management

VIGNETTE 2.11

An inpatient unit struggled with co-occurring patients who were homeless, on medication-assisted treatments such as buprenorphine or methadone, and had limited finances or family support. Only a few rehabilitation centers, residential programs, or crisis beds were either willing to accept the patient or had immediate openings. It was not uncommon for this unit to have a few patients waiting for discharge because they required a safe place to transition to while many incoming patients waited in ER beds. These aftercare options were a constraint in the system.

When looking at waste in a system, the goal is to understand what impedes the flow of value to the patient. Consider water flowing down a stream as an example. The water moves down the stream at a constant flow or demand level. When the stream runs without anything impeding flow and the supply (stream basin) matches the demand (water), there is a smooth flow and relatively few ripples in the water. As the water encounters impediments to flow, the water becomes turbulent. The impediment could be a beaver building a dam, rocks constricting flow, a gust of wind, or even a sudden rainfall increasing the demand above the supply. As the water is restricted, it moves with more speed and increased turbulence against these impediments.

The same phenomenon occurs in a healthcare system. There is a buildup of waste in a system that leads to unsatisfied patients, disgruntled staff, and a system that erodes or breaks over time. Within each system lies a natural constraint, which limits the rate at which patients pass through. No matter how much an organization tries to improve, the constraints prevent streamlined flow from occurring and cause issues with receiving the right amount of care in the right place and at the right time. Therefore, to improve flow, organizations must manage the inflow and outflow from constraints and work to prevent bottlenecks from occurring.

D. Waste in Psychiatry

Psychiatry is no different, and in some aspects, the variation encountered is much more unpredictable because the patient brings several comorbid conditions to the process. Variation examples include misdiagnosis based on presenting symptoms, the effectiveness of medications, and the various approaches to the treatment of psychiatric conditions. For example, there is a wide variety of initial treatments for patients with anxiety disorders or substance use disorders. Also, some providers do not often understand the contribution of social factors such as homelessness, poverty, or exposure to violence to the diagnosis. Further, many hand-offs in care exist for chronic psychiatric conditions, which adds to the variation experienced.

E. Within Treatment Waste

When translating the eight forms of waste into medical practice, the best way to see the waste is from the patient perspective. Waste in a system or process causes patients to experience variation from one process step to the next and from one clinician to the next. Observing and eliminating waste within processes helps to ensure variation never reaches the patient. At any point in time, if a patient experiences variation because of waste in the system, then the patient considers the system unreliable. Examples of variation experienced in general medicine include mislabeled samples, low rates of handwashing amongst healthcare workers leading to infections, errors in diagnosis, wrong-side surgeries, and incidents of sponges and instruments left behind in the patient's body after surgery.

Typically, an observer will notice multiple forms of waste acting on the process at the same time. For example, when observing a clinician providing care, there is motion waste for the provider to log into the health record, waiting waste while the system verifies bed availability, and transportation waste when retrieving the patient from the waiting room. Sometimes a provider experiences interruptions from the office to the waiting room, and this delay causes the EMR to logout the provider. Re-entering credentials is a form of defect waste. Sometimes a provider will begin the patient interview at the same time the phone rings. Answering the phone is a form of overproduction waste to the patient in the room and motion waste when the doctor leaves the room to complete the call.

Meanwhile, the patient experiences a waste of waiting. Once the phone call interruption is complete, the provider returns to the room and repeats the questions he began to ask before the phone call. During the interview, the provider is noticeably trying to document in the EMR directly while talking to the patient. The waste continues for the entire appointment, and, in some cases, the waste repeats during a single patient encounter.

Because waste is everywhere, providers do not need to look too far to find waste to improve. Once providers learn to observe for waste, they can work to spot and eliminate it. Understanding and eliminating waste effectively uses staff time because it is relatively easy to engage staff and implement improvement. The benefits in patient value outweigh the costs of the approach.

F. Between Treatment Waste

Once treatment processes begin to streamline, organizations can start looking at the steps between treatments. Communication waste manifests itself in all eight forms of waste when the handoffs from one shift to the next or from the weekend staff to the weekday staff are not sufficient. Thus, a series of wasteful activities ensue.

Further, the organization can look beyond the hospital walls and focus on the handoffs from one level of care to the next. In a psychiatric setting, most patients move from an acute level of care to a lower level of care, such as an intensive outpatient program or an outpatient clinic. Other psychiatric patients move from lower levels to higher levels and back again as their chronic conditions fluctuate during certain periods in their lives. To maximize the care continuum, the models need improvement to prevent redundancy in the provided care.

With the recent push to incorporate mental healthcare resources in primary care, there is a perpetual need to ensure mental health is attended to because it is a leading indicator of primary health. Mental health costs are rising twice as fast as general medicine (LaVito, 2018).[11] Therefore, working to coordinate care between treatment facilities will help reduce healthcare waste overall.

G. The Cost of Waste

The US requires more than double the psychiatrists in place today to handle the needs of the mentally ill (Carlat, 2010).[12] Kaplan and Porter (2011) conducted a study that provided answers on how to contain healthcare costs. He suggested working on both sides of the supply-demand equation.[13] On the demand side, he said that patients need to become aware of the cost of the care they or their loved ones are receiving. Doing so will guide patients to make better choices about the care they receive in relation to the dollars spent. On the supply side, he suggested that we must move from fee-for-service models to population health models. However, neither of these strategies will adequately provide the clinical capacity needed. If more than 40% of a clinician's time is wasted, there must be a concerted effort to reduce waste and free up enough resources to address the need.

Most of the waste focus in healthcare today is on a hospital or a clinic's administrative or operational aspects. However, there must be an equally focused effort on improving clinical effectiveness to maximize the use of clinical time to improve mental healthcare. There is a need to study every clinical practice that inadvertently adds to the length of stay, every medication provided that does not prove effective, and every documentation practice that produces idle information. It is no longer enough to provide good quality clinical practice. Organizations must focus on providing good quality clinical practice while maximizing the efficiency of the health system.

References

1. Porter M. E. 2010. "What Is Value in Health Care?". *The New England Journal of Medicine* 363(26), 2477–2481. https://doi.org/10.1056/NEJMp1011024. Accessed December 26, 2019.
2. Roca, R. P. 2015. "Value in Mental Health Care: What Is It and Who Decides?". Lecture, Sheppard Pratt Conference Center, Towson, MD.
3. Toussaint, J. S. & Berry, L. L. 2013. "The Promise of Lean in Health Care". *Mayo Clinic Proceedings* 88(1), 74–82. https://doi.org/10.1016/j.mayocp.2012.07.025. Accessed December 26, 2019.
4. Womack, J. P. & Jones, D. T. 2015. *Lean Solutions: How Companies and Customers Can Create Value and Wealth Together*. Simon and Schuster, New York, NY.
5. Gold, M.S. 2018. "Stages of Change". *PsychCentral*. https://psychcentral.com/lib/stages-of-change/. Accessed December 26, 2019.

6. Rother, M. 2009. *Toyota Kata*. McGraw-Hill Professional Publishing, New York, NY.
7. Chang, S. 2019. "Nobody Wants a Waiting Room". *NEJM Catalyst* 5 (1).
8. Ohno, T. 1988. *Toyota Production System: Beyond Large-scale Production*. CRC Press, New York, NY.
9. Aboraya, A., Rankin, E., France, C., El-Missiry, A., & John, C. 2006. "The Reliability of Psychiatric Diagnosis Revisited: The Clinician's Guide to Improve the Reliability of Psychiatric Diagnosis". *Psychiatry (Edgmont)* 3(1), 41.
10. Lareau, W. 2003. *Office Kaizen: Transforming Office Operations into a Strategic Competitive Advantage*. Quality Press, Milwaukee, WI.
11. LaVito, Angelica. 2018. "Anxiety Is Expensive: Employee Mental Health Costs Rise Twice as Fast as All Other Medical Expenses". *CNBC*. https://www.cnbc.com/2018/09/26/employers-are-starting-to-think-about-healthy-differently.html. Accessed December 13, 2020.
12. Carlat, Daniel. 2010. "45,000 More Psychiatrists, Anyone?". *Psychiatric Times*. https://www.psychiatrictimes.com/view/45000-more-psychiatrists-anyone. Accessed December 13, 2020.
13. Kaplan, Robert S. & Porter, Michael E. 2011. "The Big Idea: How to Solve the Cost Crisis in Health Care". https://hbr.org/2011/09/how-to-solve-the-cost-crisis-in-health-care. Accessed December 13, 2020.

Section III

Developing the Healthcare Workforce for Performance Improvement

I. A Newer Approach to Work

VIGNETTE 3.1a

A patient with delusions and cognitive impairment on an inpatient unit felt that he was in the hospital for several months, even though he was just admitted the previous night. He started yelling and cursing at unit staff, telling them to discharge him immediately. Within minutes, he grabbed a chair and threatened to break his way from the unit if not released right away. The attending physician asked the nurse to administer IM antipsychotic medication to help contain the patient's behavior and reduce the patient's delusions. The nurse said that she needed an emergency IM medication order because there was nothing noted in the electronic medical record (EMR). After the physician entered the necessary order, the nurse had to wait for the pharmacist's review. The physician asked the nurse to call the pharmacy and inform them that they needed the IM medication as soon as possible. It took ten minutes for the nurse to receive the IM medication from the pharmacy. Meanwhile, staff had to call a code to restrain the patient to ensure everyone's safety. The team struggled to put the patient in restraints, and while trying to do so, the patient injured two staff members.

The unit leaders Dr. Lowe, the service chief, and Ms. Jones, the unit manager, had observed this event. They brought the following questions to the unit staff's attention at the next staff meeting: (1) Could they make sure that every new patient had emergency medications for severe agitation placed on hold, ready to be delivered instantaneously to reduce the delay during an emergency? (2) Could they expedite the emergency medications approval process for new patients to prevent delays during emergencies? The staff worked to answer each question and implemented a solution.

Transforming the current mental health delivery system is an urgent imperative, and all team members working in the current system have a responsibility to transform it. In doing so, the healthcare system can deliver better patient care and improve patient outcomes. To successfully transform care delivery, front-line staff must promptly 'spot and repair' wasteful processes and redesign existing processes to create value. A question remains on how to prepare best the mental health workforce to think and act as problem solvers to transform the mental healthcare system.

Paul Batalden, a senior fellow at the Institute of Healthcare Improvement, stated, "Every system is perfectly designed to get the results it gets." Poorly designed healthcare systems are more of a norm than an exception. It is common for nurses to deal with faulty or inefficient equipment, inadequate information, or missing medical supplies, including medications. Anita Tucker, a professor at the Questrom School of Business at Boston University, suggested that nurses face such operational failures on average once per hour. In her study, she found that in a 7.5-hour shift, nurses spend an average of 33 minutes dealing with such operational failures (Tucker, 2004).[1] If the goal is a better system of care, then those working within that system of care need training, infrastructure, and the appropriate leadership support to build a culture that supports continuous improvement.

One may argue that hospitals often provide high-quality care despite being poorly designed. A good reason for this is that healthcare workers are very passionate about their profession and highly skilled at working around these operational inefficiencies (workarounds). A 'workaround' is defined as "a situation in which an employee devises an alternate work procedure to address a block in the flow of his or her work" (Halbesleben et al., 2010).[2] Workaround culture is pervasively prevalent in healthcare. There are many reasons for this. Healthcare workers compensate and provide a buffer for a poorly designed system. Some workarounds can be very creative, and some can be quite heroic.

Workarounds offer some immediate reinforcement, which gets them to become more entrenched as a recurring workplace behavior. They allow the patient in urgent need to get care quickly and smoothly despite existing operational obstacles. Such quick resolution can be immensely gratifying to the front-line caregivers and is often applauded by their managers. In the short run, the ability to provide prompt and needed care despite obstacles with limited time and resources at hand is a useful skill from a patient and the manager's viewpoint. It is perceived to be creative and patient-centered. It allows patient care to continue seamlessly without interruption. It demonstrates the caring nature of the caregiver and the resilience of the organization (Tucker, 2009).[3] However, in the long run, workarounds are people dependent and eventually fail at providing high-quality care consistently.

VIGNETTE 3.2

Nancy, a new nurse on an inpatient psychiatric unit, was passing medications to the patients. She noticed that a patient's medication bin did not have the ordered medications. This scenario was the third of its kind that she had encountered in the past week. Nancy was a diligent nurse with the reputation of having a very positive attitude and being a good problem-solver. She apologized to the patient waiting for his medications and called a neighboring unit to ask if she could borrow the same medication from another patient's medication bin. She had discovered that this was possible earlier in the week when trying to solve a similar problem. She quickly ran to the neighboring unit and retrieved the needed medication. She did not inform the pharmacy nor her supervisor about these missing medications.

The pattern of behavior, which leads to creating workarounds by trying to take care of the immediate issue, is called *first-order problem-solving*. This kind of reactive problem-solving keeps the work moving forward, but it can be detrimental to a work environment's long-term performance. It can hamper organizational learning (Tucker et al., 2002).[4]

As shared in vignette 3.2, if a staff member does not take the time to pause and think about why this operational failure occurred or what is at the root of the problem, it is quite likely to recur. These failures often stay hidden like the underbelly of an iceberg. Each operational failure has a compounding effect that can lead to more extensive safety or quality issues downstream. If there is no mechanism for communicating a quality issue, there is no investigation or remedy to remove the problem's root cause.

An improvement-minded healthcare worker will try to prevent the recurrence of failure by communicating an operational failure, investigating the root cause, and implementing improvement to prevent future recurrences. This kind of behavior is called *second-order problem-solving*.

VIGNETTE 3.1b

Dr. Lowe started tracking the reliability of having emergency medications available for every patient. After tracking the data for two weeks, she still found that in 25% of the cases, 'on-hold' IM orders were missing. In doing a root cause analysis, she discovered that in 90% of missed cases, a psychiatry resident had admitted the patient. Dr. Lowe communicated this concern to the chief resident and improved the standard admitting guidelines so that emergency IM medications were more consistently available as admitting orders. She also developed a checklist for the chief resident to review a new residents' documentation.

Ms. Jones was aware of this impressive work and worked with Dr. Lowe to empower all staff nurses to stop the attending physician if the emergency IM order step was forgotten. Together, the unit manager and the service chief worked to create a culture where any staff member could 'stop the line' to ensure both staff and patient safety.

They also worked with the Pharmacy and Therapeutics Committee and the Medical Executive Committee to get approval for a policy that allowed emergency medications to be available very quickly after an order was entered into the EMR.

> The unit's dyadic leadership also made it a practice to review every aggressive incident with injury to see what could be learned. The unit implemented a 'just culture' where the staff felt safe pointing out ideas for improvement without blaming or fearing a supervisor reprimand. Injuries stemming from aggressive incidents reduced by more than 50% over the past six months. The word spread, and soon other units became interested in emulating the practices from this unit.

This kind of behavior is uncommon in healthcare environments because workers generally feel pressed for time, stressed and overworked, and feel that they don't have the luxury of stopping their work to think about and improve their environment. In a study, pausing to fix the root cause occurred in only 7% of the situations (Tucker & Edmondson, 2003).[5]

Managers and leaders have a significant role to play in fostering a culture of continuous improvement. They need to observe the work as it is being done, solicit information about challenges faced by front-line workers, look for operational failures, and provide coaching to the front-line staff to remedy these failures. It is their responsibility to get their teams to define the optimum standards of care for their unit and monitor adherence to these standards. Also, they need to study the variation to determine the need for improvement. Managers must also encourage front-line staff to dig deeper into root causation and try to fix the cause rather than providing temporary band-aids to failures as they arise. The greater the number of front-line staff who have been sensitized and activated to engage in second-order problem-solving, the more successful an organization will be. Dedicated staff in 'quality' or 'safety' roles in large organizations are no match to the collective power of an army of problem solvers (Liker & Meier, 2007).[6]

VIGNETTE 3.3

Dr. Miller was a psychiatry resident who heard from his patient about a side effect of Gabapentin, which was given for management of anxiety after alcohol withdrawal. The patient complained of peripheral edema. He remembered seeing a case like that at his earlier neurology rotation. He mentioned it to his attending physician, and the attending praised him for his observation. He completed a literature search to see if this finding was reported in the literature and reported this to the medication hotline. This hotline was created to gather information about the adverse effects of medications in their hospital.

In addition to workarounds being ubiquitous, there is a high prevalence of and tolerance for ambiguity in healthcare settings (Spear, 2005).[7] In healthcare, roles with respect to tasks are not very clearly defined. It is not often specified who needs to do precisely what. Sometimes more than one person is found to be working on a specific task, and sometimes no one remembers to do these tasks. Such ambiguity often leads to increased variability and makes many healthcare organizations error-prone. Knowledge critical to daily work is not clearly defined, and the detailed steps of activities that staff need to know are often not spelled out, leading to an error.

VIGNETTE 3.4

Sanchez, a new mental health technician, was asked to fill in on different inpatient units when staff were absent from work. He had worked on three separate units and found his initial work experience to be quite confusing. One unit followed a checklist to help patients prepare to transition to the next level of care. The second unit had a very organized room for patient belongings, with each patient's belongings safely stored according to their room number. The third unit did not use a checklist nor had the patient's belongings neatly organized. He was surprised that such common procedures on all units did not follow standard practice and felt that each unit could learn from the others so that preparing patients for discharge became more manageable and less stressful.

One way to specify steps and specific roles for each task is to create a checklist. There is a commonly encountered resistance to adopting 'checklists' or 'standards' in healthcare (Clark, 2011).[8] The usual counter-argument is that each patient has unique needs or is particularly challenging, making practitioners generally resist following standardized best practice checklists. By rejecting attempts at standardization, the practitioner does not acknowledge the stress endured by other staff.

VIGNETTE 3.5

An inpatient team was working on setting up aftercare plans after stabilizing a homeless patient. They submitted the clinical information on Friday to a community residential program and were waiting for a response from them about an available bed. On Monday, the social worker called in sick. His job was to usually arrange and gather everything needed by the residential program (discharge documents, prescriptions, etc.). In his absence, another social worker covered the case and helped with the discharge arrangements. During this day, the residential program told the team that a bed had become available. The covering social worker quickly arranged for transport. However, while rushing around, some of the patient's belongings were left behind. Later that day, the residential program emailed the manager to complain that the discharge papers and medication supply were not sent with the patient. The discharge team did not review the available discharge checklist to ensure that all patient needs were accounted for properly. Consequently, they did not prepare the patient for a successful transition.

Operationally excellent and highly reliable organizations tend to embrace standardization and reduce ambiguity in their operations. In this regard, the world of medicine has a lot to learn from other industries such as the automotive, aerospace, and nuclear industries. Within the automobile industry, Toyota is a superlative example of high reliability. They continually lead to overall reliability as well as the resale value of their vehicles. Many have learned from and tried to emulate Toyota's success. The Toyota Production System is based on improvement science, and their culture expects continuous improvement and respect for people. After studying the workings of forty plants for four years across the United States, Europe, and Japan, researchers were able to specify the four basic rules that guided the Toyota Production System. These four rules were:

i. Work (*activities*) was highly specified as to the content, sequence, timing, and outcome.
ii. Every *connection* between customers and suppliers was direct and unambiguous.
iii. The *pathways* for each product or service was simple and direct.
iv. *Improvements* were made according to the scientific method, under a teacher's guidance, at the lowest possible level in the organization (Spear & Bowen, 1999).[9] Front-line staff embodied proactive thinking and second-order problem-solving in their daily work.

As activities, connections, pathways each are specified, it is easier to spot variations from the expected standard. Once variability is spotted, staff must immediately address it to understand why and aspire to prevent future recurrences.

Everyone working in that environment is responsible for improving the system of care. When these behaviors are applied consistently by managers and front-line staff, it enhances the performance as experienced by the patient and staff engagement. With every new cycle of work, more and more improvement opportunities are addressed, which sets the entire workgroup on a continuous improvement path.

II. The Development of an Improver

To enable an entire workforce to become a capable group of second-order problem solvers, it would take a formidable and consistent effort. Such effort seems like a herculean task, but there are examples in the United States, within and outside of healthcare.

For example, at the beginning of the nineteenth century, medical schools were mainly for-profit institutions where instruction was provided through didactic lectures, textbook readings, and memorization of facts. The Carnegie Foundation commissioned Abraham Flexner to evaluate the quality of medical education. Flexner, an educator and a former headmaster of a private school, became a catalyst for a large-scale change in medical education. He published a report after visiting and evaluating 155 medical schools in the United States and Canada, after which the number of medical schools dramatically reduced from 133 in 1910 to 85 in 1920 (Barzansky, 2010).[10] Schools became more rigorous by requiring a college degree for admission, adding laboratory work, and implementing medical students' clerkships. In these reformed schools, medical students would 'learn by doing.'

It is important to note that Abraham Flexner wanted each generation of medical educators to adapt to science's evolving needs and changing circumstances. Many of Flexner's recommendations about medical education are still being used a century later, even though the context and circumstances are very different for a new physician today.

Although Flexner never wrote anything about the healthcare delivery system (Ludmerer, 2010), the context can be a significant determinant of patient care provided.[11] Most of the illnesses encountered by today's physicians are chronic conditions, unlike the majority of illnesses that physicians were treating in Flexner's time. For medical education to change with the current circumstances, it will have to reform once again.

Another example of change that happened in the United States was the response to Germany's offensive during World War II. The US government had to rapidly produce war munitions, vehicles, and planes to support the war effort, and there was a need for skilled and experienced workers. Many skilled workers had enlisted in the military, which left a massive void in the manufacturing workforce. To deal with this void, the war manpower commission emergently set up the 'Training Within Industry' (TWI) program. It led to a massive educational effort, and about 1.6 million workers (mostly women) received certified TWI training. This effort led to increased production, diminished training time, labor-hours, and grievances (Ezez, 2019).[12] Unfortunately, the interest in TWI began to fade by 1944, as orders from the military declined and as the soldiers returned home and went back to work.

Interestingly, TWI as a training method was introduced in Japan after World War II to help with its post-war rebuilding efforts. Toyota took the lessons of TWI very seriously and incorporated the importance of workforce development into their production system. One of their master trainers, Isao Kato, had said in an interview, "You cannot separate people development from production system development if you want to succeed in the long run" (Liker & Meier, 2007).[6] Today, interest in TWI has resurfaced because organizations are finding it challenging to emulate and sustain gains from using quality improvement methods.

Any healthcare organization's leadership must be ready and prepared to make such training and development a priority to support an improvement culture. While there is some upfront cost to move in this direction, the long-term benefits on patient outcomes, the organization's performance, and staff satisfaction outweigh the initial costs.

How does an organization ensure the development of staff along this line of thinking? How can an organization assess and facilitate a worker's transformation to become a habitual second-order problem solver, or improver, in short? The developmental steps for any improver are:

i. Developing *awareness* for the need to improve systems,
ii. Fostering an *improvement mindset*,
iii. Acquiring performance improvement *knowledge*,
iv. Applying and practicing improvement *skills*, and
v. Transforming these skills into routine *habits* to carry out such improvements consistently and as a 'way of life.' The steps are illustrated in Figure 3.1.

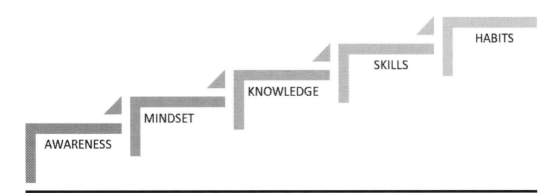

Figure 3.1 Developmental steps of an improver.

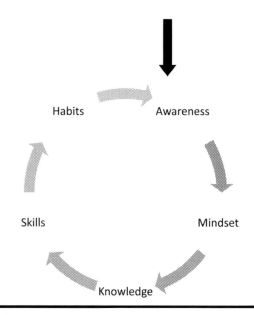

Figure 3.2   Developing improvement capability cycle.

The application of knowledge invariably leads to greater awareness and knowledge about the organization and makes this a cyclical, iterative process. This is seen in Figure 3.2.

In addition to subject matter expertise, it will take a well-developed and engaged workforce with the awareness, mindset, knowledge, and skills regarding improvement science, which are applied habitually to transform the healthcare system.

A. Developing Awareness

Learning about improvement starts with an awareness that it is not just the patients but also the care system, which is also ailing and not optimal. Professionals are well versed in the logic and the skills that are used for diagnosing and treating individuals. The same logical scientific thinking used to treat patients can also be applied to diagnosing and repairing poorly functioning or less reliable systems. The diagnostic and improvement tools vary, but it requires a similar kind of iterative learning process to care for and improve systems, as it does to improve individual patients (Ogrinc et al., 2012).[13] Think of the ailing system as akin to a 'patient' that also requires attention.

Within any healthcare system, one often encounters safety and quality problems, errors and delays, near misses, and untoward events, in addition to patient and family complaints. There is plenty of data to illuminate the gap between the desired goal and the system's actual performance. All of these are opportunities to sensitize team members and make them aware of the problems within existing systems. Systemic issues in healthcare are ubiquitous. Once an individual becomes aware of the different types of waste, they can find opportunities all around them to eliminate waste and enhance value. We will discuss various tools in section four, which help surface and 'diagnose' waste in systems.

Medical students spend most of their time learning the right generalizable evidence or a plethora of 'best practices.' It takes an average of seventeen years for research evidence to reach clinical practice (Morris et al., 2011).[14] Even after evidence comes to clinical practice; such evidence is not reliably adopted. 'Best practices' are developed within hospitals and health systems. Many best practices get published in reputed journals, and yet, they don't become accepted practice. This lag of adoption ought to give any leader some pause because even after they know what works well, there is a quality gap motivating an entire team to adopt research evidence or the 'best practice.' As was stated in section one, only 57.7% of patients suffering from depression received the recommended care, whereas, for the group of patients struggling with alcohol dependence, only 10.5% of patients received the recommended care. Such quality gaps are common in healthcare.

Having the right research evidence is not enough for the research findings to be adopted uniformly. The context in which this best practice or evidence is introduced can be a significant modifying factor in how successfully and reliably it is adopted. The skill of implementing best practices consistently in different contexts requires a specific set of knowledge and skills that is often not taught in medical schools or residencies. A manager or leader becomes aware of this variable degree of acceptance and adoption, and it often becomes an impetus for seeking performance improvement knowledge and skills. The ability to take the best generalizable scientific evidence and implement it reliably in clinical settings requires 'a separate set of knowledge and skills.'

This missing link in healthcare has been described as the 'connector' (Ogrinc et al., 2012).[13] The connecter pays attention to the local context in which a new 'best practice' is introduced. The structures, processes, and culture of each work environment matter and affect the practice's adoption. Every attempt to close the gap increases the awareness that work is made up of interconnected processes, the importance of understanding systems and not just individuals, and the need to apply improvement science methods.

Every new environment where best practices are implemented is the beginning of a new learning cycle. Whether expecting healthcare professionals to wash their hands or implement a checklist, implementing any new idea with new practitioners poses unique challenges. Each of these challenges acts as an iterative learning opportunity. Every challenge increases the awareness of the individual who desires to close the quality gap.

VIGNETTE 3.6

Thelma, the unit manager on an adult inpatient unit introduced a new discharge process in the morning staff meeting. The process involved getting all necessary items ready for discharge the day before discharge. She explained why this was important and informed the staff that another unit had reduced errors, complaints, and costs by using this new process. They had demonstrated improvement in satisfaction scores as well as their 'discharge by noon' metric. She had hoped to emulate their success in her unit as well. She allowed her staff to ask questions and clarified their concerns. Later in the day, she sent the new process instructions steps for discharge preparation to staff across all shifts if they had to carry out a discharge. She then asked them to send her their questions and concerns in case there were any. At the end of the first week, she found out the process was followed correctly 85% of the time on the day shift, 50% of the time on the evening shift, and only 20% on the weekends. She was not sure why there was such a variation. She decided to consult her improvement specialist in her hospital and ask for their help.

Any attempt at improving a system's performance helps build the understanding that the way the system has been set-up can be a significant determinant of the patient experience and patient outcomes. Through learning, staff gradually learn that an existing process is amenable to redesign and change. This insight is very empowering and can catalyze positive change. Organizations that support their staff with the proper resources can transform systems for the better.

Courses that teach improvement science to incorporate hands-on activities are great opportunities to cultivate such an awareness quickly. If awareness is the precursor, then the desire to assume responsibility for the problem and improve the system is the required next step. An improver has to cultivate such a mindset.

B. Fostering an Improvement Mindset

Certain qualities and attitudes are desirable to help an individual along the improvement journey. Staff must have 'enthusiasm, optimism, curiosity, and perseverance' as they begin their improvement journey (Jones et al., 2019).[15] These qualities are not always inherent but can be gradually cultivated with the right kind and support. These qualities also help when individuals or leaders face barriers to change and can be counterbalancing forces to apathy, cynicism, resistance, and burnout. The ones who are good at improvement have a positive mindset and can remain resilient even in the face of challenges (Lucas, 2015).[16] They are open to new ideas and invite 'critical scrutiny of their thinking.' They embody a spirit of collaboration and see strength in diverse points-of-view. They seem to have a proactive approach to change (Covey, S.R 2013).[17] There is a desire to learn from all experiences, whether successful or not. Also, they epitomize a balance between thinking and acting (Watanabe, 2009).[18] Such individuals seem to embody the desire to change the status quo.

Another important aspect is the ability to reflect inwards, to see how an individual or system is falling short of providing a value-added experience. If one adopts the stance to look for someone else to blame or expect someone else to change first, it is not very helpful. Such a view does not inspire individuals or teams to start on a path of improvement. In 'Fixing Health Care from the Inside, Today,' Steven Spear (Spear, 2005) highlights how some hospitals are not looking outwards toward the insurance industry or the government or technology to solve their safety or quality problems. They are looking inwards and applying improvement methods to reduce waste and improve value. They are not only saving costs but also improving safety and quality in the process.[7]

Once there is an awareness of problems, a desire to change, and an improvement mindset, knowledge of performance improvement methods comes in very handy. If every system is perfectly designed to get the results it gets, one needs to think about changing the system where results are suboptimal. The Institute of Healthcare Improvement describes the three essential drivers of system-level improvement: Will, Ideas, and Execution (Nolan, 2007).[19] If the awareness and mindset give the improver the will and ideas to change the system, they need a body of knowledge to execute this complicated endeavor.

C. Acquiring Performance Improvement Knowledge

W. Edwards Deming provided a foundational framework for understanding systems and also providing some fundamental principles of how to go about changing systems. This framework, titled 'System of Profound Knowledge,' was formulated by him in 1993 at the latter end of his career. One of the reasons to examine this four-part framework is that it correctly orients a leader to see quality problems through a system's lens and not just individuals (Deming, 1994).[20] There are many parts of the system that interact with each other, and changes made in one part of a system can affect others. Secondly, when a quality gap is seen in variation from an expected standard, it is crucial to understand when to act on this variation and when not to (knowledge of variation). All variations inform us about the current nature of the system in question. Third, the framework helps leaders build knowledge about the system by making predictions and learning from the gap between prediction and actual results (theory of knowledge). Finally, all technical changes introduced in systems have to deal with the human side of change (psychology). It is hard to successfully change systems without learning how to deal with the challenge of getting others to change. Many transformation efforts fail, not because of the shortage of technical ideas, but because there is an under-appreciation of the adaptive challenge when dealing with others' psychology. Hence, in addition to subject matter knowledge, this system of profound knowledge is beneficial for improvement. It has far-reaching applications and is capable of impacting both the product and service industries. A foundational theory provides a framework for quality improvement work, management principles, and leadership philosophy.

Deming's philosophy's fundamental aim was the empowerment of the individual with dignity, knowledge, and skills so that they can contribute to the long-term success of the organization. According to Deming, management's purpose was to foster this kind of learning and development to intrinsically motivate individuals to do their best and contribute to the organization's success (Aguayo, 1991).[21]

As an aside, Deming was a summer intern at Western Electric, where he became interested in the work of Walter A. Shewhart (Best, 2006).[22] Shewhart had developed a three-stage process for mass production (specification-production-inspection). Over a few decades, this three-stage process evolved into a four-step cycle – the Plan-Do-Check-Act or PDCA Cycle (AKA, Plan-Do-Study-Act or PDSA Cycle). Deming popularized this cycle. Today it is also referred to as the 'Deming's Cycle.' Learning and building knowledge is built into Plan-Do-Study-Act Cycles and is key to improving systems.

Deming's 'System of Profound Knowledge' addresses fundamental principles that are incorporated within various performance improvement methodologies. As depicted in Figure 3.3, the first aspect begins with an appreciation for a system.

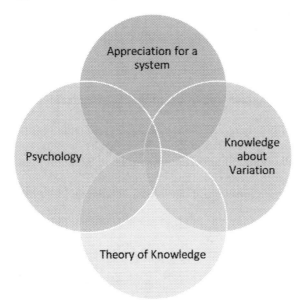

Figure 3.3 System of profound knowledge. (Adapted from Deming, 1994.)

1. Appreciation for a System

> A system is an interdependent group of items, people, or processes working together toward a common purpose. (Langley et al., 2009)[24]

An organization is a system united by a common purpose, which has many interrelated connections and interactions. Even though they may appear to have discrete departments or 'silos' managed by different entities, all the departments should work toward a common aim. When departments only think about and optimizing their own needs, it often comes at the expense of other departments and can sub-optimize the whole system. When different departments collaborate well and align toward a shared aim, a well-integrated organization can achieve breakthrough results. An aligned and collaborative workforce raises the quality of an organization's product or service and improves overall morale.

VIGNETTE 3.7

Dr. Costa, in his first six months as a service chief of an inpatient psychiatric unit, worked on improving the utilization of available beds on his unit. His Chief Medical Officer had informed him that there were tremendous needs and long waits in the emergency rooms (ERs) at neighboring hospitals for available inpatient beds. When he reviewed the admission criteria for his unit, he felt they were significantly restrictive. He focused on making it easier for challenging patients to be admitted to his inpatient unit. It took him some time to gain the trust of his physician and nursing teams. He made himself available to discuss any problematic cases in daily staff meetings, and he made himself available for curbside consultations. Each week, he provided quick five-minute tutorials on topics that he felt would alleviate his staff's anxiety and improve their competence over time. Their CEO informed him one day that the neighboring hospital ER was appreciative of this, and boarding in the ER had reduced. As a result of his efforts, patient satisfaction went up. Dr. Costa kept a close watch on this unit's performance to ensure safety and quality levels were sustained as they accepted more challenging patients.

The management team's job is to optimize the system and ensure that people work well within various departments. Deming attributed most of the problems arising in an organization, not to individual performance but to how the system is designed and managed. He believed it was the responsibility of management to recognize and fix systemic problems.

Outcomes can be improved by working on the processes within any system. A system thinker understands the interconnectedness of these processes in a system when trying to improve. Operating a service organization reliably and safely requires the optimum orchestration of many processes within different departments. Accomplishing this in any organization requires good leadership. A leader optimizes the contribution of each department to help reach the overall aim of the organization. For instance, the leader understands the importance of thorough housekeeping staff in preventing infections or the importance of kind, compassionate, and engaged mental health technicians in preventing violence. Every staff member in the mental health organization contributes equally to achieving good quality outcomes. The importance of this fact cannot be understated, and a good leader understands this well. Section five covers the role of leadership in greater depth.

One way to achieve awareness and optimize a system is first to visualize it. A method that helps visualize all the activities, pathways, and connections in the same sequence that a customer moves through is called process mapping. We will go review process mapping in some greater depth in section four. Visualizing the flow allows organizations to achieve 'clarity,' build 'focus,' and visualize waste much more clearly. Process mapping also helps everyone understand the interconnectedness and interdependence of various components and how their role is imperative to process steps further downstream.

2. *Knowledge about Variation*

There is a need to understand and reduce variations from standards to improve the system's performance. Variation is the dispersion from the mean or nominal value. As variation or dispersion from nominal increases, waste in a process increases. In other words, the more the system does not behave as it is expected to, the greater the chances of there being quality issues. There can be considerable variation in a patient's hospital stay given the number of steps in the process and the number of staff involved.

Given that Deming was a statistician, he emphasized the use of data to understand and reduce variation. First, it is essential to measure the system's performance over time with a balanced family of measures. Health systems are complex; hence multiple measures are needed to understand how different components of the system and how the entire system functions. In doing so, a leader recognizes that, at times, parts of the system behave predictably and stably. At other times, they see that other parts of the system act in a more unstable, unpredictable, and erratic manner. By questioning and getting to the root cause of these variations, they understand their system's true nature.

Deming stressed the importance of using statistical thinking to respond to variation optimally. Now that clinicians and administrators have access to more data, they would not overreact if they learned how to interpret data correctly. Sometimes making small and incremental changes can lead to huge improvements. However, not all changes lead to uniform improvements. Sometimes, they can lead to unintended consequences, as changes made in one part of the system can unpredictably affect other parts of the system. Often, actions taken by leaders can increase variation in the system. A good understanding of how to interpret data can help managers ensure that reliable improvement has occurred after making changes to the system.

VIGNETTE 3.8

Dr. Pollard, a new medical director, went to a leadership meeting and learned that the medical record deficiency rate (the percentage of incomplete medical records) of all the doctors on her unit last month was 9%. She felt a little embarrassed and decided to do something about it. Dr. Pollard went back to her team of doctors and asked them to be more diligent. She received feedback from an experienced colleague and mentor that the rate of deficiency in the entire hospital had improved over the last six months from an average of 18% to 14%. Her own unit's deficiency metric had improved from a mean of 13% to a mean of 10% over the last six months. This month's rate of 9% in her unit was better than most of the hospital units.

This senior colleague informed her that usually, whenever there were upcoming accreditations or regulatory surveys, such messages about more attention to documentation increased in frequency, which leads to short-term improvements in the deficiency rate. After the surveys are completed, the clinical staff relaxes their record completion efforts, and the rate climbs up again. However, in most cases, unit deficiency rates are predictable. He advised her to look at a run chart instead of discrete monthly numbers without context and said that he would be available if she had any questions.

Embarrassment quickly turned into a learning opportunity for her unit. She became intrigued by a new way of looking at data and now felt a sense of urgency that made her want to learn more about run charts. She decided that she would not be so reactive in the future and wanted to learn to calmly guide her team to improve.

Walter Shewhart pioneered a theory that helps in understanding variation better. He identified two types of variation (Best, 2006):[23]

i. Common Cause Variation (chance-cause variation)
ii. Special Cause Variation (assignable-cause variation)

Common Cause Variation is random variation inherent to a stable process. This variation is small, within statistical limits, predictable, and the outcomes still meet clinical requirements.

For instance, a clinic director impressed upon staff the value of punctuality and how punctuality improved patient show rates and overall patient satisfaction scores. After receiving agreement from all practitioners during a recent retreat, each practitioner started their day within five minutes of the specified time. Minor differences of a minute or two are examples of common-cause variations. Several issues can prevent a clinician from starting at the same time every day. Sometimes minor delays occur with the best of intentions. One day a clinician might have been delayed because their computer is slow to start, and then next, a clinician may be delayed as they took a couple of minutes helping a family with wayfinding. This common cause variation is considered noise in the system. It affects everyone, and it is not too significant. It is not easy to alter unless there is a fundamental change to the system.

Special Cause Variation is the variation that is not inherent to the process. It is not ongoing, does not affect everyone, is not predictable, can significantly affect outcomes, and usually occurs due to exceptional circumstances.

Continuing with the previous example, a clinician checking her phone while walking toward the clinic slipped on a wet floor and fell. The slip resulted in a bad sprain and made it hard for the clinician to walk. The clinician decided to go to urgent care for treatment and learned that she had fractured her ankle. The office manager canceled the clinic for the day, and the office manager apologized to all the patients because there was no one else who could cover the clinic. This scenario would be considered a special cause variation because it was a one-time unpredictable event.

Common cause variations indicate a predictable process, whereas special cause variations indicate an unpredictable process. Trying to adjust a system based on a common cause variation as if it is due to a special cause is a mistake, just as it is to ignore special cause variation and let go of an opportunity to solve a problem. One can make things worse if one keeps trying to adjust the process in response to common cause variations. According to Deming, around 95% of all process variation is due to common causes. *Tampering* with the process and making adjustments every time one sees small common cause variations can worsen variation.

3. Theory of Knowledge

Continuous improvement of a system requires ongoing learning. Learning about a system happens in the following sequence of steps. (1) Articulating a theory about the system, (2) Making predictions about the system based on the theory, (3) Testing this prediction, and (4) Checking to see if the prediction was entirely correct, partially correct, or incorrect. Trying to understand the variance in the short and long-term between the prediction and actual performance in the system's context leads to learning. It causes the practitioner to dig deeper to understand the variance in the system's performance from the predicted outcome. This kind of reflection results in a better understanding, a deepening of existing knowledge, and new knowledge about the system. This learning is akin to the Plan-Do-Study-Act Cycle (Berry, 2006).[23]

Setting goals for improvement requires making predictions based on theory and experience. The theory keeps going through revisions based on the results of the tests and experiments conducted on the system. The application of the theory leads to knowledge about the system. Not all changes made to the system lead to improvements. Therefore, measurement is a crucial feature of any improvement process. Measurements give credence to the usefulness of the changes made to the system. Treatment of any patient is a prediction based on a theory, which is the diagnosis. Both laboratory tests and the response to the doctor's empirical interventions inform the doctor about such interventions' effectiveness.

VIGNETTE 3.9

Dr. Crosby is a new child psychiatrist who starts a part-time outpatient psychiatric practice in a particularly underserved area. The decision was based on the premise that business would be profitable in this area due to the lack of competing providers (this is her theory). Dr. Crosby thought she would be happy if she got one new patient a day until she became well-known in this area (her prediction). Due to the pent-up demand in this area, she got three new patient calls in each of her first two weeks of opening the practice. She felt encouraged by this initial response (testing her prediction). She rationalized the lower than expected number in the initial two weeks because she was new in this area. The number of new patients she received in weeks 3 and 4 dropped to an average of two patients (checking with respect to prediction). This low response got her worried. She concluded that she might need to market herself to get the community to know her better (new theory). She hoped that it would help her get a steadier stream of new patients (prediction). After investing some money in marketing, she would have to test and see if her prediction came true.

Concerning improvement, it is essential to clearly define terms and think carefully about operational definitions (Langley et al., 2009).[24] This is important for measuring, judging whether a particular test is successful or not, and also communicating the meaning and impact of change. For instance, if someone measures tardiness in staff arrival time to work, what needs to be specified is what degree of delay is acceptable and what constitutes being late.

Evidence of improvement is demonstrated through the use of measurements. Staff sees that the improvement process makes their work more streamlined and easier through visualized charts and tangible outcomes. Once they experience this, it becomes easier to get buy-in for future improvement activities. Also, engaging staff from other areas before, during, and after the improvement process helps engage others in the learning process while implementing change and making adoption easier. It is important to use improvement activities to make work 'easier, better, faster, cheaper, and in that order' (Derington et al., 2019).[25] This is especially important to engage as many people as possible to improve and learn about the system. A team will not support or want to learn if all actions lead to adding more work to their daily duties.

Once a process or part of the system is working predictably, it is crucial to create a 'standard work' document. This document specifies the steps of the process, the key points, and the reasons why a particular step is undertaken. We will elaborate on this document in section four. Such standard work documents become the repository of knowledge about the working of a system. These become useful in orientation, training, performance evaluations, managing staff transitions, and succession planning. As mentioned earlier, successful organizations have activities, connections and pathways more precisely specified and roles clearly defined. Standard work documents aid learning, create new knowledge and preserve such knowledge for use in the future. They are essential aids to see how a process sticks to or varies from a standard, especially if there is an unpredictable or unsafe event.

Theories about the system also get tested when a team tries to cascade improvements to other areas. What may appear easy to the pilot team that developed and tested an improvement idea may be thought of as burdensome or unnecessary change by other teams. Hence, measurement and proper communication of ideas are crucial to getting others to accept new ideas. Encouraging others to interact with the proposed change, soliciting their feedback about the ease of use of the new method, and incorporating their ideas about adapting the change to their context is essential before getting them to accept the idea to be cascaded fully.

Participating in improvement events and activities emphasizes the value placed on learning. Over time and with continued participation in such improvement activities, staff feels empowered to solve more operational problems using similar methods. At the same time, the manager or team leaders coach staff to be less reactive, use empirical thinking and help them grow from their learning process. On the other hand, if changes are made without forethought, proper prediction, and testing, or without relying on measurements, it stops the learning process. This empowerment to engage everyone in learning is also vital for the morale of the workers.

All four elements of Deming's system of profound knowledge are interconnected. In solving problems, team members develop an appreciation of their system, and they learn to reduce variation over time. This reduction makes their processes more stable, reliable, and predictable. An environment that is free from fear, safe for staff to question the status quo, and respecting staff participation and wisdom is also an environment that fosters growth and learning of the staff. The organization that builds its knowledge is better able to predict its performance. Learning and development of the workforce are vital for the well-being and growth of the organization. From a psychological perspective, this approach taps into the team's intrinsic motivation, who feel a greater sense of engagement, pride, loyalty, and involvement with their work.

4. Psychology

> A leader of transformation, and managers involved, need to learn the psychology of individuals, the psychology of a group, the psychology of society, and the psychology of change. (Deming, 1994)[20]

Whether enacting change by oneself, with a small team, or within a large organization, understanding psychology comes in handy. In many organizations, fears, unresolved interpersonal differences, or conflicts often lead to stalled improvement efforts or resistance to change. Managing change amongst groups of individuals is as important as coming up with technical solutions to problems.

When embarking on changing people, there is an appreciation that *each individual is different*. Each person has their own needs, ambitions, temperament, and motivations and each of them interacts with the system differently. These differences create variation and indeed affect outcomes. Every manager and leader's job is to understand and respect these differences amongst individuals and learn how to optimally work with them. A particular clinician might consider it essential to be exhaustive in her documentation because she is somewhat obsessional and risk-averse. Another clinician who just had a baby may be eager to get home early and hence tries to be very concise in her documentation to be expedient. Some employees may only think of their job to get a paycheck and support their family, whereas others may derive their life's purpose from it. These variations may lead to different degrees of engagement toward each of their jobs and differences in performance.

It is imperative to understand what motivates people and what is truly important to each of them. Rather than assuming, a leader should try to understand the motivation of a team's behavior.

VIGNETTE 3.10

Dr. Qadir, the service chief, wanted to adopt a daily management huddle on his unit at 8:30 AM, necessitating that all team members attend this huddle. This huddle looked at safety and quality problems daily. Someone from management also would attend this huddle to help remove any systemic barriers to improvement, and they had suggested 8:30 AM as the time. It was also crucial to quickly get an idea about anything on the unit that made it hard for teams to care for their patients. Such communication enabled Dr. Qadir, the unit manager, and the management representative to overcome these barriers.

Dr. Qadir was having a hard time getting two of his fellow physicians to attend. One detested anything to do with administrative tasks. He had an antipathy for anything non-clinical and grumbled about such a request. The other physician was into fitness and liked to arrive at work around 9 AM after his morning gym routine.

Motivation can be intrinsic or extrinsic. Intrinsic motivation means doing something because it is inherently enjoyable, satisfying, or interesting. Extrinsic motivation means doing something because it leads to a separable outcome in reward, recognition, or avoidance of punishment. Deming suggested that the role of management is to create an environment that could unleash intrinsic motivation. An intrinsically motivating activity is one where the activity itself fulfills the personal and social needs of a person (Langley et al., 2009).[24] Leaders can take time and explain why improvement work is necessary and how it is in keeping with organizational values. Engaging the workforce in improvement activities helps the staff grow, helps them find meaning and purpose, and shapes their identity. It also helps them be part of the shared identity and vision of the organization. A workforce engaged in making an organization better feels a sense of belonging and ownership.

Individuals vary in their degree of motivation and the type or orientation of their motivation (Ryan & Deci, 2000).[26] Intrinsic motivation can be increased or decreased by one's home, school, or work context. Intrinsically motivated tasks satisfy innate psychological needs of relatedness, autonomy, and competence. Any approach by a mentor that makes a mentee feel more connected, autonomous, or competent increases their intrinsic motivation. The mentor needs to continually challenge, provide optimal feedback, and not be too harshly critical to help their mentees grow and flourish.

Conversely, any rewards or threats to facilitate improved task performance can diminish intrinsic motivation as they tend to reduce the sense of autonomy. The commitment to do something can diminish once rewards or threats are withdrawn. If leaders can tap into the strengths, interests, and passions of their individual they lead, they can unleash a significant amount of creativity, energy, and innovation.

Many activities that workers engage in are not necessarily driven by intrinsic motivation but by external motivation. Also, individuals can approach actions because of external motivation, either with interest or with disinterest. A considerable degree of tasks expected at work can be uninteresting. The relative degree of autonomy perceived in completing the task driven by external motivators can increase the person's engagement level in completing the task. Anything that can help employees internalize and integrate values and regulations can improve their investment in following those values and regulations. Once internalized, there is a more significant commitment to completing the task. Hence, it helps when leaders explain why specific changes are essential for the organization. Once employees understand why and if it aligns with their own beliefs and values, it leads to better adherence to regulations.

Another point that Deming makes in his fourteen key points for management is the need to *drive out* fear so that everyone can work effectively. Fear is the opposite of trust. Fear can paralyze improvement efforts and also rob a workplace of the joy, creativity, enthusiasm, and innovation needed to make an environment where improvement thrives. A good leader can motivate individuals to give their best to organizations, but this will not be seen with managers or leaders who believe in a 'command and control' management style. Individuals have to feel free to air their differences of opinion, question practices and policies, and co-design workplaces. They are the nearest to work and have a keen sense of steps that add value and wasteful steps and need modification.

Sometimes in healthcare, when regulations do not entirely make sense or are not in keeping with current challenges, the work environment needs to support efforts to minimize time and effort taken to do the tasks that meet those regulations. Sometimes regulations can be interpreted by the administration in a very risk-averse manner, leading to extra work that is heaped upon an already overburdened workforce. Staff needs to see and closely examine regulations to prevent added waste in a day's work. Once again, it is essential to remember that making work easier first is the best way to foster intrinsic motivation. If the employee has to do something that feels imposed, at least the employee needs to feel that management has made an effort to make such work less burdensome.

VIGNETTE 3.11

When Dr. Vaz came to work at an institution, she found completing the master treatment plan for the patient to be burdensome. It felt like a perfunctory exercise to her because everything expected in such a plan was already present in other parts of the record. She knew it was something required by regulations. She spoke to her supervisor, who validated her feelings and suggested that she look at the template critically and think of ways to simplify it. She noticed the 'strengths and weaknesses' section asked for five patient strengths and weaknesses. All ten fields were assumed to be mandatory. Nurses and doctors were filling in those areas with sentences that added very little value because they felt that they did not have a choice. For instance, under the category of 'physical strengths,' she saw that a colleague had written that the 'patient is ambulatory.' She found this to be a great example of how completing all those fields had turned into a meaningless exercise.

She asked to examine the regulations that informed treatment planning. Interestingly, all she could find in the regulations was that it is essential to identify the strengths of patients during treatment planning. Someone had overzealously interpreted them to create five separate categories of strengths and weaknesses. She suggested the reduction from ten mandatory fields to one field for identifying a meaningful strength. Her supervisor helped to implement the new change. As a result, she felt empowered and genuinely saw her supervisor as an ally who was eager to make everyone's work experience less burdensome and more meaningful. She felt safe to bring up future concerns.

According to the organizational theorist Russell L. Ackoff, leadership requires an ability to bring the will of followers into consonance with that of the leader to follow him voluntarily, with enthusiasm and dedication (Ackoff, 1998).[27] An environment plagued by fear causes a level of leadership distrust and becomes very detrimental to such enthusiasm and commitment in the workforce.

It is also vital for individuals in the workplace to speak up about unsafe conditions and report human errors without fearing punishment, retaliation, or retribution. It indeed has to be balanced with personal accountability. The idea is to create a psychologically safe environment to improve patient safety. Individuals need to feel comfortable calling out errors, safety concerns, near misses, and sentinel events so that the system can learn from such occurrences. The focus is on open reporting, participating in learning and improvement activities to design 'safer' systems.

A system should aim for a 'Just Culture.' It is not entirely a blame-free culture with no accountability, nor is it a punitive environment where individuals are blamed for all errors. A 'Just Culture' recognizes that often the system and not the individual are at fault. On the other hand, errors could also be unintentional or risky, reckless, or malicious actions. They could result from impaired judgment because the caregiver was impaired due to substance use, cognitive problems, or psychosocial issues (Leonard & Allan, 2010).[28] The caregiver's response is based on analyzing their behavior and comparing their behavior in that situation with a caregiver with similar skills and knowledge. Their behavior would help them decide on an appropriate response. After analyzing the event, it may be agreed that the employee may need counseling or corrective action, or the system itself may need to be error-proofed or redesigned.

Deming stated, "Management's overall aim should be to create a system in which everybody may take joy in his (or her) work." (IHI Multimedia Team, 2017).[29] In the context of staff burnout, more joy is an important aim for any leader in healthcare today. Many factors contribute to burnout, and many may have to do with not the employee but the experience of the organization's culture. Efforts to deal with burnout can help to reduce barriers to joy. Such actions are essential for staff engagement and lead to better patient experience, quality, safety, and productivity (Perlo et al., 2017).[30]

Working to improve systems suggests the need to work with the human aspects of change. There is a need to determine what must change and how the change will affect staff. Communication about proposed changes and reasons why change is being considered is crucial—measuring the effects of change before and after changes are implemented to share the benefits. Individuals respond better when they come to know the impact of their improvement efforts. Everyone likes to be informed, involved, and engaged in the change-making process. Involving others draws out the ideas, strengths, and talents of everyone on the team. It is a great way to get buy-in for the change process.

D. Applying and Practicing Improvement Skills

Once there is an awareness of the need for improvement, an improvement mindset, and the knowledge of improvement methods, practitioners, must learn to apply and practice these skills. The practitioners have to move from this conceptual knowledge (knowing that) to working knowledge (knowing how) (Batalden & Davidoff, 2007).[31]

Performance Improvement knowledge is best acquired through experiential learning. Experiential learning has been described as a four-element cycle:

i. Learners first get involved in a new *experience*. Such involvement is done through direct observation of work or through practical demonstrations or simulations to see how abstract ideas come alive in real-life situations. This involvement is a crucial step to awaken awareness. For instance, learning about waste, standing in a corner, and watching other staff on a unit can make the person who is conducting the observation aware of how well or poorly the unit is set up to easily help the staff carry out their jobs. Are materials that are needed to be stored in an organized fashion? Do nurses have to walk a lot in between steps as they go about taking care of multiple patients? Do the staff know what needs to be done in different situations? Can information needed for daily work be found easily?

ii. The second element is to *reflect* on the experience. Having an experienced coach or a mentor is vital for this step. They can point to observations or highlight key ideas to help the improver learn the essence of the concept that is being demonstrated. After having seen demonstrations, the improver can also try to apply these principles to improve processes by themselves or their team. For instance, does organizing all the supplies needed for a manual restraint save time for the nursing staff and reduce the staff's chances of getting hurt?

iii. The third element is to *integrate these observations* with sense-making concepts and mental models. Learning about waste also nudges staff to think about value and where value can be found in their work processes. How can staff preserve value, and how do they grow value? If face-to-face time with patients is what adds the most value, what comes in the way, and how can staff think of ways to increase such time?

iv. Finally, the improver can *apply* these newly acquired concepts back again in real-life situations to become proficient at this newly acquired skill. The improver might then ask, is there anything else that needs reorganization, which might also save more time and increase care quality? For example, after seeing a few wastes demonstrated, does the improver develop a deeper understanding of waste, and do they begin to find wastes in other areas at work? What is also very important here is that the workplace empowers its employees to make changes and provides leadership support to enable their development as improvers.

Active, hands-on learning from coaching is preferred rather than passively gathering knowledge from experts. It requires repeated cycles of applying improvement skills and reflection. It is the most efficient way to learn. One learns more from doing rather than from listening, reading, or viewing audiovisual presentations. Adult learners learn more effectively with a hands-on approach to learning. They retain much more if they can apply new skills and knowledge to a problem at hand. Improvement methods embody the scientific method. The scientific method is best learned through experimentation.

Medical professionals are used to this active way of learning in their practicums and clinical rotations. Reading about depression or schizophrenia pales compared to viewing manifestations of these on a film about these kinds of patients, with a knowledgeable instructor acting as a discussant. Better still is learning about them through interacting with patients. The practitioner gets to understand the various manifestations of these disorders and the heterogeneity of these conditions. Through interacting, they learn how to talk to someone who is extremely delusional or very agitated. It is not easy to just get this by reading.

Similarly, it is one thing to learn about a concept such as standardization or reduction of waste. It is another thing to get different individuals and teams to minimize waste in their daily workflow to incorporate these ideas. It is a complex undertaking, and there is no substitute for experiential learning.

Many of the technical improvement and change management skills require practice because they do not come naturally. Most healthcare practitioners do not learn these skills in their professional schools. A deeper understanding of these principles only emerges once they start practicing and applying these skills to different problems in various situations, contexts, and with diverse groups of individuals. Improvement has been described as a 'contact sport.' Practitioners learn best by doing, and they understand both from their successes and failures.

Today, individuals can find ample opportunities for such experiential learning in their daily work. A simple way to get started is to 'count something' (Gawande, 2008).[32] When practitioners count something that indicates the reliability of a process or how their team's daily work ultimately affects an overall outcome, they become aware of the gap between the desired performance and actual performance. Trying to get to the desired level of performance by dealing with all the barriers is an excellent way to start learning about improvement. Usually, such improvement toward an ideal state takes a few cycles of doing and learning and teaches them valuable lessons about improvement.

E. Developing Performance Improvement Skills into Routine Habits

In their paper, 'Habits of an Improver,' the authors suggested that as the field of improvement science has grown, there is now a plethora of tools and techniques available (Lucas & Nacer, 2015).[33]

The risk of such availability is that busy professionals can think of improvement as just a set of techniques, which they either have no time to learn or may assume can be delegated to the quality improvement department. The authors seemed to suggest a specific pedagogy of improvement science, which will be necessary to prepare the workforce to improve mental healthcare systems. They highlight the central role communication has in the work of improvement, and they identify dimensions or habits of improvers that need to be developed.

In addition to developing such curricula that might prepare the workforce, attention will have to be paid to creating space and time for professionals to learn these skills. They will need an infrastructure, which will enable and encourage them to keep practicing these skills to develop into habits.

Typically, as mentioned at the beginning of this chapter, healthcare professionals can engage in first-order problem-solving. They can be habitually reactive, engaged in firefighting, and adept at creating workarounds. These reactive habits are also reinforced as they solve problems and get the patients what is needed at the moment. However, as was discussed earlier, such habits weaken systems over time. Changing these habits will require changing the behaviors and routines of healthcare professionals.

In his book 'Toyota Kata,' Rother introduced Toyota's improvement and coaching behaviors and routines (Rother, 2009).[34] 'Kata' are like practice drills that by frequent repetition become second-nature. Based on his research of their management methods, he concludes that by encouraging the use of such improvement and coaching habits, Toyota has created a culture that believes in surfacing problems. The culture also encourages the deliberate application of the scientific method by their entire workforce to all of the issues they encounter. Creating a workforce that is so well trained in problem-solving is what has led them to be a leader in quality. Coaching is one of the central tasks of any leader at Toyota. Each worker is assigned a mentor who ensures that the worker uses tools, engages in improvement routines, and habitually uncovers and solves problems.

Another example of a routine to encourage an improvement mindset is described as 'stop the line.' Workers on the assembly line are encouraged to pull an 'Andon cord' (a mechanism to stop the assembly line) whenever they encounter a situation that is not according to a specified standard or whenever they see a problem. Pulling an Andon cord leads a senior team member to promptly find the root cause of the problem and help the worker learn how to solve such problems. The idea is to stop the line often early on to spot and solve problems, but as those problems are solved, the variation is less and less, and therefore there is not the same need to stop the line. In addition to doing their work, the workers are being taught to systematically get into the habit of learning to solve problems using the correct method. A reduction in the number of times the 'Andon cord' is pulled during a shift gets the leadership concerned. The assumption is that problems are not being uncovered and that learning is not occurring. Such an approach seems very different from what is seen in healthcare settings, where issues are often hidden or worked around.

Fostering a continuous learning environment and culture also requires leadership to manage differently. Management must foster problem-finding and problem-solving, learning, and creativity in the workforce. Decision-making and delegation of responsibility have to be pushed down at the lowest level possible so that staff can learn by doing and not depend on leadership for every little step in their day's work. Leadership has to demonstrate proactive problem-solving and lead by example. They cannot delegate such an undertaking to a department. They have to encourage and model such behaviors through their support of a learning and problem-solving culture. We will explore this topic further in section five.

III. Preparing the Medical Professional to Learn Performance Improvement Skills

Providers need to be engaged so that they initiate, participate, and get involved in this monumental task of transforming our mental healthcare system. Medical, nursing, and pharmacy schools have not uniformly and systematically taught performance improvement skills. There are gaps in the existing educational system at every stage of a practitioner's development, which does not help prepare providers to think about improving quality and safety. Practitioners get trained in the science of medicine and in skills that help them take care of individual patients but don't get trained in skills required to improve and sustain systems (Aron and Headrick, 2002).[35] Systems have also grown bigger and more complex over time. Methods and procedures that were put in place to make the system run smoothly initially may not be adequate to manage the current day complexity. They may be overdue for a closer examination and redesign to optimize currently available resources and be ready for present-day challenges. Providers need to learn the skills that will allow them to keep redesigning their existing systems to keep with the ever-changing and evolving context. Training has to focus on creating 'competence' (defined as what providers know can do in terms of knowledge, skills, and attitude) and also 'capability' (defined as the provider's ability to adapt to change, generate new knowledge, and continue to improve their performance) in providers (Fraser & Greenhalgh, 2001).[36]

Consider, for instance, how this applies to the development of physicians. In 1999, the Accreditation Council for Graduate Medical Education (ACGME) and American Board of Medical Specialties (ABMS) jointly identified competencies for the development of resident physicians in six domains – patient care, medical knowledge, practice-based learning and improvement (PBLI), interpersonal and communication skills, professionalism and systems-based practice (SBP). The coming together of an accrediting body and a certifying body to implement these competencies helped them take hold to shape Graduate Medical Education. The idea was to come up with competencies that were not overly prescriptive (Batalden et al., 2002).[37] The competencies would (1) apply to all specialties and encourage conversation across specialties; (2) use measurement; (3) recognize the continuum of medical education; and (4) adopt an improvement rather than a simple minimal threshold model of accreditation.

It was also expected that education programs would collect data, demonstrating the resident's ability to care for patients and show that they can perform effectively in healthcare systems (Swing, 2007).[38] Based on the Dreyfus Model of Knowledge Development (which was developed by commission for the US Air Force to describe the development of knowledge and skill level of pilots), trainees would move through the following stages: novice, advanced beginner, competent, proficient, and expert (Carraccio et al., 2008).[39] Graduate medical education would help physicians progress from the advanced beginner stage as medical school graduates to the competent stage as physicians. As skilled physicians, each trainee would be expected to learn to plan the approach to patients while under the guidance of a supervisor.

The curricula and faculty needed to support all of these competencies are not easily and uniformly available everywhere. PBLI and SBP were the two new competencies. They were hard for residents and faculty to conceptualize (Ziegelstein & Fiebach, 2004).[40]

Components of PBLI include establishing learning and improvement goals, identifying and performing appropriate learning activities, systematically analyzing practice, and implementing changes to improve practice.

VIGNETTE 3.12

Colin, a pharmacist, analyzed the number of controlled substances available in the automated medicine cabinets on inpatient units of a psychiatric hospital. From his analysis, he learned that patients waited on average 26 times longer for an initial dose of a controlled substance if the cabinet was not stocked with the medicine. If the number of controlled substances stored could increase, not only would patient wait times improve, it would also tighten the controlled substance supply chain and lower the risk of diversion. He calculated that nurses and pharmacists spend more than two thousand three hundred hours in the hospital keeping track of controlled substances and transporting the medications that were stored outside of the automated medicine cabinet over the past year.

A 'mirror' metaphor was used at a training program to explain PBLI (Ziegelstein & Fiebach, 2004).[40] PBLI is thought to be like holding up a mirror to improve the trainee's practice. Chart audits and resident learning portfolios are examples of such activities. They could be used to see how much each resident practice varies from expected norms. Peer review for physicians is another such activity. They need to identify areas of proficiency and areas in need of improvement. This kind of awareness can come from faculty and patients' feedback as well as other team members. Systematically collecting and studying data about a physician's practice can also be very instructive. Baseline data can suggest an improvement, and follow-up measurements of those same metrics after making changes can indicate if the change has led to an improvement (Berwick, 1996).[41]

Today, many practitioners are employers of hospitals, group practices, or healthcare systems. Even those who practice in solo private practices may have to work with pharmacies, laboratories, hospitals, and insurances, making them aware of the complex nature of the overall healthcare system. System-based practice as a competency allows providers to become knowledgeable of and responsive to the larger context of the healthcare system. It will enable practitioners to learn how to use various system resources to provide patient care (Dyne, 2002).[42]

Components of SBP included working in inter-professional teams to enhance quality and safety and participating in identifying system errors, amongst others.

VIGNETTE 3.13

Thelma, a pharmacist, decided to reduce the use of antipsychotics to manage the behavioral and psychological symptoms of dementia (BPSD) in a geriatric inpatient unit. There was heightened attention to this practice all around the country. Around 97% of dementia patients exhibited BPSD at some point in the course of their illness. There were no approved medications for treating BPSD.

The pharmacist was able to work with the multidisciplinary team to identify the root causes and interventions necessary to reduce inappropriate antipsychotic use. The interventions led to a 10% rate reduction in overall antipsychotic prescribing in the geriatric unit.

The metaphor of the 'village' (as in 'it takes a village to raise a child') was used to explain SBP at the same training program. Focusing on daily improvement huddles or trying to collectively reduce readmissions are reminders to residents that they are one part of a large health system. Trying to understand how to improve safety and quality through a rapid improvement event, root cause analysis, or failure modes and effects analysis could be other examples of such activities. It is only participating in such activities that make practitioners think about systems, variation, and the need for improvement. Even current ways of healthcare reform or payment reform and the current emphasis on population health or the triple aim (Berwick et al., 2008) makes practitioners think of systems.[43]

In 1998, Don Berwick, the former President and CEO of the Institute of Healthcare Improvement, wrote, "We believe that the prognosis for the healthcare system is good if physicians will contribute actively to improving the system as a whole. If we are wrong, our agenda at least gives professionals something more pleasant to do than complain. More importantly, if we are correct in stating that the seeds of fundamental improvement in healthcare systems lie within the reach of physicians, then physicians can best exert their influence by recognizing the problems to be solved and then doing everything in their power to assure that the solutions they help develop are technically proper, ethically sound, and effective." This appeal to improve healthcare systems applies not only to physicians but also to every other healthcare professional today.

Any practitioner interested in transforming the mental health system has to go through these developmental steps of awareness, developing a mindset, acquiring knowledge and skills to initiate and habitually practice these improvement skills. It would enable them to be proactive and take these steps toward improvement. The next section of the book summarizes a structured problem-solving method to help anyone improve the performance of his or her system. The method incorporates the Plan-Do-Check-Act logic as its basis. Individuals who want to embark on a project to tackle any kind of safety, quality, or delivery problem can utilize it. It is the most actionable part of the book. The vignettes in the next section demonstrate how such tools can be put into action.

References

1. Tucker, Anita L. 2004. "The Impact of Operational Failures on Hospital Nurses and Their Patients". *Journal of Operations Management* 22 (2): 151–169. Wiley. doi:10.1016/j.jom.2003.12.006.
2. Halbesleben, Jonathon; Savage, Grant & Wakefield, Douglas, et al. 2010. "Rework and Workarounds in Nurse Medication Administration Process". *Health Care Management Review* 35 (2): 124–133. Ovid Technologies (Wolters Kluwer Health). doi:10.1097/hmr.0b013e3181d116c2.
3. Tucker, Anita. 2009. "Workarounds and Resiliency on the Front Lines of Health Care". *Perspectives of Safety*. Agency for Healthcare Quality and Research. https://psnet.ahrq.gov/perspective/workarounds-and-resiliency-front-lines-health-care. Accessed February 24, 2021.
4. Tucker, Anita; Edmondson, Amy, & Spear, Stephen. 2002. "When Problem Solving Prevents Organizational Learning". *Journal of Organizational Change Management* 15 (2): 122–137. Emerald. doi:10.1108/09534810210423008.
5. Tucker, Anita L. & Edmondson, Amy C. 2003. "Why Hospitals Don't Learn from Failures: Organizational and Psychological Dynamics That Inhibit System Change". *California Management Review* 45 (2): 55–72. SAGE Publications. doi:10.2307/41166165.
6. Liker, Jeffrey K. & Meier, David P. 2007. *Toyota Talent*. 1st Edition. McGraw-Hill Education, New York, NY.
7. Spear, Steven J. 2005. "Fixing Health Care from the Inside, Today." *Harvard Business Review* 83 (9): 78.

8. Clark, Cheryl. 2011. "Gawande on Checklists: Why Don't Hospitals Use Them?" *Health Leaders*. https://www.healthleadersmedia.com/clinical-care/gawande-checklists-why-dont-hospitals-use-them?page=0%2C4. Accessed June 13, 2019.
9. Spear, Stephen & Bowen, Kent. 1999. "Decoding the DNA of the Toyota Production System". *Harvard Business Review* 77 (5): 96–106.
10. Barzansky, Barbara. 2010. "Abraham Flexner and the Era of Medical Education Reform." *Academic Medicine* 85 (9): S19–S25.
11. Ludmerer, Kenneth M. 2010. "Commentary: Understanding the Flexner Report." *Academic Medicine* 85 (2): 193–196.
12. Ezez. 2019. "History of TWI | WWII beginnings | Re-introduction in the US". *Twi-institute.org*. https://www.twi-institute.com/search/History/. Accessed July 26 2020.
13. Ogrinc, Gregory; Headrick, Linda & Moore, Shirley, et al. 2012. *Fundamentals of Health Care Improvement: A Guide to Improving Your Patient's Care*. Joint Commission Resources, Oakbrook Terrace, IL.
14. Morris, Z. S.; Wooding, S. & Grant, J. 2011. "The Answer is 17 Years, What Is the Question: Understanding Time Lags in Translational Research". *Journal of the Royal Society of Medicine* 104(12), 510–520. https://doi.org/10.1258/jrsm.2011.110180.
15. Jones, Bryan; Vaux, Emma & Olsson-Brown, Anna. 2019. "How to Get Started in Quality Improvement". *BMJ* k5408. doi:10.1136/bmj.k5437.
16. Lucas, Bill. 2015. "Getting the Improvement Habit". *BMJ Quality & Safety* 25 (6): 400–403. doi:10.1136/bmjqs-2015-005086.
17. Covey, S.R., 2013. *The 7 habits of highly effective people: Powerful lessons in personal change*. Simon and Schuster.
18. Watanabe, Ken. 2009. *Problem Solving 101*. Vermillion, London.
19. Nolan, Thomas W. 2007. "Execution of Strategic Improvement Initiatives to Produce System-Level Results." *IHI Innovation Series White Paper*. Institute for Healthcare Improvement, Cambridge, MA.
20. Deming, W. Edwards. 1994. *The New Economics for Industry, Government, Education*. Massachusetts Institute of Technology, Center for Advanced Engineering Study, Cambridge, MA.
21. Aguayo, Rafael. 1991. *Dr. Deming: The American Who Taught the Japanese About Quality*. Simon and Schuster, New York, NY.
22. Best, M. 2006. "Walter A Shewhart, 1924, and the Hawthorne factory". *Quality and Safety in Health Care* 15 (2): 142–143. BMJ. doi:10.1136/qshc.2006.018093.
23. Berry, B. L. 2006. *There Is a Relationship Between Systems Thinking and W. Edwards Deming's Theory of Profound Knowledge*.
24. Langley, Gerald J; Moen, Ronald & Nolan, Kevin, et al. 2009. *The Improvement Guide: A Practical Approach to Enhancing Organizational Performance*. John Wiley & Sons, New York, NY.
25. Derington, Catherine G.; Jordan B. King; Kelsey B. Bryant; Blake T. McGee; Andrew E. Moran; William S. Weintraub; Brandon K. Bellows & Adam P. Bress. 2019. "Cost-Effectiveness and Challenges of Implementing Intensive Blood Pressure Goals and Team-Based Care." *Current Hypertension Reports* 21 (12): 91.
26. Ryan, R. M., & Deci, E. L. 2000. "Intrinsic and Extrinsic Motivations: Classic Definitions and New Directions". *Contemporary Educational Psychology* 25 (1): 54–67.
27. Ackoff, Russell L. 1998. "A Systemic View of Transformational Leadership." *Systemic Practice and Action Research* 11 (1): 23–36.
28. Leonard, Michael W. & Allan Frankel. 2010. "The Path to Safe and Reliable Healthcare." *Patient Education and Counseling* 80 (3): 288–292.
29. IHI Multimedia Team. 2015. "Like Magic? ("Every system is perfectly designed…")". http://www.ihi.org/communities/blogs/origin-of-every-system-is-perfectly-designed-quote. Accessed June 18, 2019.
30. Perlo, Jessica; Balik, Barbara & Swensen, Stephen, et al. 2017. *IHI Framework for Improving Joy in Work*. Institute for Healthcare Improvement, Cambridge, MA.
31. Batalden, Paul & FrankDavidoff. 2007. "Teaching Quality Improvement: The Devil Is in the Details." *JAMA* 298 (9): 1059–1061.
32. Gawande, Atul. 2008. *Better: A Surgeon's Notes on Performance*. Macmillan, London.

33. Lucas, Bill & Hadjer Nacer. 2015. *The Habits of an Improver: Thinking About Learning for Improvement in Healthcare*. The Health Foundation, London.
34. Rother, Mike. *Toyota Kata*. McGraw-Hill Professional Publishing, New York, NY, 2009.
35. Aron, David C. & L. A. Headrick. 2002. "Educating Physicians Prepared to Improve Care and Safety Is No Accident: It Requires a Systematic Approach." *Quality and Safety in Health Care* 11 (2): 168–173.
36. Fraser, Sarah W. & Trisha Greenhalgh. 2001. "Coping with Complexity: Educating for Capability." *BMJ* 323 (7316): 799–803.
37. Batalden, Paul; Leach, David & Swing, Susan, et al. 2002. "General Competencies and Accreditation in Graduate Medical Education." *Health Affairs* 21 (5): 103–111.
38. Swing, Susan R. 2007. "The ACGME Outcome Project: Retrospective and Prospective." *Medical Teacher* 29 (7): 648–654.
39. Carraccio, Carol L.; Benson, Bradley J. & Nixon, James L., et al. 2008. "From the Educational Bench to the Clinical Bedside: Translating the Dreyfus Developmental Model to the Learning of Clinical Skills." *Academic Medicine* 83 (8): 761–767.
40. Ziegelstein, Roy C. & Nicholas H. Fiebach. 2004. ""The Mirror" and "The Village": A New Method for Teaching Practice-Based Learning and Improvement and Systems-Based Practice." *Academic Medicine* 79 (1): 83–88.
41. Berwick, Donald M. 1996. "A Primer on Leading the Improvement of Systems." *BMJ: British Medical Journal* 312 (7031): 619.
42. Dyne, Pamela L.; Robert W. Strauss & Stephan Rinnert. 2002. "Systems-Based Practice: The Sixth Core Competency." *Academic Emergency Medicine* 9 (11): 1270–1277.
43. Berwick, Donald M., Thomas W. Nolan & John Whittington. 2008. "The Triple Aim: Care, Health, and Cost." *Health Affairs* 27 (3): 759–769.

Section IV

Improvement Methods for Mental Health Organizations

The previous chapter focused on the need to enhance the clinician skill set that will enable a greater focus on innovation and improvement. This chapter will provide an improvement toolbox that clinicians can use to focus on health outcomes as well as improvement in quality, service delivery, and cost.

I. Plan-Do-Check-Act Cycle

There are several approaches to improvement. However, the one method that can improve value without the need for expensive consultants or extensive training is Shewhart's Plan-Do-Check-Act (PDCA or PDSA) cycle. The PDCA cycle is a shortened version of the scientific method and was popularized by Deming (2018) in the 1960s to improve focus on quality.[1] The PDCA process in Figure 4.1 represents a circle with arrows that continuously drives teams toward improvement. The PDCA improvement process is an iterative approach to learning and improvement that clinicians can utilize for any problem-solving activity, including designing new processes that currently do not exist.

VIGNETTE 4.1

The Medical Director of a hospital decided to improve the timeliness and cost of discharge summaries. Every doctor dictated their discharge summaries and sent them to outpatient providers as a helpful method to ensure continuity of care once a patient left the inpatient setting. However, the costs for developing and transcribing discharge summaries were extensive. The Medical Director examined the process and noted that each summary was completed two weeks after a patient was discharged from the hospital. The outpatient providers complained that they were getting the summaries after the first appointment with the patient or sometimes not at all. The medical director decided to improve this process's quality and gathered feedback from multiple stakeholders and outpatient providers about what they would like to see in a discharge summary. A new standardized discharge summary template was created in the electronic medical record (EMR), which was considerably shorter in length using their feedback, reducing the time to complete and transmit to the outpatient provider. After the first round of improvement, the medical director learned that the discharge summaries were completed in 45% less time on average and saving 33% in transcription costs.

A change may or may not produce the desired outcomes for a process. The PDCA framework allows a project leader to experiment with small incremental changes over time, which provides a learning lab in the workplace without the need for expensive research studies or lengthy approval processes. While there is also a need for designing new and improved processes that reduce large pockets of waste, introduce technology, and advance the entire system forward, these lend themselves to a design process outside of a PDCA incremental improvement cycle. As shown in Figure 4.2, as the scope of change grows, the resistance grows with it. For our introductory purposes, the goal is to provide a safe way to introduce small process changes to allow for learning.

Small teams also benefit from taking part in the learning process. A team can provide input on what changes to try and then determine how the trial affects their work. Giving all workers a chance to interact with, question, and provide feedback on a change is an invaluable employee engagement tool that incorporates people into the improvement process. By involving workers in a small-scale change, the initial resistance to change is reduced, which allows for learning to occur.

The diagram in Figure 4.3 depicts the iterative nature of improvement.

If there was ever a diagram that depicted the entire process in a simple visual, this is it. Continual improvement is like rolling a barrel up an inclined plane. After the first PDCA, the

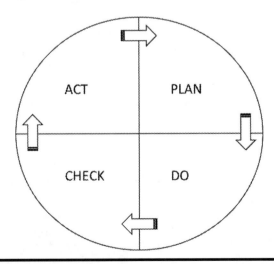

Figure 4.1 PDCA cycle.

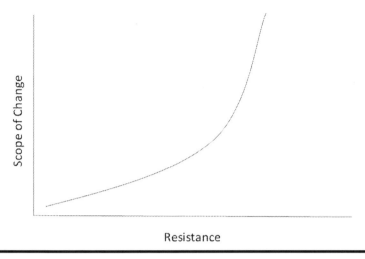

Figure 4.2 Scope of change vs. resistance.

process shifts to a new level of performance. To sustain a process at a new level of performance, a control, depicted as a wedge, prevents the barrel from naturally rolling back down the inclined plane. A control is a method by which a team standardizes and adheres to the new change. When implementing change, all workers must train on and follow the new plan to prevent backsliding. From that point on, a new round of learning can begin to determine how the process can improve further. With each new learning, a new wedge or control is set in place to continually move the project team toward an improved level of performance.

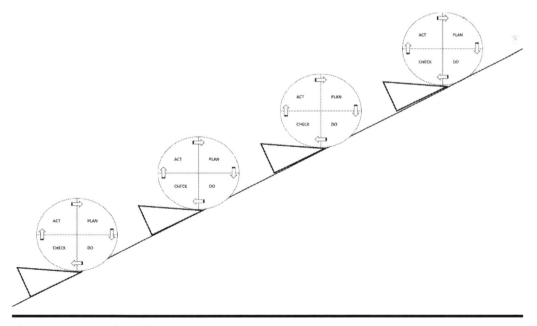

Figure 4.3 PDCA iterative process.

VIGNETTE 4.2

An inpatient unit decided to examine safety on their daily performance improvement huddle. During this daily five-minute ritual, all the clinicians of this inpatient team would gather and analyze the performance of a pre-selected process. As a team, the unit staff decided to focus on safety every day. Inspired by seeing a multi-point inspection done by her car mechanic, the service chief of this unit came up with the idea of creating a multi-point checklist. This checklist was developed by reviewing all safety concerns commonly seen on this unit in the past year. She and the unit manager asked the charge nurse of each shift to conduct this multi-point review of all potential safety concerns at the end of each shift. The idea was to engage the staff of each shift on weekdays and weekends to focus on safety. Each safety concern was reviewed every day in the morning during the daily unit meetings. If any safety events were brought up, there would be a brief discussion of the situation and the background of the event. Based on a brief root cause analysis (RCA) of the safety event, the team would then decide on an action plan to prevent similar unsafe situations in subsequent shifts. As new safety concerns were addressed and mitigated, staff members began to see the value of this brief daily improvement huddle. The participation and engagement of the staff grew over time. The hospital leadership team visited the unit during the huddle once a week and interacted with the team. The leadership team would take on any system-level concerns or barriers for follow-up and resolution.

II. Standard Work

A basic example of a control used to stabilize new levels of performance is a standardized work practice. A standard work document is the beginning and the end of every improvement process. Without a standard, there can be no improvement (Ohno, 1987).[2] Standard work allows a team to study the process and determine how they can improve further. Thus, the goal is to consider standard work as the one best way to complete a process (Graupp & Wrona, 2011).[3] By following the new standard, teams can learn where the waste is and then work to create a new best way. For instance, the standardized admission note template is a standard established by consensus based on best-practice guidelines. Every provider knows what the requirements are to complete a note. If a particular section is left incomplete, the headings in the EMR make it easy to pick up what section is missing. Should the standard change, a team can create a new heading and add it to the admissions template as a new standard for every subsequent admission note.

It is important to note that while Figure 4.3 depicts the improvement process as a barrel rolling up the hill to three new positions, it does not mean that all improvement will happen in three iterations. Improvement can happen in one iteration or twenty iterations. The goal of improvement is to determine where to focus next. In some cases, continuing efforts on improving the existing process are necessary because several variables are acting on each step in the process. In other cases, there comes the point where the process is running as optimally as possible, and the focus needs to switch to another more pressing need. A team needs to collectively determine where they are with process improvement and how much further they have to go. Once all low-hanging fruit has been picked, this will open up space for teams to reinvent themselves. Innovative thinking can then inform further improvement.

Innovation in a healthcare system, for instance, can be seen with a never-ending push to reduce the length of stay in hospitals. While the process has been optimized over the last 20 years, there is still a need to focus on it as each hospital stay is associated with considerable costs. If several iterations have improved a process to an optimal level, then it becomes time to consider breakthrough design changes that can alter the paradigms of existing care practices. For example, tele-triage, proactive flu shot clinics, and screening for mental health issues during routine primary care visits are just a few design changes in care that can dramatically offload the burden that hospitals face. Such changes will help reduce costs and avoidable high-cost interventions such as hospitalizations.

III. PDCA vs. Research

A primary concern when improving in a healthcare environment is making changes to processes that affect the patient. A patient may experience increased variation because of one or more changes. Thus, it is important to highlight the differences between the PDCA process and a clinical research project. The intent of PDCA is not an alternative to clinical research. We also do not recommend bypassing an organization's research process from a clinical perspective with PDCA. A research project is one where changes in clinical practices, medications, and so forth are studied with a robust measurement system and a review board to protect human subjects. The PDCA process is best for reviewing administrative processes in organizations to determine where wasteful steps are taken by staff that do not add value to the patient. For example, when looking at the flow of patients in the morning, the doctor pulled patients out of group therapy to ask them how they were doing even though the group leader required them to provide the same information just an hour prior. In this example, the process caused a duplication of effort because the system of care was not designed with the patient in mind, and the documentation was not timely enough to let the doctor know how patients were feeling.

VIGNETTE 4.3

The team on an inpatient was very concerned about the opioid epidemic. The team decided to send home every patient admitted after an overdose, who had an opioid use disorder, or who was on opioids chronically for pain, with a prescription for Narcan (intranasal naltrexone), which had been suggested by the research and best practice guidelines. They decided to use the PDCA process to ensure that this vital step was not forgotten. Every physician agreed that it was the right thing to do, but making it into a reliable practice required multiple rounds of feedback and improvement.

IV. A3 Thinking

The best approach to exploring the use of the PDCA framework is with the A3 problem-solving tool (Shook, 2010).[4] There is no mystique around the A3. A3 is a paper size and represents an 11 × 17 sheet of paper. Toyota developed the A3 approach to allow individual factories to fax a project summary to other Toyota factories and headquarters in Japan. At that time, the A3 size was the largest size of paper that could be sent via fax. Therefore, they utilized it as a simple,

Project Title	
Why? / Why Now?	Solutions for Root Causes / Gaps
Customers / Stakeholders	Experimentation (who / what / where)
Process Map / Baseline Data	Improvement Confirmation
Goal	Lessons Learned
Root Cause / Gap Analysis	Follow-up Action Plan (who, what, when)

Figure 4.4 A3 problem-solving tool.

effective project management tool to employ across their organization. The A3 format is shown in Figure 4.4.

The A3 process flows through an entire problem-solving activity and is consistent with the PDCA process. The entire left-hand side of the A3 is considered the plan phase, while the right side of the A3 is split between do, check, and act phases. Each section builds on the previous sections to improve process outcomes.

A. Plan

The plan is the most critical step in the improvement process. The goal of the plan is to define the project adequately and its relative importance, determine the scope and complete the necessary steps of change management and data collection upfront before formally launching improvement. Projects fail 90% of the time due to poor initial project planning. Often, project leaders will get through the plan, do, and check phases, realize they have not made an impact in performance, and revert to the plan step. Thus, there is a considerable need to focus on the plan to ensure the project setup is correct. A well-known quote attributed to Abraham Lincoln is, "Give me six hours to chop down a tree, and I will spend the first four sharpening the axe."

1. Project Title

The Plan process begins with a project title. While titling choices may not seem important, wording matters. The first common mistake is lengthy titles that do not help convey a clear and concise understanding of the project. Therefore, the recommendation is to keep the title to six words or fewer. For example, a rather lengthy title for an improvement project was "Reducing the off-label use of antipsychotic medications to mitigate the health risk in the dementia population." This title assumes the reader knows what off-label use means and would cause questions related to the words 'off-label' rather than merely focusing the reader on reducing the use of such medications. A more streamlined title would be "Reducing antipsychotic medication in dementia treatment." The improved version is simple and straightforward and does not cause the reader to question the title. Every section of A3 is supposed to succinct. It is mean to be used for communication to the team and organization, both for learning and improvement, hence both brevity and visuals help.

A second issue seen in project titles is the use of a pre-determined solution. For example, "Reducing falls on an inpatient unit by installing handrails" provides a pre-determined solution of installing handrails. There is no need to run through a problem-solving activity given a pre-determined solution. Further, sometimes the title may not be well understood at the outset of a project. Lack of clarity about titles is not uncommon. As a project leader works through an improvement activity, the title should be refined. When looking at the data for falls, they mostly occur in the bedroom at night when a patient was walking to and from the restroom or getting out of bed. Based on the data, an improved and scoped title could be "Reducing falls within inpatient bedrooms."

2. Business Case

Once the title is set, the next step is to complete a business case. The business case helps to provide the reason why the potential project is about to begin. There are four basic questions to ask when conducting a business case. The first question is why we are engaging in this project. It is vital to link the project to the organizational mission, values, strategic objectives, and philosophy when developing the 'why.' By connecting a project to an organization's core foundation, we heighten its importance and acceptance as a project.

Second, the 'why' also helps to determine how an improvement project links to the patient. An excellent way to understand this is to consider customer requirements. To quickly reiterate what was discussed in Section II the value or benefits received from a customer perspective is to safely receive the right quality service at the right time for the right cost. Five major strategic objectives emerge from this definition of value – Safety, Quality, Delivery, Cost, and Morale (SQDCM). Using the five pillars is a way to align organizational improvement toward the customer by connecting the improvement project to the strategy. SQDCM are all pillars of strategy and can be found in all strategic plans in one form or another. From this construct, we can link both the organization's mission to a strategic objective, which provides the burning platform for the project. Consider Figure 4.5 as an example of a project tie-in to the strategy.

The 'why' statement in this example is, "Safe care for patients on the geriatric inpatient unit is a top priority for our organization."

Once the 'why' is answered, the next question to address is "why should the organization pursue this project now?" Answering this question helps grab the attention of the reader and provides a sense of urgency. For example, "One area of concern is the rate of falls resulting in patient injury." Anyone and everyone within the healthcare setting can rally behind reducing patient injury, and within two sentences, any remaining cultural, organizational, or people resistance to beginning this project is likely to decrease.

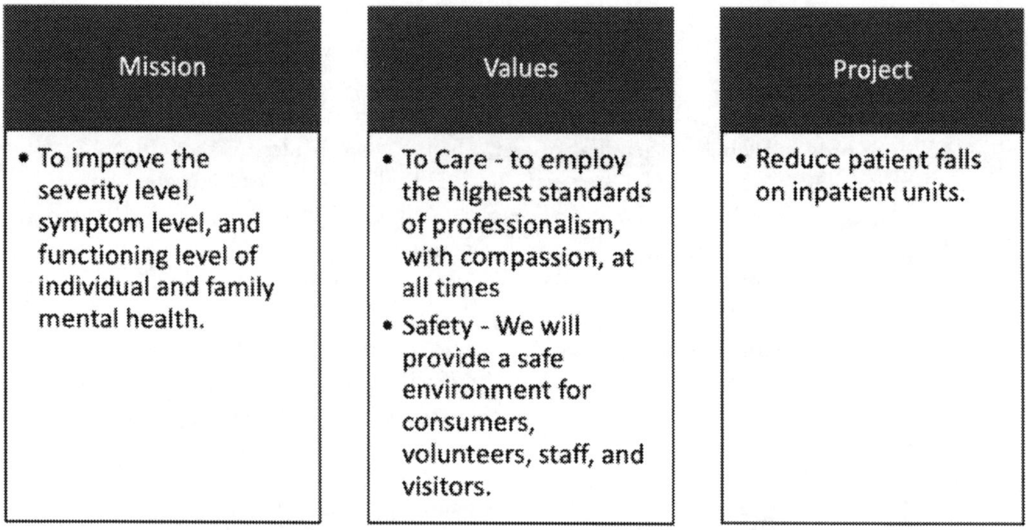

Mission	Values	Project
• To improve the severity level, symptom level, and functioning level of individual and family mental health.	• To Care - to employ the highest standards of professionalism, with compassion, at all times • Safety - We will provide a safe environment for consumers, volunteers, staff, and visitors.	• Reduce patient falls on inpatient units.

Figure 4.5　Mission and values connection to process improvement.

The third question is, "how will the organization benefit from this project." The reason for this question is to add business support for the project. Culture and behavior are great starting points but typically not enough to encapsulate the importance, especially when it comes to those in charge of accounting for all of the dollars entering and exiting a business. As with any business, there are a limited number of resources and hundreds, if not thousands, of projects that need to be completed. Establishing a business reason helps to move the project up on the priority list. For example, "The fall rate over the past year has increased costs of care by 25% and prolonged patient length of stay by 30 days." Utilizing real data helps all team members understand the business need for a project and ensures adequate support. Falls also increase morbidity and mortality, and it certainly would not be good for any hospital business to have worse outcomes concerning those measures.

The final question of the business case is to ask, "What are the consequences of not pursuing this project?" The 'do nothing' alternative is considered to ensure there is reasonable cause to engage in the project, and this project is the best use of limited resource time. For example, "By not pursuing this project, we will continue to experience patient injuries, higher lengths of stay, increased morbidity and mortality, and risk reputational damage."

Piecing this example together into a paragraph and adding the A3 WHY/WHY NOW section would become:

> Safe care for patients on the geriatric inpatient unit is a top priority for our organization. One area of concern is the rate of falls resulting in patient injury. Over the past year, the fall rate has increased costs of care by 25% and prolonged patient length of stay by 30 days. By not pursuing this project, we will continue to experience patient falls with injury, higher lengths of stay, worse morbidity and mortality rates, and also risk reputational damage.

This simple but elegant statement gives the reader a great sense of what the project is and why the need.

VIGNETTE 4.4

Here is another example of a business case:

> The Adolescent unit was committed to establishing a safe environment. A problem area for both patient and staff safety was locked door seclusion (LDS). By reducing LDS, patients would spend more time engaged with staff in therapeutic activities, and staff would enjoy fewer injuries as a result of hands-on, aggressive patient behaviors.

3. Project Y

The next concept to consider is the measurable outcome for a project. The measurable outcome is denoted as 'Project Y.' This is not to be confused with the why or purpose of the project. The Y is simply the outcome and comes to us via basic mathematics. In simple terms, a project leader wants to understand all of the variables (Xs) that contribute to the outcome (Y).

In an earlier example, Project Y is 'patient injury rate.' Having this metadata on patient injury rate is essential for an organization to determine if safety is improving, declining, or staying the same over time.

VIGNETTE 4.5

Here is another business case from a few years ago:

> Frequently, patients were admitted as inpatients to the hospital without sufficient proof of insurance. This phenomenon had increased over the past four years since the hospital stopped financial screening for emergency room transfers as part of being compliant with regulations. As the potential for more insured patients to be admitted to hospitals was imminent with the opening of the Healthcare Exchange that year, the hospital thought that it was an opportune time to improve the processes related to the collection and communication of insurance information as close to an admission as possible. By improving this process, the hospital would reduce its bad debt, and administratively denied day rate, and experience increased patient revenues. Allowing the current processes to continue would contribute to ongoing financial losses for inpatient care. The estimated annual cost of this problem in denied days was an imprecise $50,000. The cost of labor and rework was much higher.

Using insurance card capture as a proxy for accurate insurance information, the hospital improved procedures piloted on the adult service line and hopes to increase the capture rate by 40%.

In this case, the Project Y was the 'annual cost due to several denied inpatient days.'

4. Scope

Developing a scope helps to set the natural boundaries for a single project. The boundaries allow a project manager and an improvement team to achieve greater focus. If the team begins with a Project Y of patient injury rate, what is the clear focus? Patient injury is too broad. Briefly, considering all variables influencing injuries in a healthcare setting, there are hundreds of variables. Each variable may be subdivided into several variables, and those variables may be subdivided further. For example, segmenting the data to just focus on patient falls is one way to limit the scope. Further segmentation might limit the scope to the geriatric population where patient falls are more prevalent. The cost of falls in this population is more significant to the patient and the organization.

The second aspect of scoping is to determine where the project will take place. If there are multiple hospital sites with geriatric patients, will this be a project encompassing all of these locations or just one? We recommend choosing a single location to learn from because the larger the area or the more areas involved, the harder it is to implement changes and study the effects of changes.

As a project leader considers the scope, several pitfalls tend to derail projects. The first pitfall is scope creep. Scope creep happens when a simple small project team starts to notice all of the waste and variation within the process, and they slowly expand the project focus to be inclusive rather than exclusive. Project teams must protect against scope creep and evaluate each new data point to determine if it pertains to the original business case. Suppose an expanded aspect is recommended by a team member but is out of scope for the project. In that case, it's best to document the concern and determine if the project can move forward, knowing a team can address the concern in the next PDCA cycle.

The second pitfall is timing. When teams come together to improve, they want to see results that are either effective instantaneously or in a relatively short amount of time. If the project scope is too large, the project will tend to stay open for a very long time, and actions drag on over multiple months traversing several committees and meetings before implementation. It is not unheard of that projects without good scoping tend to turn into committees that meet for years. A PDCA project aims to limit action implementation to a maximum of 3–4 weeks from start to finish, although newer project leaders may take up to four months to complete their first project.

The third pitfall is expensive projects. As expected, costs increase for a given project, organizational barriers cause substantial resistance to the change process, making it hard to manage change. Second, expensive projects that are not defined well or miss providing better outcomes will cause the organization to ask questions and re-evaluate the effectiveness of the PDCA approach. The best way to manage this issue is to start small and fail cheaply.

VIGNETTE 4.6

After trying to persuade the organization to spend $70K for a new quality management software system and failing to generate enough support, a team scaled it back to start by piloting the same software in a small area for just $2.5K. After implementing the scaled-back version, others understood and appreciated the value this software system provided and soon asked for an expanded launch.

The fourth pitfall is too many people on the team. When developing teams, it is important to utilize an ideal team size of six to eight people. The reason for more than six is to ensure adequate representation for all stakeholders. The reason for eight or less is to prevent different personalities from affecting the teaming process and focusing on improvement. Another important point that in addition to projects leading to improvement, these are also experiential learning opportunities. With each project, participants become more skilled at solving the next improvement challenge.

The final pitfall is to rely on high technology as an approach to solve a problem. Once a project engages the IT group of an organization, the project is relegated to IT prioritization and project management, programming time, and software implementation. Each IT process in the queue will affect the ability to implement in the period required, not to mention that each IT project adds to the project's expense. It is best to come up with the best way for each process through quick PDCA experimentation and optimizing that process before subjecting the process to automation. If broken processes are automated, waste just gets multiplied all the faster.

Thus, the overall approach within PDCA is focused on action. Big systems require scoped thinking. While being specific is essential, it does not diminish the effectiveness of a project. A small project can have an enormous impact. An excellent example of scoping is the creation of a platform where students at a local college could communicate with one another. This one single project to connect students on campus turned into Facebook with over a billion users worldwide.

When scoping a project, it is essential to consider both customer requirements (external to the system such as patients or families) and stakeholders (internal customers to the system such as nurses and administrators) feedback. Customer requirements ensure the project hits on all aspects of a process that are critical to quality. Stakeholder feedback helps to ensure the scoping is correct. Further, stakeholders help assess the willingness of those who work within a process to focus on improving. Generating feedback from customers and stakeholders is essential in the change management process and helps ensure adequate support for a project before developing and implementing solutions.

VIGNETTE 4.7

A unit manager wanted to engage his team in daily improvement huddles to get them to learn the PDCA thinking process. As part of COVID-19 precautions, inpatients were supposed to isolate in single rooms for the first three days of their admission to the unit. He wanted to ensure no delay in the transfer of these patients to double rooms after the first three days if the patients were asymptomatic. The unit manager had seen delays in this process. He decided to work with the day shift staff to scope the project and learn about any barriers from their workday. Any successful interventions could then be adopted or adapted by subsequent shifts.

5. Project Management

While this chapter is not meant to be a project manager guide, some tips can help scope a project. First, every project has a beginning and an end. Establishing these targets is essential to determine how much time is allotted to move through the steps outlined. Projects can also be segmented into milestones or gates for the project manager and team to pass through. The PDCA process has natural milestone markers in each phase of the process. Providing timing on the Plan section, the Do section, the Check section, and the Act section help shape the project's overall timing.

Just like scoping, there are a few pitfalls to watch out for when managing a project. First, a project manager (a facilitator that helps guide the team toward implementation) must ensure all stakeholders are communicated with before the project starts, during the project, and after the project is completed. Second, the project manager must recognize that the management of the project rests on their shoulders. Third, each project must have an executive sponsor (a senior leader who will support the project and help allocate resources) to ensure organizational support at the organization's highest levels. Fourth, as tasks are developed, it is crucial to establish an owner (a team member who takes on the responsibility to complete the action) and a due date for each item and gain the commitment of those assigned to complete the task. If the team is not progressing, then the project manager and the executive sponsor work to remove any barriers in the way. As issues are discovered within the management of a project, a project manager must address them quickly or risk a loss of focus on the problem.

6. Measure

Before starting the observation process, the project manager must first determine what to measure. The output or Project Y is already known. However, it takes too long to decide on how a single change will affect the output in many cases. Thus, it becomes critical to establish metrics to determine if a specific change leads the team toward improvement.

A metric is a standard of measurement that helps a project manager define the starting point, track results during a project and the entirety of the project. It also helps depict the improvement in a graphical form. A word of caution here is only to choose metrics that have an impact on Project Y. The number of metrics may be one or several, depending on the project's size and scope.

A metric also helps to ensure we have not compromised the process we are trying to improve. For example, if the goal is to improve efficiency and shortcuts are developed that impact quality or safety, then there is an adverse effect on the patient. Thus, a balanced set of metrics helps determine if a team's changes provide the correct results without compromising other essential metrics.

To generate measures further upstream from the outcome, a team must determine process measures and input measures. A process measure helps to understand process stability. For example, if a nursing assessment for suicidal ideation is too subjective and the scoring changes from one assessor to the next, there is an issue with process repeatability. We must address this repeatability question as an initial PDCA because the ability to consistently perform on a process measure upstream will help determine if process changes yield an improvement in outcomes downstream. If the process is not reliably done from one cycle to the next, it becomes hard to know if the team is following the one best way as a baseline for improvement.

An input measure helps to determine whether a variable is acting on the output. For example, if a patient is incapable of providing credible answers to a risk assessment if they are psychotic, agitated, or delirious, the nurse will receive erroneous data. The assessment will not produce the desired results. As a second example, if the emergency department does not provide information to the nurse about a recent event that triggered a patients' aggression, then the ability to anticipate the patient's next bout of aggression will be compromised.

In the case of the falls example, if most of the falls are happening when a patient gets out of bed, a team can review a process metric of nursing response time to bed alarms and an input metric of ensuring that all bed alarms are operational.

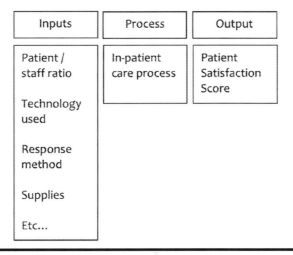

Figure 4.6 IPO diagram.

Each process has inputs (I) or variables that act on the process, process steps (P), and outputs (O) or variables that show the outcome of a process. See the IPO Figure 4.6.

The input variable is the closest leading indicator we have to a good patient experience. Hence, it is so essential to understand the input measure and utilize it within the improvement process. For example, a team might start a project by understanding the outcome of a patient survey. However, suppose the survey suggests that the response time is lacking or the communication is unclear to the patient. In that case, focusing on the input variables of the response method or measuring response time and reasons for delays helps to enable a better process and thus lead to better outcomes.

VIGNETTE 4.8

The output measure for a particular team was improved staff morale. The unit manager asked her nurses to tell her about the most significant stressors and dissatisfiers of their day's work. The nurses were engaged employees, committed to their jobs, and cared for their patients. They felt comfortable sharing their concerns with the manager. One of the common concerns they brought up was their inability to take a lunch break on certain days of the week. The manager knew that it was one small thing for the overall staff morale, but she thought it was an excellent input measure to work on as it was something she could control.

7. Observation

Observing the process is the next step in the process. Observation helps us learn what is occurring during the process that might be causing some of the variations. It is the best way to uncover waste. In Lean terminology, it is referred to as 'going to the Gemba.' In Japanese, the word 'Gemba' means 'the actual place'; in other words, the 'place where value is created' or the workplace. Taiichi Ohno, one of the developers of the Toyota Production System, was known for creating an 'Ohno circle.' He would draw a circle and ask a new worker to stand there for hours and observe the workplace to see if they understood how value was created and if they could spot waste in the process. If the answers were unsatisfactory, the new worker would be expected to stand there for a few more hours to try to come up with a satisfactory observation. He wanted workers to be in the constant practice of acutely observing reality at the site of work.

The value of this observation is to prevent us from jumping to conclusions too quickly and ensuring we have a thorough understanding of the facts by asking the right questions. Observation also allows the team to investigate together and gain a comprehensive understanding. While having subject matter experts on the team is helpful, there is inherent importance in achieving objective evidence through observing the process for oneself. Keep in mind that even the best subject matter experts can manifest thinking in certain fixed paradigms that objectively prevent them from thinking about the process. This is especially true if they describe a process from their mind and not basing it on actual observations. Observation merely is helping a project team understand the observable facts.

A corollary to this is that if we do not know where we are, we will not know how much further we have to go. From a patient perspective, do they flow through every process step in their treatment setting seamlessly without any issues, or are there opportunities for improvement where problems occur during their care? The only way to understand the variation is to 'go to Gemba.' 'Going to Gemba' means to go to where the work is happening and observe.

VIGNETTE 4.9

An IT administrator was interested in ensuring that newly trained employees utilized the new video-conferencing telehealth application right at the onset of the COVID-19 pandemic. Some early adopters were doing well with it. Other units were struggling, and she could not understand why. She asked a physician who was working from a remote location (from a unit that was resisting using this technology) to share her desktop so that she could see the nature of the technical difficulty firsthand. Only when she went into the physician's default settings for the video-conferencing, the administrator realized that the settings had to be configured differently. Also, the volume on the mobile device was low and did not lend itself to a satisfying conversation if there was no headset available. After she was able to put in solutions based on her actual observations, the IT administrator began to understand the clinical staff's resistance.

8. Process Map

Several tools within the Lean toolkit help project teams document the 'as is' process and uncover 'waste.' First, and most importantly, a process map is used in many improvement projects to document the current process. Process mapping is a technique where a business process or workflow is

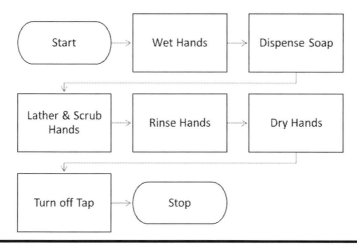

Figure 4.7 Process map example.

converted into a step-by-step visual diagram. An example of a process is shown in Figure 4.7. For reference purposes, an oval depicts the start and stop of the process. A rectangle depicts a process step. The arrows indicate the flow from one step to the next. Other shapes not shown here include the diamond, which represents a decision step in the process, a circle that connects process maps on multiple sheets of paper, a D-shape which depicts a delay in the process, and a file folder shape which helps to highlight paperwork at a given step.

A common question from first-time project managers is how detailed or specific should the process map be. At first, it is important to keep the process map at a high level highlighting 5–7 essential steps within the process. Mapping the process while observing helps to flush out any missing process steps. It becomes apparent when a team draws a map from observing the process versus when the team draws a map in a conference room or sitting at their desk. Those that observe the process tend to have more detail and understanding of how the actual process works.

The steps to mapping a process are the following:

i. Select the process to map
ii. Determine the starting and stopping point of the process
iii. Define the output
iv. Define the customer
v. Determine the inputs to the process
vi. Determine the suppliers of the inputs
vii. Draw the map (5–7 steps)
viii. Validate with stakeholders

To help understand the steps of process mapping, consider the handwashing process on an inpatient unit. The output is clean hands. Next, when determining hand hygiene requirements, it is crucial to know who the customer is. In this case, the customer is the patient and requires as sterile an environment as possible to prevent any unintended complications. The inputs are

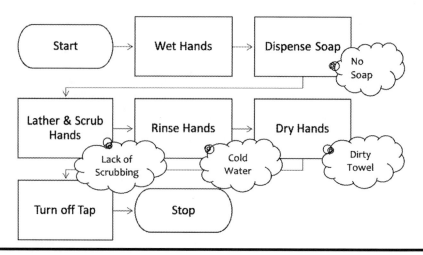

Figure 4.8 Example process map with storm clouds.

soap, water, sink, and towels. The suppliers of soap and towels are the housekeepers; the water and sink are supplied by the facility and maintained by the facilities team. Understanding the suppliers to the process helps a project team ensure they engage all critical stakeholders in the performance improvement process. The starting point is wetting your hands, and the stopping points are turning off the tap.

Sometimes, when mapping a process at a high level and observing it, a team can see the waste within the process. For example, observations might show different amounts of soap and water being used within the handwashing example, or the time it takes to lather, scrub, and rinse, vary from one user to the next. If the variation is apparent after observing the process, an additional shape to use in the process map is a storm cloud shown in Figure 4.8. A storm cloud highlights any observable issues that need to be addressed.

A few process-mapping tips include:

i. Clarifying process boundaries to ensure the process map is complete.
ii. Including subject matter experts (those who perform the process steps) who know the current process.
iii. Using the verb-noun format to keep the map verbiage clear and concise.
iv. Combine and eliminate any duplicate steps to clarify all process steps in the flow.
v. Organizing the steps in the order in which they happen.

9. Sub-Process Map

A sub-process map highlights more detail about a given step in a process map. For instance, in the handwashing example, if there is observed variation of inadequate scrubbing in the lather and scrub process step, a sub-process map can help show the detail at this step. A sub-process map for lather and scrub is shown in Figure 4.9.

A swim-lane sub-process map can also help when a process involves multiple people or departments. Swim-lane maps help a project manager understand which discipline owns each step in the

Methods for Mental Health Organizations ■ 109

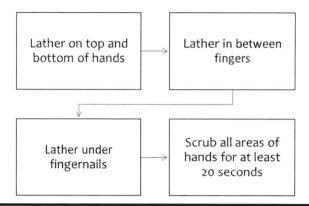

Figure 4.9 Sub-process map for lather and scrub step.

process. For instance, when looking at the process to capture clinician charges after a group home visit, the swim-lane process map might look like the following example in Figure 4.10.

Sub-process maps and swim lane maps are also very helpful when trying to understand how much time each process step takes and where waste exists in the process. In most processes that cross between two or more departments, there are usually significant delays in processing information. For example, a clinician will first see all of her patients and then fill in her charge tickets at the end of the day. The administrative assistant may not start the review process until the next morning with a pile of tickets on her desk for review. Thus, a process that should take mere minutes ends up taking several hours to complete the entire process.

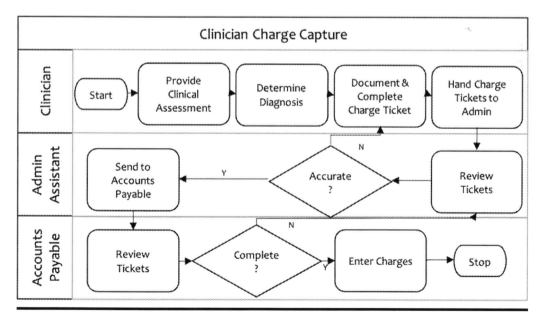

Figure 4.10 Swim-lane map example.

When capturing the detailed steps in a process, there is an opportunity to classify each step as valuable or wasteful from the patient's perspective. As elaborated in section two, a project team needs to understand three types of work: Value-Added work, Value-Enabling work, and Non-Value-Added work.

- *Value-Enabling*: Tasks that are not essential to the patient but allow the value-added tasks to be done better or faster. In the example in Figure 4.10, the value-enabling step is documenting the note, completing the charge ticket by the clinician, and entering charges by the finance office.
- *Value-Added*: A task that the patient is willing to pay for because it captures the service provided and is completed the first time correctly. In the same example, the value-added steps are the clinician providing the assessment and diagnosing the patient.
- *Non-Value-Added*: Steps that are considered non-essential to produce and deliver the product or service to meet the patient's needs and requirements. Patients are not willing to pay for these steps. In the above example, delivering the charge ticket by the clinician, reviewing for accuracy, sending the charge ticket to finance by the administrative assistant, and reviewing the charge ticket again by the finance office are all non-value-added steps. A patient would argue that poor process design resulting in auditing information is not their responsibility.

The diagram in Figure 4.11 helps to differentiate the value-added (VA) from the non-value-added (NVA) and the value-enabling (VE).

The goal is to preserve value-added steps, simplify value-enabling steps, and eliminate the non-value-added steps. In this example, using a charge capture method from the EMR would streamline the process and take several steps and time out of the process. An improved process might look like Figure 4.12:

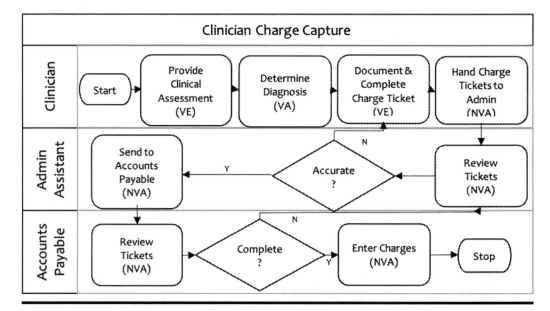

Figure 4.11 Waste and value in a swim-lane process map.

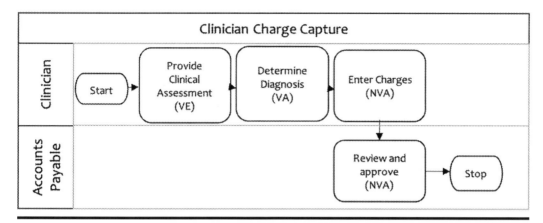

Figure 4.12 Improved process map for clinician charges.

After this first round of improvement, while the entire assessment process is shown as value-added, there are several pockets of waste (completing documentation, reviewing documentation, and sending documentation to finance) within this step. This process takes over an hour to complete, and when initially developing the flow of data entry into the EMR, the clinician workflow was impacted. The goal of improving processes is to ensure each professional is working at the top of their license and organizations are efficiently and effectively utilizing their highly skilled resources. To ensure this is achieved, project teams must work to eliminate the non-value-added, reduce or streamline the value enabling steps and preserve the value-added steps.

10. Time and Motion Study

Time and motion studies help determine how much wasted time and wasted motion there is in a process. To set up a time study, first ensure the process under review is repeatable. For example, there is a clear understanding of how the process works, and the staff completes the process in the same way each time. If the process step alters from one patient to the next, this will cause an issue when determining the time for individual process steps. Second, conducting multiple time trials for the processes is important to ensure the correct time is collected. We recommend the time-keeper conduct as many time trials as it takes to get a sense of the process, determine if the process is repeatable and where the waste is.

Time studies also capture wait or idle time, delays, rework, and time waste due to inspections. From this data, organizations start to understand the amount of staff time spent on waste versus the amount of time spent on the value-added activities within the process. This data gives an improvement team great insight on where to improve the process potentially.

11. Spaghetti Diagrams

A spaghetti diagram is a visual depiction of staff and patient transportation and motion waste within a given process. If a process under study does not have movement within it and everything within the process happens in an office, then a spaghetti diagram will not provide significant insight. However, if the process under study is more extensive in scope and requires staff and patients' movement, then this kind of visual may help highlight waste within the process. For example, when observing a doctor completing their rounds in a nursing home setting, it was found that the doctor wasted up to two hours and walking over a mile during the day to try and locate each patient on the schedule.

To develop a spaghetti diagram, the project manager can use a blank piece of paper or use graph paper to provide a simple layout of the process under study. As a staff member begins the process and moves, the idea is to draw the path of movement on the paper. From there, drawing the walking path is continued until the entire process is complete. The patient movement needs the same approach. Use different colored inks can map the movement of different individuals. Once finished, a project leader can approximate the total linear feet walked by the staff member and/or the patient to complete the process. An example of a spaghetti diagram in action is provided in Vignette 4.10.

VIGNETTE 4.10

An inpatient unit was moved from an older hospital building to a newer hospital building. In doing so, the supplies required to do admission assessments on the older unit got spread out in the newer space. This move led to an increased amount of time needed to complete an admission and added to the amount of waste. A charge nurse for the unit decided to do an improvement project to address this issue. Figures 4.13 and 4.14 depict the spaghetti diagrams for the process.

By locating and organizing the supplies needed for admissions in a smaller and more contained space, the charge nurse reduced the number of steps in the process. This change led to less time spent on doing assessments and more time becoming available for other value-added tasks – the time to complete the admissions process improved by 65% and the distance traveled by

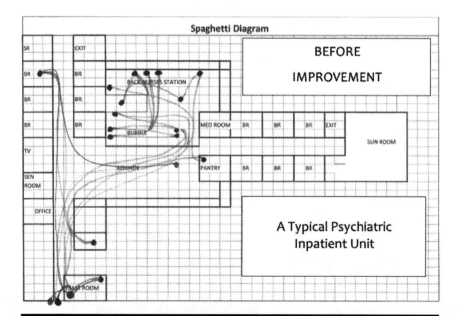

Figure 4.13 Before improvement spaghetti diagram.

Methods for Mental Health Organizations ▪ 113

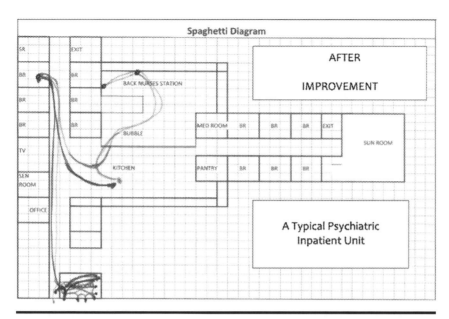

Figure 4.14 After improvement spaghetti diagram.

89%. The estimated savings was approximately $25,000 a year in nursing time. When the charge nurse presented this project, nurses on other units wanted to do the same on their respective units. Figures 4.15 and 4.16 show the organization completed as a result of this project.

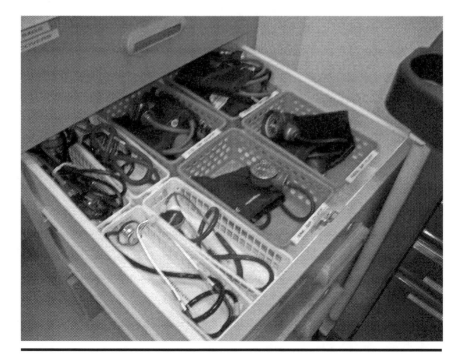

Figure 4.15 After improvement example.

Figure 4.16 Result of improved organization based on spaghetti map.

12. Measurement for Improvement

Measurement is a vital aspect of the improvement process. It helps define the starting point of a project or how well a process performs once a project team makes changes. It helps provide objective evidence to stakeholders and customers alike. Moreover, it helps drive support for cascading improvements to other areas of the health system that may also benefit from project outcomes.

When considering measures, a project team must keep it simple. There are two types of data used for measuring performance, discrete data such as frequency or counting and continuous data such as time, weight, or distance. In general, project managers opt for continuous data. Discrete data requires as much as three times more data collection, and there is usually not enough time to collect and sift through this data. A simple way to determine if a measure is a discrete or continuous measure is to ask the question, "Does a half make sense?" For example, hospitals' seclusion frequency data is a discrete measure because either someone is in seclusion or not. Half of a seclusion does not make sense. Hospitals also measure the time spent in seclusion, which is a continuous measure because time can be cut into half-hours or half-minutes.

Although discrete data is prevalent in healthcare, improvement practitioners prefer continuous data because it reduces the amount of data and time needed to analyze a process. A normal curve is a type of continuous probability distribution that allows a project team to understand a variable. Consider Figure 4.17, where the normal curve is shaped like a bell (aka bell curve) with a large hump in the middle and two symmetrical tails on either side of the middle hump.

When focusing on improving a process, the first and main goal is to determine if the data collected adheres to the normal curve properties. If the variable in question does not adhere to the normal curve properties, it is considered unpredictable. The first question is to understand why a variable

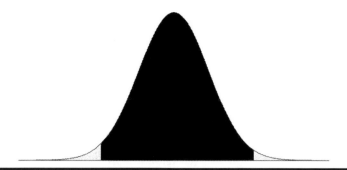

Figure 4.17 Gaussian (normal) curve.

is unpredictable. Is there any data missing from the dataset? Is the definition of variable understood to measure it accurately? Is there a special cause acting on a dataset that is skewing the variable? For example, collecting data from equipment to measure vitals that has not been calibrated for several years may cause errors in the data. The good news is if special causes are acting on a dataset, they usually give project teams a good starting point on where to improve. For example, calibrating the equipment to measure vitals will ensure the equipment is not the source of unpredictability.

There are three main summary metrics used to approximate the Gaussian curve – the mean, the median, and the mode. Each of these measures helps to understand the center and spread of the dataset. The center is a single data point derived from the dataset, and the spread is where all data points are in relation to the center of the dataset. The mean is defined as the average of a dataset. What is the average length of stay? What is the average number of times the clinician misses documenting the suicide assessment for a patient? What is the average frequency of admissions or discharges? The mean is a great start at understanding the current state and developing a baseline. However, the mean by itself does not necessarily provide precisely where the center of the dataset is because there could be one or two data points that are outliers from the rest. For example, when polling a class full of students about how many siblings they have, some would say three, others would say none, and the average of less than or equal to two is expected. However, if by chance there was one student in the room with ten brothers, then that would skew the average to four or five even though the rest of the class averaged two. Outliers can skew smaller datasets more significantly, so another measure is needed to understand the dataset's center.

To help understand how centered the mean is for our dataset, a team can use the median. The median is the middle number of a dataset. To determine the median, if teams can place each data point in order from lowest to highest and then take the middle number as the median, they would find this is a better approach to understanding where the center is. While the median is helpful where the mean might not be, the dataset must be normally distributed. For instance, Likert scales do not conform to the normal distribution, and therefore a median or mean would not prove helpful.

To help us answer the question of centeredness, a team can use a third summary metric called the mode. The mode is the number that repeats the most often. Typically, this is the center, but not always. In some cases, there might be more than one mode in the dataset, which would counter the claim of adhering to Gaussian curve predictions.

When looking at any one metric, it is difficult to understand the center on its own. However, when the mean, the median, and the mode are approximately the same, then a team can confidently say the data is acting predictably.

Why does this matter? There is an old saying that "Lean is about shifting the mean." When trying to compare data from before implementation to after implementation, adhering to normal or Gaussian properties is essential to determine with any level of confidence that the team has indeed made a change that shifted the mean to something better. An astute reader might question if shifting the mean equates to quality improvement. Not necessarily. If a team is reducing the time it takes to complete a process, the mean will go from 5 minutes to 1 minute, but it does not necessarily equate to reducing defects. To understand the quality component, a team must look at the shape of the normal curve. Is the curve tall and narrow or short and wide? A short wide curve would indicate one or more variables are acting on the dataset.

Lean is also about reducing the waste of defects, balancing the amount of work content amongst team members within a process, and equally balancing work content between process steps. This view aims to achieve a steady patient flow at an even rate, which prevents wait time and waste in the system of care.

It is important to note that customers experience variation. For example, an outpatient office may have a mean wait time to get an appointment of two weeks. For a new patient who waits for four weeks, we can study the new wait time and understand why there is such a large deviation. The patient and their family will typically experience every frustrating minute, hour, day, and week of a wait because it is human nature to want service when requested rather than when a provider is available.

As a second example, if the room temperature for the first ten hours of the day was forty degrees, would a patient feel comfortable? If the temperature was then raised to one hundred degrees for the next ten hours of the day, would the patient feel comfortable? If we had two data points like these, one would conclude that the mean was seventy, the median was seventy, and the mode does not exist. Another would conclude that we only have two data points and need more data. In the meantime, the customer experiencing these temperature changes may conclude that the hospital does not know what they are doing. While this example is fictitious and not very realistic, it illustrates an essential point for organizations to look beyond the mean, median, and mode and understand the underlying causes of the variation as it exists.

Variation is simply the accumulation of all data points that deviate from the norm, the standard, or the mean. Variation exists in every process. Some variation is inherent in the process (common cause variation), while other variation is due to external circumstances not intrinsic to the process (special cause). Lean is primarily focused on special cause variations and gaining control of processes. Thus, a majority of improvement can happen with simple lean tools. As a project team works to improve common cause variations or move from a flat wide curve to a tall narrow curve, a more robust measurement system is required to understand all of the variation acting on an output.

The intent of providing all the content in this chapter is not to make each person into a statistician but to highlight the importance of measurement. Also, it would help to tell the story of improvement. The goal of improvement projects is to provide evidence or proof that a new way is indeed better. The best way to provide this evidence is with data.

13. Measurement Tips

    i. It is essential only to document the metrics that affect a project's outcomes. Measurement overload can lead to analysis paralysis, and project teams need to move through projects quickly.

    ii. Developing a family of measures is also important and may include both continuous and discrete measures. A family of measures should consider the output, process stability, and the input variables acting on the process. Another example of a family of measures is structural measures, process measures, outcome measures, and balancing measures. Usually, outcome measures are what many are interested in, but they are often much farther away from the locus of control. Also, outcomes can be determined by more than one variable, so it can be much harder to study.

VIGNETTE 4.11

An inpatient team started measuring instances of dissatisfied patients or families on their unit. From a couple of months of data, they felt that there were too many instances where the patients or their families were unhappy about their care. They got overwhelmed and demoralized looking at those numbers.

They were advised to look at one or two variables to control to see if the overall outcomes improved over time. The team decided to focus on initial orientation to the unit and a mechanism to address complaints regardless of the time of the day or shift. Gradually the team began to take one commonly occurring problem after another and focus their attention only on improving a few problems at a time, such as nurse responsiveness and food temperature. As they came up with standardized ways of tackling common problems, the overall satisfaction scores began to trend positively.

14. Visual Representation of Data

Visually representing data visually allows stakeholders to absorb the information as presented without immediately moving into a resistive mindset. If a project leader was just verbalizing their data, the ability to listen and understand would be somewhat limited. If a project leader were to speak about it and provide tables or spreadsheets with a lot of data, there would be less resistance in a group setting, but participants may not see any patterns in the data. For example, is the metric under question increasing or decreasing over time? Is there a track record of stability in the process under study? And so forth. Presenting a visual chart or graph while discussing the data is the most effective method. It would lead to more acceptance, less argument, and even reduce the project leader's own bias. A visual display of data would also help us to ask more informed questions and helps to align customers, stakeholders, and leaders when concluding.

A few graphing charts are highlighted and represented in Figure 4.20. The goal is to select the chart that will help to understand the current state best.

A *Pie chart* is a visualization for portions of a complete dataset. For example, the Pie chart in Figure 4.18 shows the percentage of dietary order accuracy.

Bar charts (column charts) help visualize categorical data when the intent is to make inferences from comparing the bars or columns. For example, the column chart in Figure 4.19 provides a comparison of quality performance for several clinics during a recent quarter. A team might question why Clinic D is performing so poorly when compared to the other clinics.

Run charts help to understand how a measure is performing over time. Run charts are usually depicted in daily, weekly, or monthly time periods. Run charts also help us see trends or patterns in

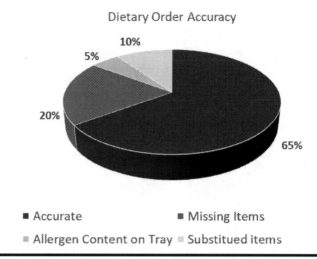

Figure 4.18 Pie chart example.

our data. For example, the chart in Figure 4.20 shows a run chart of patient-to-patient assaults on a unit specializing in psychotic disorders. The data shows a nice improvement trend over four months.

A project team may question why the numbers have improved from January to April. Is it due to a change in process or practice? Or, did the average daily census decline during the last two months? Such questioning leads to an understanding of what truly is causing the numbers to improve.

A *Pareto chart* is a column chart depicted in descending order from left to right and a corresponding cumulative frequency run chart accumulating to 100% of the dataset. The Pareto chart is a visual of the Pareto principle developed by Vilfredo Pareto that 20% of the categories cause 80% of the problem. The Pareto principle allows a project team only to solve the variables that will make the most significant impact. An example Pareto chart in Figure 4.21 shows why patients do

Figure 4.19 Column chart example.

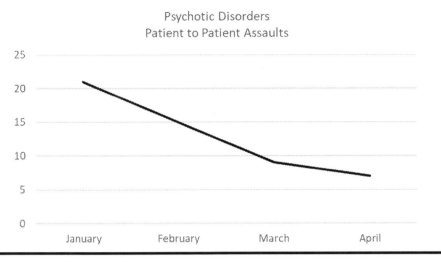

Figure 4.20 Run chart example.

not show up for appointments. From this example, the team can understand the root causes of patients forgetting appointments because this accounts for 50% of the total problem.

A *Histogram* is a column chart depicting groups (classes) of data to visually depict the normal curve of a dataset. Histograms are very useful at summarizing large sums of data into a single chart. For instance, if a team wanted to understand the depression scores of patients admitted to a clinic, they can then use this data to compare to the distribution after discharge. Figure 4.22 provides an example histogram for depression scores before treatment.

Scatter charts help to depict the relative relationship between two variables visually. For example, if a team wanted to understand if there is a relationship between exercise and mood, they can

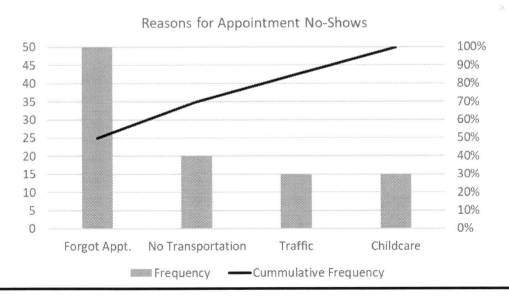

Figure 4.21 Pareto chart example.

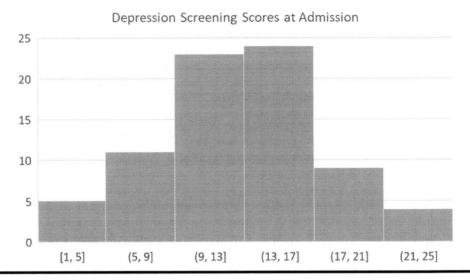

Figure 4.22 Histogram example.

use a scatter plot to determine if a relationship exists. While more advanced statistical analysis is required to assess the strength of any relationship, a project team can infer that there may be a relationship and use this data to ask further questions. For example, the fictitious Scatter plot in Figure 4.23 may indicate that mood improves with the duration of exercise.

A project team can question the length of exercise, the type of exercise, and so forth. Although this is a fabricated chart, it is easy to see how numerous questions can be developed from a single chart.

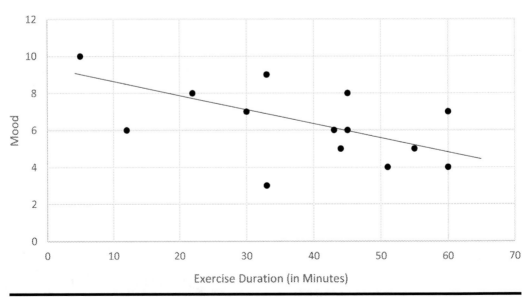

Figure 4.23 Scatter chart example.

VIGNETTE 4.12

An administrative staff member found that many patients coming from or going to the partial hospitalization program ended up in his office by mistake. The program office was in the middle of a large hospital, and patients were getting lost on their way. They ended up in front of his office, looking for directions. He reviewed the problem, tabulated the number of times patients ended up in front of his office and identified where they were trying to go. He found many patients were losing their way during the day and could not find their way back to the program. He decided to tackle this problem and improve wayfinding for partial hospitalization patients.

After completing a patient survey, he tabulated the results on a Pareto chart to summarize the responses in order from greatest importance to least importance. As shown in Figure 4.24, The two most important locations for patients were finding their way back and forth from the cafeteria and rest-

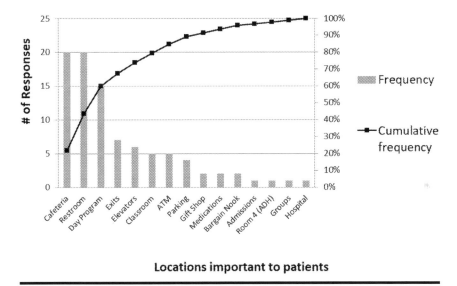

Figure 4.24 Using Pareto chart to focus improvement efforts.

rooms to the partial hospitalization program.

He developed a few temporary signs and received approval to hang them until the in-house marketing team had time to create improved signage. The number of patients who ended up in front of his office dropped by over 90%.

When visualizing data, it is vital to use a chart that helps a project team question and study a problem. If a chart does not help a team learn, then consider using an alternate chart that allows the team to get a better picture.

15. Goal Setting

Setting a goal for a project is the logical next step in the problem-solving process. The goal is something that helps a project leader and project team stay focused on achieving improvement. Without a goal, the project leader does not know when to stop one project and start another.

When developing a goal, the best method is utilizing the 'SMART' acronym; the goal must be specific, measurable, attainable, relevant, and time-bound. *Specific* suggests the measure is clear and concise, and anyone on the team can understand how it is defined. *Measurable* suggests the goal can be objectively and quickly measured in real-time. *Attainable* suggests the goal can be reached by the end of the project deadline. *Relevant* indicates that the goal supports the outcome of the project we are undertaking as well it is aligned to the strategic objectives, mission, values, and values of the organization. *Time-bound* suggests the project team can achieve the goal within the time allocated for the project.

There are several schools of thought on how to establish a goal. Some prescribe the mantra of zero defects or 100% compliance. However, it is best to leave 'all or nothing' goals as a vision to strive for but not as a single project goal. If a project were to go after an absolute goal, the project would stay open for several months if not years, and the people involved in the project would lose interest, momentum and would end up moving on to other work. An additional supporting point for this is to consider that each organization has hundreds if not thousands of processes that are all in need of refinement or improvement over time. With a select group of people working on improvement, an organization must work to get the biggest bang for the buck.

When setting goals, it is also important to remember that perfection is the enemy of good. If a team can improve one process to 100% or a team can improve a hundred processes by 80%, an organization will benefit more from the latter. This mantra helps to move organizations along the change curve faster, knowing there is always time to come back and complete a second and third PDCA. Suppose a project team does not know how much improvement they are trying to achieve. In that case, this will become clearer as the project team identifies the amount of wasted time in the process and determines how much improvement is possible.

16. Root Cause Analysis

Once the project manager and team have collected baseline data, mapped the process, and questioned the data, it becomes time to determine what is causing the outcome or Project Y to fall short of the goal. To complete this part of the investigation, a team will employ an RCA. An RCA helps prevent the project team from jumping to conclusions too quickly and ensuring there is adequate focus on fixing deep-seated system issues rather than focusing on issues at the surface by developing more wasteful workarounds.

Getting to the root cause is primarily accomplished through using a cause-effect diagram and a five-why analysis.

17. Cause-Effect Diagram

A cause-effect diagram is a visual tool that logically organizes possible causes for the problem the team is trying to address. The logical organization of causes is completed using an affinity diagram where like (or similar?) causes are grouped together. The most common groupings

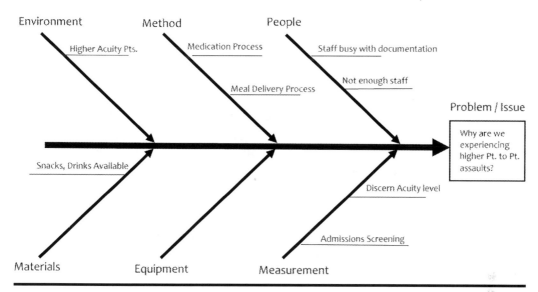

Figure 4.25 Cause-effect diagram example.

are people (staff, contractors, administrators, etc.), method (processes and procedures used), measurement (what, how, and reliability of the measurement process), equipment (machines, preventive maintenance), materials (supplies, delivery) and environment (anything outside our system impacting our system of care). An example cause-effect diagram is shown in Figure 4.25.

The visual nature of the cause-effect diagram helps a project team determine all of the possible causes for an effect and acts as a focal point during this discussion. The grouping titles can be altered depending on the project. For instance, instead of an 'Equipment' category, a team might need a 'Patient' category. The idea is to not use the groupings verbatim but to use them to organize thoughts. The most common approach for cause-effect diagrams in an improvement project is to write the issue the team is trying to solve in the form of a question using the box on the right-hand side of the form. The questions come from the baseline data collected. For example, why is there an issue with a step in our process map; Why does our data indicate we are experiencing major variation in a specific department; and so forth. Getting a team to answer these questions with potential causes helps with both team alignment and focus. It also enhances the learning and engagement of the team as a whole to first uncover the main issues and then work toward solutions.

Some cause-effect diagrams are very detailed with more than forty causes while others have a few causes on them. If a process has only a few, then it might be wise to explore each one. However, if a process has a high number of potential causes, there will be too many for the team to review during a single PDCA. To narrow down the focus in this case, the team should vote on the most likely of possible causes of the problem which will allow the project manager to rank the causes in order of priority. Once the causes are prioritized, the suggestion is to select the top three causes and bring each into a 5-why analysis.

18. 5-Why's

A 5-why analysis will help project teams to determine why a possible cause could be affecting the output. It is a method of iterative questioning. The answer to each 'why' becomes the basis for the next 'why' question. Asking 'why' five times helps to get a team to a root cause. The reason for conducting a 5-why analysis is to prevent the team from offering premature solutions without discovering the real root cause. For example, when a unit runs out of blankets, their solution is often to call a neighboring unit to get a needed blanket. By working around the process, the team hides the issue and does not learn to get to the root. An additional question might be, "why did the unit run out of blankets?" Continuing to dig into the problem helped the team discover if they had the right level of blanket inventory and further found that the supply team lowered the number of instances they deliver blankets to the nursing unit. This example was discussed in section three as *first-order* versus *second-order* problem-solving.

However, there is no set rule that the root cause will be reached after five whys. Sometimes it takes three whys, and sometimes it takes seven why's, but typically five helps to ensure a team reaches root causation. When conducting this analysis, it is essential that the first why works to answer the question "why is the possible cause effecting the output?" The answer to the first why becomes the question for the second why. The answer for the second why becomes the question for the third why and so forth. Thus while the cause-effect diagram gives a team the breadth of potential causes, the five why analysis helps a team dig deep into one specific possible cause – an example of the five why analysis is shown in Figure 4.26.

Notice in the example above that each why builds on the previous why until root causation is reached. The team could have blindly come up with a solution to the problem for that particular transfer. However, the 5-why process helped solve a problem for all future staff transfers, which could have been an ongoing source of staff frustration.

---

5 Why Worksheet

Problem Statement: A team member is having trouble accessing the network.

Why is the team member having trouble with network access? Because they lost access.

    Why loss of access? Because the information technology team removed their access.

        Why did IT remove their access? Because the information technology group received an automated message that the team member was terminated.

            Why did they receive a message of termination? Because Human resources transferred the team member and it triggered a termination notice.

                Why do internal transfers cause a termination notice to be sent? Because the current system setup cannot distinguish between a transfer and a termination.

Figure 4.26 5-Why analysis example.

> ## VIGNETTE 4.13
>
> A local nurse manager wanted to reduce staff injuries. After reviewing the data, she found patients were scratching the staff on their arms. The nurse manager developed a predetermined solution before completing an RCA and implemented arm guards to all nurses and nurse technicians. The staff did not appreciate this 'improvement' because arm guards were uncomfortable and did not solve the main problem. After stepping thru a 5-why analysis with the team, they discovered the main issue was adolescent patients with long fingernails. They felt that if they manicured patients' fingernails, the problem would go away. After implementing a nurse-led group activity to manicure nails, both patients and staff enjoyed the activity, and, more importantly, arm scratches were reduced by 98%.

A question that often comes up is "how does a project team know that they have reached root cause?" The root cause is reached when a team can enact a solution that will prevent a problem's recurrence. An important clue that the team identified a root cause is when a system issue surfaces. For example, there was no formal process to deal with long fingernails, or there was no distinction in the employee database that separated transferred employees from terminated employees.

When the last why suggests there is a need for education or training, a team must continue to ask an additional why to determine why the training or educational part of the system is not transferring the knowledge or why such training or education was not provided in the first place. It may also lead teams to question how the education system is designed. Just having asked team members to sit through verbal instruction or PowerPoint presentation is not training as it is often assumed. This will focus on fixing the training system rather than relegating the group to a continual retraining loop. Further, suggesting that a team member needs more training may indicate that a team member is at fault. However, the PDCA process and much of Deming's philosophies suggest that people are rarely the problem. It is the system leadership to set up the organization so that the employees have a good chance of being successful. We must always look to the system-level issues and drive systemic improvements if we seek improved results.

B. Do

The next phase of the PDCA cycle is the 'Do' phase. At this point, a project team has completed the required communication, brought a team together to review the baseline information, measured the current condition, completed a process map of the process under question, and completed an RCA. The next steps are to develop solutions and conduct small scoped experiments to determine if those solutions help improve the process. Some use the word, countermeasures, instead of the word, solutions, as the word, solution, suggests finality. In contrast, countermeasures assume that what may work for today's context may have to be changed tomorrow. The first step in the 'Do' Phase is brainstorming.

1. Brainstorming

Brainstorming is a step where a project team works to generate as many ideas as possible. Brainstorming is a team-based approach, usually ad hoc, that helps discover both small scoped solutions and breakthrough solutions to the problem. Brainstorming is a necessary step because there are typically multiple solutions to a single cause. A team must explore various solutions to ensure they have the best chance at selecting the most effective and impactful one as a pilot.

VIGNETTE 4.14

A project manager wanted to improve the compliance of completing master treatment plans. A master treatment plan is a multidisciplinary note completed by the nurse, social worker, and psychiatrist. The data showed that doctors were not achieving the necessary sign-off by the deadline, causing non-compliance. After completing a five why analysis, the root cause showed no automated method within the electronic health record to notify a doctor of a signature needed before the deadline passed. However, during the brainstorming session, the team noted that the doctor's signature was the last step in the process. There was an issue with all disciplines knowing the standard practice when completing their step in the process. They found that patients arriving on Thursday did not have a completed treatment plan before the weekend. Covering weekend doctors were not aware of each patient's details and could not complete the work. This kind of occurrence led to a situation where the treatment plans were well past their due date for completion. After brainstorming solutions that included flags in the EMR, escalation emails to the doctor's supervision, and more auditing, the best solution was to complete the treatment plans for late week arrivals within the same day, which reduced the delinquency rate.

Thus, exploring multiple potential solutions is necessary to help a team achieve the results they seek.

A few major points about brainstorming:

i. Brainstorming in a group setting helps to engage all members of a team. Staff engagement exponentially increases during a brainstorming activity because the focus is on generating solutions to a known problem rather than complaining about a problem that leaders are ignoring. Solutions also tend to build on prior suggestions of the team members, and the brainstorming process uses the collaboration of everyone's ideas collectively.

ii. Brainstorming is also fun because it allows participants free reign in developing quirky, out-of-the-box ideas. Sometimes these ideas may not work. Other times, these ideas, when tweaked, facilitate a rich array of creative solutions and innovations that help to reshape and improve processes.

iii. Brainstorming works to bring the diversity of a team's experience into play as well. This diversity helps to explore several solutions that help in deciding the final solution.

iv. Brainstorming can help a group achieve buy-in from involved team members. In general, team members are more committed to improvement if their ideas are acknowledged, and they are involved in developing solutions.

v. A quote attributed to Albert Einstein suggested, "When everyone is thinking alike, then nobody is thinking." The main point is to get people to think and to challenge each other in productive ways.

2. Try-Storming

Creativity and change go hand in hand. Creativity requires teams to change. Change causes teams to be creative. However, most people do not like change because it involves risk and uncertainty. This leads people to resist even the most basic of changes. In some cases, teams will brainstorm great solutions and then brainstorm their way out of those solutions all within the same brainstorming activity. Thus, sometimes brainstorming can cause a team to get stuck. To channel creativity and encourage forward momentum during the change process, a team can use a concept call try-storming. Try-storming means just that, to try an idea on a small scale and learn from it. Does it help to improve the outcomes the team seeks? If yes, then continue and enhance. If not, then modify or change solutions. Try-storming also helps teams get unstuck because they will have data to show the team and the organization. Also, it becomes a great way to engage those working within the process on what went well and what improvements are needed. For example, when working to improve a storage room organization, a group may try a new labeling approach or use different colored tape on the floor to identify homes for medical equipment such as a wheelchair. After implementing a new visual system, they can then use this try-storm to learn what works and what does not. Try-storming leads to insight. Insight leads to innovation and breakthroughs. Ten ideas to boost creativity are:

  i. Play 'the angels advocate' first. What is good about the ideas that people are providing? A team always has time to turn down ideas later on after they tried a solution.
 ii. Generate and foster a creative environment as a leader. An effective facilitator of a brainstorming session is always looking for and listening to staff suggestions for improvement.
iii. Be supportive rather than defensive and maintain a forward motion.
 iv. Remove the automatic 'No' response. Doing so will shut off people from thinking about solutions in the future. It is better to write down all thoughts and ideas and not be dismissive of staff.
  v. Defer judgment while thinking up ideas. Sometimes an idea on its own does not help us, but two ideas, when connected, allow us to develop a robust and workable solution.
 vi. Challenge all assumptions because they tend to lead a project team down the wrong path.
vii. Find the creative people on your team. They can help jump-start an effort to find solutions to a problem.
viii. Continue to ask why things were set up the way they were or how a work practice came into existence. In many cases, the procedures put in place were set up long ago by other leaders trying to address a problem, as it existed then with the understanding and resources available at that time. However, as systems grow over time, the past solutions do not support today's business needs.
 ix. Protect ideas from scrutiny. Even the slightest eye roll or yawn will not make team members feel good about their contributions.
  x. Be a risk-taker and enjoy taking the lean leap. Remember, those who never take risks never venture very far.

It has been said that when Thomas Edison was creating the lightbulb, he failed hundreds of times. Improvement scientists do not consider each trial a failure. Instead, each trial is a point of learning that helps a team to achieve a solution that works.

When brainstorming with a group, as the facilitator, it is essential to ask questions rather than the one developing ideas. Asking questions will give the group enough space to think for themselves. Sometimes, leaders make mistakes during this activity and start inserting their solutions to problems. Improvement is a path to learn and a path of self-discovery. If a leader forces their own opinions, thoughts, or solutions, the team's ability to come together around a solution is compromised. Thus, it is recommended that the facilitator act impartially toward helping the team move forward through the PDCA process through good Socratic questioning practices.

As a final thought on brainstorming, there will be many ideas out of scope, too lofty, or just will not work. To address this concern during a project, deploy a parking lot for these ideas. A parking lot is a simple flip chart paper that allows a project leader to write down out-of-scope ideas for consideration later. This process helps to prevent alienating a team member should one of their ideas not be written down and helps to gain acceptance for those whose ideas were not chosen.

3. Pilot Study

Pilot studies are scoped experiments to determine the feasibility of solutions. Scoping an experiment to assess the efficacy of a solution on one unit, one shift, or even one clinic helps reduce the waste of cost and time when trying to improve. They also help the team learn and gain acceptance as a team considers implementing a system-wide solution later on. When implementing a pilot study, consider answering the following questions before getting started.

   i. What (solution) will you try?
   ii. Where (area) will you try it?
   iii. When (timeframe) will you try it?
   iv. Who will try it?
   v. How often will you collect data?

4. Change Management

Change takes place every day in the business world as well as in everyday life. Change is constant, and the world will change around us even if we decide not to. It is up to individuals to realize that the team either improves or risks being left behind. For example, Kodak was once a huge and prosperous organization. They hung their hat on the concept of the film. The more film they sold, the more profits they made. However, when a young creative thinker at Kodak came up with the digital camera, they decided not to invest in it because they thought it would ruin their film-based business. Kodak ended up locking themselves out of developing the future because they were stuck in the past. Their stock went from trading at $50–$100 per share with a few stock splits over the years to be almost worthless.

As an additional example, Uber is a relatively new company that helps anyone with a car make money, driving people around town using a simple, user-friendly app. This approach opened up the taxi business to anyone with a license and a car. People are no longer relegated to using a restricted service, run by restrictive union rules, and prone to anonymous drivers who may or may not be friendly toward their passengers. Within just a few short years, a taxi medallion in New York City worth millions is now worth one-tenth of its former value. They did not see this wave coming. Also, while there are currently new rules in place to help protect taxi drivers, it will only be a matter of time when new software comes out that allows people to connect to people to circumvent these rules. Thus, change happens, and teams can choose to invest their time and resources to prepare for and adapt to change, or they can choose to be left behind. An example in mental healthcare is the push toward integrating mental health counseling and treatment into primary care, thus reducing the cost of care over a patient's life.

There are both external factors and internal factors of change that can affect an organization's viability. From an external perspective, the following is a list of external actors.

i. *The Nature of the Workforce*: Workers today are focused on the quality of life, working hours, flexibility, and working from a park bench, coffee shop, or home. Prior generations did not exercise expectations of a work-life balance in the same way as today's workers.

ii. *Technology*: Today, technology advances workplace processes. Advancements allow data capture, data reporting, and data visualization to happen in real-time, thus allowing organizations to make better decisions. The COVID-19 crisis facilitated psychiatric practices and hospitals to quickly adopt telehealth platforms (enabled by insurance companies and loosening of regulations) to keep their services accessible and functional.

iii. *Economic*: Our national economy and the global economy play into the changes we see. Based on the types of services offered, how well do organizations handle recessionary periods? Are organizations diverse enough to weather the storm? Should organizations re-prioritize based on national needs, pressures, and resources? Otherwise, they could end up losing funding for a service needed by their customers or not be as helpful to their patients. For example, many first-line medications become unavailable due to shortages. Pharmacies have to improvise and quickly offer alternatives, or else patients are unable to get effective treatment.

iv. *Competition*: How do organizations grow service offerings without increasing costs? In the service sector, staff salaries are the primary driver of cost. Organizations need to find more efficient ways to complete the current work to make the staff flexible enough to focus on new work. A common mistake made is merely asking the staff to do more. The first step must be to make the current job easier to do before adding on tasks.

v. *Social Trends*: How do trends in society help or hurt an organization's service offerings? How can the organization tap into these trends and utilize them to its advantage? A great example of a social trend is the use of TikTok. There is a broad audience for teens and preteens making fifteen-second videos that are fun and informative. How can mental health institutions use such platforms to engage teens struggling with depression or addiction?

vi. *World Politics*: The continued push toward globalization and standardization makes it difficult to maintain the status quo. However, the goal is not to preserve the status quo but to continually improve the system of care.

Thus, with all of these factors and more playing out every day, organizations must understand why people resist change to prevent an organization from imploding. A few common resistance factors to consider:

i. *Habit*: people resist change when it takes them out of their comfort zone. Organizations must teach their people to tolerate some discomfort to allow the change process to work.

ii. *Security*: People tend to resist change if it threatens their job security. Thus, teams must reduce this anxiety when implementing improvement practices and ensure that staff will be guaranteed a job even if their current position is no longer needed.

iii. *Salary*: People will resist change if there is an adverse change in their base salary or compare like jobs and find others are being paid more for less work.

iv. *Fear of the Unknown*: If a person is afraid they cannot learn the new method, they will naturally resist change.
v. *Selective Information Processing*: People tend to hear what they want to hear and pay attention to only those things they select as necessary. Thus, changing will be a struggle unless there is a common understanding and staff can understand the big picture.

From an organizational perspective, there are yet a few further factors to consider:

i. *Structural Inertia*: organizations have built-in structures for stability. When confronted with a change, an organization's structural inertia will help pull the group back to the baseline state.
ii. *Limited Focus of Change*: An organization is made up of interdependent subsystems. If we change one subsystem without considering the other subsystems, we will find the change not sustaining itself.
iii. *Group Inertia*: If one member of a group agrees with the change, but the rest of the group disagrees, the one supporting member will resist as well.
iv. *A Threat to Expertise*: Changes in organizational work patterns, such as outsourcing work, will cause resistance.
v. *A Threat to Establish Power Relationships*: A change in a leader's authority will change the organizational hierarchy and cause different behavior patterns. There needs to be a carefully laid out plan for people changes, especially leadership changes, to keep an organization functioning. Positive outcomes from improvement efforts can be fragile and prone to being erased unless proactively protected during leadership changes.
vi. *A Threat to Established Resource Allocations*: if a change reduces a departmental budget, then that department lead will naturally resist or scrutinize further changes to the status quo.

When a project team utilizes the PDCA process, communicates through discussing stakeholder feedback, observes the current state, completes an RCA, brainstorms solutions, and conducts pilot studies, the combined activity reduces barriers and resistance to change. PDCA requires communicating the need for change, requires participatory decision-making, and requires building cohesive teams. It helps to delegate control to lower levels in the organization. If leaders delegate responsibility, the implied benefit is front-line ownership and empowerment, which leads to process improvement. When considering everything needed to make change possible, the PDCA process using the A3 tool ensures success. This is why PDCA is a universal tool for making a change in any setting and any process.

5. Action Plans

Once the brainstorming activity is complete, it becomes necessary to have a deliberate plan of action. An action plan is a document that summarizes all of the changes we will make within the process. An action plan is shown in Figure 4.27.

For successful action plans, here are a few tips:

i. Determine if the action needs to be piloted or experimented with before large-scale implementation.
ii. Only assign one project team member per action item to prevent ambiguity and assign responsibility.

Issue	Action	Owner	Due Date	Status
Staff lost access to the network.	Regain Access	Joe Deen	10/12/2020	Complete
	Place a flag in the notification system for transferring team members to prevent access problems for future transfers.	Barbara Snow	11/30/2020	Open
	Validate new flag system to with next 5 transfers	Larry Campbell	12/31/2020	Open

Figure 4.27 Action plan example.

iii. Allow the action item owner to provide the project manager with a due date. This due date helps ensure the action item owners hold themselves accountable to complete the action as committed.

iv. As errors pop up, new barriers arise, or new data is learned, update the action plan accordingly, and continue the PDCA process.

When the team is at a point of making changes, it becomes important to be deliberate, focused, and to move with speed. We recommend the team use all available time to implement. Remember, there are 24 hours in a day and seven days a week, and the work does not have to stop at 5 pm on a Friday. Also, ensure that stakeholders are engaged in helping to make changes. This approach will help the team learn about what went well and what we need to fix. This participative approach further cements buy-in to the changes.

C. Check

The Check in PDCA is to assess the new change once it is in place. It is important to do another round of observations with the team to determine the impact. These observations include a new process map where applicable, new time study data where needed, and an understanding if the output measure has improved.

When completing the Check process, it is vital to the team and the larger group working within the process to see the data collected or the 'score' so far. Seeing the data will help them determine if processes are improving or not. If improving, then there is a general feeling of accomplishment by the team. If no improvement, the team enters a loop where they must learn what went wrong, ask why, and then decide if they want to re-evaluate the solution, tweak the solution, or change to a different solution entirely.

Thus, measuring the results and providing the improvement confirmation box on the A3 helps showcase the improvement when sharing with the team. If there were any measurement errors, this would be an excellent time to correct those errors and ensure the data is reliable. In the end, the team needs to see the final score. A completed A3 is shown in Figure 4.28.

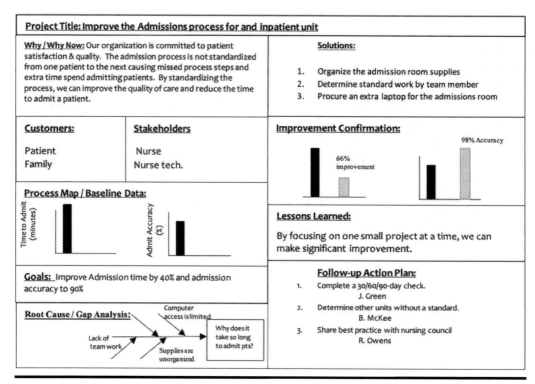

Figure 4.28 A completed A3.

The last part of the Check process is to determine any lesson learned by the team. It might be a lesson learned about following the A3 process or about the results from the project. All lessons learned are important to add to the A3 for the current PDCA team to reflect on and future teams to study. An important note here is not all lessons learned are positive. There are times when a project fails to meet the expectations of the team. However, a team never fails as long as there is continued learning.

D. Act

In the Act section of the A3, the team must take action with an experiment if it indeed showed improvement. We must now work to develop an action plan that incorporates the changes into the larger process or system. There is a simple three-step plan to get this accomplished.

  i. Develop the new Standard Work (Standard operating procedure and gain acceptance by the larger group).
  ii. Develop a monitor and response plan to prevent backsliding.
  iii. Develop a cascade plan to adopt or adapt improvements to similar areas in the health system.

These three elements formulate a process for sustainment. Sustainment is a crucial element of the change process. If a team recognizes that they are permitted to slide back to their original state, the most change will not take hold in an organization. Therefore, sustainment must be treated with the same level of focus that was placed on the project plan phase.

1. Standard Work

Standard work is the cornerstone of any process. As Taiichi Ohno, the father of the Toyota production system, once said, "Where there is no standard, there can be no improvement." Every process has a basic standard that every staff member follows. However, if there is not an established standard, then the first step is to develop one. A standard allows a team to study a process, learn where the waste is, and make small incremental improvements to the standard. Without a standard to follow, making small changes can lead to faulty data analysis or, worse yet, patient dissatisfaction. Thus, standards are both the first step when reviewing a process and the last step when ensuring maintenance of change as it prevents backsliding.

Standard work is defined as an organized sequence of steps assigned to workers. When considering the sequence of steps, workers must learn the process steps, the key points within each step, and the reasons why for each key point. Adult workers need to know why they are to follow the steps in the exact order they need to follow them. If this knowledge is not transferred correctly, the worker will devise their shortcuts to get through the process and workday with minimal effort.

Standard work is a window into seeing the waste within the system. A team can determine how much time is spent waiting during a process step or between process steps. A team can also determine how much motion or how much transportation waste there is. Moreover, all of this knowledge helps teams to develop an improved process.

Standard work helps to control variation. Variation in process steps can occur from unit to unit, nurse to nurse or shift to shift, or even from weekend staff to weekday staff. Standard work helps to prevent much of this variation in multiple processes experienced by the patient.

Standard work also helps with the transfer of knowledge to new hires or float staff to understand how to do the work. In healthcare, turnover and rotating staff to cover spikes in demand is expected. Standard work helps address the ongoing training concerns, allowing staff to provide the same level of care. Figure 4.29 is an example of standard work for cleaning an exam room.

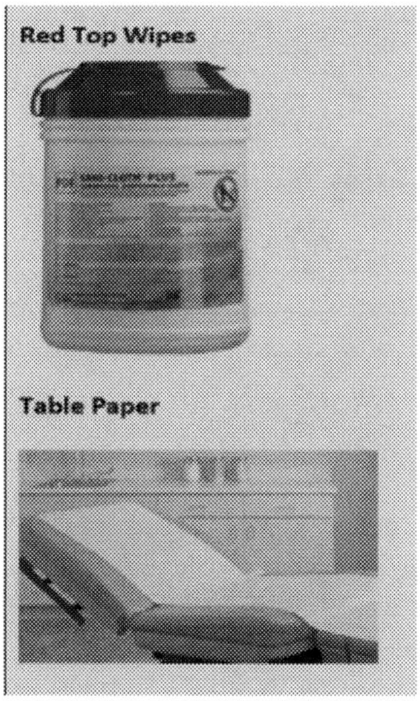

	Major Step	Key Point	Reason Why
Red Top Wipes	1. Remove paper after use	Complete after each use	To maintain cleanliness
	2. Wipe Down Exam Table	Use red top wipes & leave to air dry	
	3. Add new paper to exam table		
Table Paper	4. Stock room with supplies	Don't forget the Gloves	Most frequently used item
	5. Clean all surfaces	Chairs, counters, phone, & floors	
	6. Sign off on cleaning log	Charge nurse to check logs each shift	Ensures accountability

Figure 4.29 Standard work example.

In summary, standard work can provide many benefits to organizational systems. However, there are some common misconceptions in healthcare.

  i. "Standard work treats people like robots." Completing the process the same way by each team member helps to understand better where the waste is so the team can improve the system of care.
  ii. "Standard work is too rigid or regimented to work." Standard work is the 'one best way' a team knows about today. As the team learns and improves, they create a new standard work, which becomes the new 'one best way.'
  iii. "Standard work will not help because people will continue to do things their way." When implementing standard work, the workers affected must agree with the new standard for it to be successful. Communication is necessary, and so is leadership to ensure that staff is held to an agreed-upon standard. How will a team know which is the 'best way' for the service provided unless they standardize it?
  iv. "Standard work will not help because doctors were trained by different schools of thought." Healthcare organizations should create standard work in the eyes of the patient, not in the eyes of the way their staff were trained. Finding and agreeing on the best way helps eliminate the variation, provides improvement across the system of care, and provides patients with the consistency they need irrespective of whom they are cared for by or when they access the system.
  v. "Standard work will prevent me from being creative." Standard work helps channel creativity by first focusing on the largest amounts of waste, releasing time for care within the system, maximizing the benefit to the organization and the patient. By wasting fewer resources and time, providers can have more flexibility to handle variations brought forward by the patient with their creativity once all standardized steps have been completed.

2. Monitor and Response Plan

A monitor and response plan helps to document and control the process once improved. The overall goal is to prevent the team from backsliding, which can happen based on all external and internal forces acting on a single process. The plan documents how the organization will measure performance and, when that performance does not meet the standard, to follow up and address any known problems. An example monitor and response plan for the exam room cleaning process is shown in Figure 4.30. In this example, the monitoring occurs by the charge nurse, and the follow-up occurs during daily team meetings the following morning.

3. Cascade Plan

When a new 'one best way' is developed, sharing the best practice and asking other like areas to either adopt the new standard work or adapt the new standard work are the final steps for a single improvement project. A cascade plan summarizes the opportunity another area can gain from implementing a best practice. An example cascade plan for the exam room cleaning process is shown in Figure 4.31.

The cascade plan and implementation steps should be included on the A3 in the follow-up actions box in the bottom right corner. Once these items are completed, the first PDCA is complete.

A final note at this point is to ensure there is a celebration with the team. Change is hard, and sustaining improvement is harder still. Therefore, to continue to develop a team's resilience toward improvement, celebrating small wins along the way will show a great deal of appreciation to the team.

```
┌─────────────────────────────────────────────────────────────────────┐
│                      Monitor & Response Plan                        │
├─────────────────────────────────────────────────────────────────────┤
│ Measure #1: Cleaning Compliance                                     │
│ Definitions: Number of times the exam room was cleaned properly     │
│ Data Collection Frequency: At the end of each shift by charge nurse │
│ Monitor Method: Team review at morning huddle until 100% compliant  │
│                                                                     │
│ Measure #2: Stock room with Supplies                                │
│ Definitions: Number of times the exam room was out of supplies      │
│ Data Collection Frequency: Tally during day, Charge Nurse collects  │
│ tally totals at end of day                                          │
│ Monitor Method: Team review at morning huddle until achieving zero  │
│ stock outs                                                          │
└─────────────────────────────────────────────────────────────────────┘
```

Figure 4.30   Monitor and response plan example.

V. PDCA and Kata

PDCA is a continuous journey. When going through the first incremental improvement, most project managers realize three to five other improvements that could be made with enough time. Each of these is its own PDCA. However, once we get into those improvements, each of those leads to three to five more. The best way to approach the PDCA process is to incorporate PDCA into a daily routine of a health system and continually strive for improvement.

```
┌─────────────────────────────────────────────────────────────────────┐
│                           Cascade Plan                              │
├─────────────────────────────────────────────────────────────────────┤
│ Cascade #1: Unit 2B                                                 │
│ Opportunity: Exam room not cleaned properly after each use          │
│ Method (Adopt or Adapt): Adopt                                      │
│ Cascade Successful: Yes                                             │
│ Translation Barriers: None                                          │
│                                                                     │
│ Cascade #2: 3C                                                      │
│ Opportunity: Not using red top wipes                                │
│ Method (Adopt or Adapt): Adopt                                      │
│ Cascade Successful: Yes                                             │
│ Translation Barriers: None                                          │
└─────────────────────────────────────────────────────────────────────┘
```

Figure 4.31   Cascade plan example.

As discussed in section three (Rother, 2009), Katas are choreographed movements, drills, or patterns practiced every day.[5] The concept behind Kata is practicing every day makes them a habit. When Kata is formed as a habit, they become second nature, and people cannot imagine operating without using such a pattern. Thus, if we desire to get our organizations to improve, the organization must practice every day.

Kata, from a lean perspective, helps provide a drumbeat to improvement. If leaders ask the right questions repeatedly and work to answer those questions, we will know how to improve naturally. The most basic Kata questions form what is known as Improvement Kata.

Improvement Kata questions include:

i. What is the target condition?
ii. What is the current condition?
iii. What did you try?
iv. What did you learn?
v. What is the top causes or issue preventing us from reaching the target condition?
vi. What will you try next?
vii. What do you expect to happen?
viii. When will we have data?

Notice the improvement Kata resembles the PDCA process and the A3 process. By asking these basic questions throughout the workday, we can slowly build a culture where our staff asks these questions for themselves and continues working toward improvement.

References

1. Deming, W. E. 2018. *Out of the Crisis*. MIT Press, Cambridge, MA.
2. Ohno, T. & Kimoto L.M. 1987. *The Toyota Production System*. Monterey Institute of International Studies, Monterey, CA.
3. Graupp, P. & Wrona, R.J. 2011. *Implementing TWI: Creating and Managing a Skills-based Culture*. CRC Press, Boca Raton, FL.
4. Shook, J. 2010. *Managing to Learn: Using the A3 Management Process to Solve Problems, Gain Agreement, Mentor and Lead*. Lean Enterprise Institute, Boston, MA.
5. Rother, M. 2009. *Toyota KATA: Managing People for Improvement, Adaptiveness, and Superior Results*.

Section V

Leading a New Kind of Workforce

Given the challenges discussed in Section I and the need to improve the healthcare system as we know it today, healthcare organizations need a new kind of workforce that can:

i. Recognize problems (or waste) within the course of one's daily work (Ezez, 2020),[1]
ii. Engage in on-the-spot *repair* efforts,
iii. Redesign broken or burdensome workflows and processes, and
iv. Innovate newer ways of delivering care.

As discussed in Section III, performance improvement capability is a key competency for individuals and leaders. Given that each mental health organization has limited resources and an ever-expanding complex array of needs, a leader's role is to foster *a learning organizational culture*, which encourages the elimination or reduction of waste while it preserves or enhances value. The end goal is ensuring an organization stays viable through continuous improvement. An improvement-minded culture enables viability through building resiliency and flexibility into a workforce. Ongoing continuous improvement also frees up valuable resources that could be partially invested in building such skills in individuals, teams, and the overall culture.

This chapter begins by articulating the leadership behaviors and skills needed to facilitate and nurture an environment for developing an improvement-minded culture. This is followed by a discussion focused on exhibiting a leadership style that creates a motivated workforce where creativity and innovation take center stage. We illustrate this by delineating leadership attributes that can hinder improvement and those that can facilitate improvement. Optimum leadership is a vital prerequisite to the development of high-performing organizations. The chapter closes with suggestions of where a clinician or leader could begin their improvement journey, whether in an entry-level role, at the helm of a large organization, or somewhere in between.

I. Leadership and Culture

A leader is defined as anyone in charge of people or who directs the work of others. A leader is not just an appointed person or a title. It connotes a person that exhibits a balanced constellation of certain desirable behavioral qualities. *Leadership,* therefore, is the total of what a good leader manifests.

A leader's primary role is to manage and improve the system. With this simple premise in mind, consider the diagram in Figure 5.1. High-performing leadership gets unleashed in the context of four foundational interdependent behaviors.

First, a leader gains the trust of those they work with. Second, a leader works to develop strong interpersonal relationships. Third, the leader builds a well-balanced team and fosters teamwork.

Figure 5.1 Foundational interdependent behaviors for high-performing leadership.

Fourth, the leader gives appropriate and timely feedback to ensure that the team members progress and grow. Such behaviors enable an environment where high-performing leadership can thrive.

A. Building Trust

Trust is the most crucial element for any working relationship to form or exist. Without trust, a positive and forward-moving relationship does not develop. Employee satisfaction is multifactorial. However, in an age where purpose trumps a paycheck, trust is the primary reason why some workers engage when others do not or why some workers stay with an organization while others seek new opportunities. Without trust, the ability of a leader to successfully manage and sustain change becomes compromised. Once a leader loses the trust of a team member or trust in a team member, a relationship takes time and significant effort to rebuild. To build, maintain, and grow trust, a leader must commit to earning trust every day through respect for others.

Continuous improvement efforts cannot flourish without respect for others. Offering respect to team members is a sure way of gaining trust, which builds over time like a bank deposit. As team members' trust keeps growing gradually, it offers a steady stream of currency for the difficult work of improvement, which can then move rapidly and smoothly. The converse is true as well. Improvement work will encounter a great deal of resistance and barriers if trust is not established.

Fear works against the development of trust. Workplace fear is an emotion caused by a belief that someone or something is a threat. It could arise out of insecurity or inexperience of a leader or result from a very harsh and punitive leadership style. It can also be seen in situations where leaders are not patient-centered but ego-centered. W. Edwards Deming wrote about driving out fear in his fourteen points on Quality Management (Deming, 2018).[2] A leader gains trust by removing fear from those they work for, those they work with, and those they lead. They foster an environment of psychological safety. Fear can and will enter a team member's thought process at any point in time, from the first moment of interaction to the last and anywhere in between. Fear takes on multiple forms within the workplace. A few simple examples of how fear develops and manifests in the workplace include:

   i. A team member is left out of meetings and begins fearing for his/her job security.
   ii. A leader preys on a specific team member during staff meetings.
   iii. A leader favors one employee over others in the group.
   iv. A team member isolates themselves and does not collaborate with their peers.
   v. A leader is quick to discipline and place blame on team members for system-level errors.
   vi. A leader does not allow errors to be reported lest there are criticisms about their department.
   vii. A team member fears being reprimanded if they point out work that does not meet expectations.

These examples and other manifestations of fear can disrupt productive work, impair safety, and prevent the improvement of a system as a whole. To temper the fear of team members, a leader must learn to communicate clear intentions, be forthright with information, whether good or bad, seek to understand all information and lead in a way that eliminates fear. The more a leader pushes toward addressing system issues and drive out fear, the more trust is enabled within the workforce.

It has been written that healthcare workers experience intimidating behaviors that might prevent them from reporting safety problems. The Institute of Safe Medication Practices published the results of its 'Workplace Intimidation Survey.' The survey represented the process of receiving, interpreting, and acting on medication orders. About two thousand nurses and pharmacists reported a variety of behaviors that made them uncomfortable. These included a failure to return calls or pages and to respond to requests with impatience and condescension. This kind of response made the nurses and pharmacists avoid calling the physicians and also ask someone else to contact the physician (Ezez, 2004).[3] Leadership would have to demonstrate a zero-tolerance for intimidating and disruptive behaviors and work to create an environment where anyone can feel safe to bring up concerns that could impact patient safety.

An easy way to begin building trust is by always leading with purpose. Over the last century, various thought leaders and modern-day writers all believe that leaders who consistently lead with a clear purpose tend to capture the most employee trust. When looking back at the last 30 winners of the annual Malcolm Baldrige award for Performance Excellence, all of these organizations highlight a strong sense of purpose. For example, Memorial Hermann Sugar Land in Texas leads with purpose and requires each employee to develop individualized 'why not me' statements. A 'why not me' statement is a personal proclamation of how each individual in that health system aligns with the mission. When team members take the time to recognize how their role in an organization ties to the purpose of the organization, a sense of pride and ownership can develop. Without it, there will always be limited engagement with the work. The employees need to be made aware of the big picture and how their contribution fits into it. Also, by believing in the inherent potential and capability of those on the front line, a leader essentially says, "I value you, and I believe what you have to offer will be a significant contribution and will make a difference to our organization." This leadership proclamation shares power with the employee, who then gets energized to devote their best to the organization as they feel valued and trusted.

An organization's purpose statement is also known as a mission statement. A mission statement must have the basic components of why the organization exists. A great example is CVS, as its mission statement reads, "Helping people on their path to better health" (Lopez-Trigo et al., 2015).[4] It's easy to see CVS is focused on its customers. This statement not only helps consumers understand whom they are supporting with their business, but it allows employees to identify who they are working for, what their focus needs to be every day on the job, and why. CVS's mission statement is so clear that it led them to remove tobacco products from their store shelves. In short, it would be hard to help people find a path for better health if CVS was also supporting unhealthy smoking habits. A clear statement also enabled CVS leaders to make better decisions for the customer rather than merely focusing on profits. As they continue down this path with services like flu shots, nicotine replacement therapies, linking acute care to their pharmacies, and so forth, they will become even more valuable to their communities and more trusted by their employees. Thus, a leader must be clear with their purpose and begin and end every conversation with purpose because a clear purpose is a cornerstone to building trust in an organization.

Leaders will find that they have to build trust with each new group or employee they lead. Trust is not a given, and it is not a right for a new leader to expect it. Instead, it must always be earned. To earn employee trust, a leader must use consistency, accountability, and discipline. Consistency allows organizations to improve outcomes at an even pace over time rather than have an erratic or reactive approach to improvement. Consistency is built on knowing the values of an organization and living them in everything a leader does. Employees emulate their leaders, and by experiencing consistency from the leader, they respond favorably.

Accountability is often misunderstood. Accountability is not just about holding others accountable for doing their part. If employees do not know what they are accountable for, then this is a training issue, not an employee issue. When employees understand their accountability but are not meeting expectations, this is a leadership issue requiring some coaching to get employees back on track. However, a more significant aspect of accountability emphasized here is a leader's self-accountability. Holding oneself accountable and having employees hold themselves accountable to get the job done and improve is considered the holy grail of building trust.

Discipline is about continuing to move forward despite being tempted to abandon course with every crisis, overcoming obstacles that are in the way, and always doing what is right in the face of adversity. In many organizations, there are situations where employees are much disciplined in their approach to the workplace, but they work for a leader who is not disciplined themselves. Such a leader can lead to fragmented focus, misalignment, and the erosion of trust. To help improve discipline, many leaders create a vision of where they see their organization going in the near future and work every day to stay on the journey toward the vision. Discipline, therefore, is the link between the vision and accomplishing the vision. Yes, there will be crises and stressors in an organization. Still, a guiding document like an operating plan or even a simple action plan helps to provide discipline and rigor in work. The work of improvement is like the work of prevention. It is essential, it slowly strengthens the organization, but it can take time. Hence, a long-term vision, consistency, accountability, and discipline become key behaviors that help create a healthy improvement culture. It requires persistence and steadfastness from the leader. As Deming says, constancy of purpose.

In summary, trust is the most critical aspect of leadership, and the best leaders know that there is a reciprocal relationship between the leader and the employee. Effective leaders do not focus on fear tactics to get their employees to submit to their will. Instead, they promote the components of trust built on purpose, meeting people where they are, providing time and space to step outside the process and reimagine it, and ensuring there is an established and effective dialogue. These factors are developed through working with consistency, accountability, and discipline. As a leader works to improve, a strong foundation of trust sets the frame for achieving results.

B. Developing Strong Interpersonal Relationships

When considering what a leader must accomplish, the list of responsibilities is tremendous. Addressing safety concerns, ensuring good quality of services offered, meeting budgetary requirements, providing excellent customer service, and training staff are all part of the leadership expectations. Each of these organizational needs can only be accomplished through proper interactions with staff. A leader has to leverage their team's power to meet these responsibilities, so there must be an effective working relationship between the leader and those they lead. An average leader has good relationships with some employees, poor relationships with others, and a host of employees somewhere in between. However, the simple truth is, there are always relationships.

To determine the relative strength of relationships, most organizations utilize an annual survey mechanism as a gauge. However, relationships need tending frequently, and waiting for a yearly survey does not help the employee or the leader determine where to improve. Thus, a more frequent relationship gauge is required for effectiveness.

We introduce a concept here called the *leader-team member* relationship line. Consider the diagram in Figure 5.2.

A strong relationship between leader and employee enables acceptance, resilience, and results. A weak relationship line between leader and employee leads to disengaged, unaligned team members working on their priorities, thus generating weaker results. The problem that all leaders face is that the leader-employee relationship line is invisible. It is out of sight and often prevents clear leader focus and attention. Yet, with increased complexity and demands placed on healthcare workers, this relationship line's strength should be a top priority for effective leadership.

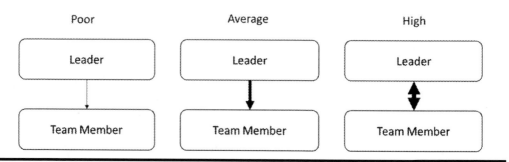

Figure 5.2 Leader-team member relationship line.

To properly tend to the relationship, there are several key components. First, there is a need for a leader to *be straightforward with an employee and let them know what they expect.* Employees will not understand expectations unless leaders are clear about them. As with any communication, the time and place for such a conversation are important. Leaders should not embarrass an employee in front of others. Instead, they should take the employee aside and discuss expectations openly and honestly. A very effective way to deal with ambiguity is to write down objectives for an employee in a very clear and unambiguous manner. The act of setting goals that are specific, measurable, and have a clear due date goes a long way in setting the tone. A key point here is to not shift the responsibility or work around the employee. Instead, leaders need to work to get them on the right track and to help an employee focus on the right things. When expectations are established between a leader and an employee, the employee will either rise to the occasion or weed themselves out of their role.

VIGNETTE 5.1

Holly, a dedicated employee, wanted more from her role at her state government agency. She found committee work to be draining, often void of purpose, goals, and results. She felt these monthly committee meetings to nowhere were stressing her mind and her heart. Her strengths included analyzing and troubleshooting problems, and the committees she engaged in did nothing but talk for an hour with no actions to move the group forward. Holly wanted out of this committee. She asked her supervisor if there were other assignments she could be reassigned to utilize her analytical and problem-solving strengths in a more meaningful way.

Second, a leader must *appreciate their employees.* A good leader does not wait for annual performance reviews to provide recognition. Instead, he or she gives kudos, and thanks as progress is made. Leadership is not very different from parenting. 'Affectionless control' is detrimental in the end. A good well-tended relationship between a leader and team members, where they feel safe to reach out and speak up, always fosters a better work culture. In this age of highly specialized knowledge, a leader cannot know everything and cannot keep their attention on all parts of an organization. Ultimately, if team members feel connected and care for, they will pass on that sentiment to the people they serve.

When recognizing the progress of team members, it is also important to understand that not everyone likes to be recognized in the same way. Some team members want private discussions. Others enjoy receiving credit in front of the team. Yet others like a small gift or a simple thank you. Leaders who are building trust and rapport must ensure recognition preferences are understood in advance. The employee impact of giving credit where credit is due enables movement along the hierarchy of needs from survival and safety to belonging and esteem. The number one reason why people leave organizations is that there is not enough appreciation in the workplace. Thus, an effective leader must prevent this from occurring by appreciating staff and their contributions to the mission.

VIGNETTE 5.2

Mary was a nursing leader who went above and beyond the call of duty, often working late nights and weekends to get the job done. She was an excellent nurse and provided excellence in care and service to her patients. She demanded that her team become excellent in delivering care and emphasized staff development in clinical care and improvement science. Mary worked to appreciate those staff members that showed promise and made progress. She would take them to lunch, give them extra praise during team meetings, shower them with gifts, and even promote her key employees when opportunities arose.

The third key to establishing strong relations is to *let employees know in advance about changes* that will affect them. As discussed in the previous sections, change affects people, and the natural response to most any change is to resist. The best way to get employees to change is to bring them into the conversation early on. Most leaders already know the direction they are going in. However, it is incumbent upon the leader to first meet their employees and build a bridge to where the leader wants them to be. It is also important to give team members some notice and time to allow each employee to digest the information, ask questions, and internalize it. Most employees tend to realize that not all change is a bad change. Also, given the right setting and approach, leaders can manage through any team member resistance without causing disruption or delays to work.

VIGNETTE 5.3

Jody White was an exemplary employee in a large home health company and ran a top-performing department within the organization. One day, she was called into a meeting with several of her peers and her supervisor. Her supervisor discussed that he wanted to make some changes and laid out a plan to move most of Jody's team to another leader in the room. Jody was distraught and insulted that such a significant change was not discussed with her in private before a joint meeting with her peers. She felt left out of the conversation and hurt. She felt change was happening to her department without first being discussed with her. Jody lost confidence in and respect for her leader and began questioning the leader's leadership style in her mind. She thought hard about the changes proposed and wanted to know the real reasons behind the change and the big picture. She had plenty of ideas of how she could help the organization, which she then became uncomfortable sharing as the trust between her and the leader had been significantly eroded.

The fourth key to strong leader-employee relations is to *make the best use of each person's abilities*. A leader must know and understand their employee's strengths and utilize them to ensure the job is as rewarding and challenging as possible. If the job does not challenge the employee, complacency will set in, and employees become stuck in a fixed position working fixed hours and not stretching to exceed performance goal targets. Thus, tapping into hidden strengths and using employee strengths on different projects is essential for full engagement.

The last aspect is to *truly understand your employees*. Each employee must be treated as an individual. Each of us deals with family concerns, health concerns, financial concerns, and a host of other issues. It is important to recognize that people bring their lives to work with them every day. Employees spend forty to fifty waking hours per week in the workplace, almost half of all awake hours in a single year. Thus, it is impossible to compartmentalize the personal from the professional completely. A leader should ask each employee in a one-on-one interview how things are going for them, how they like the job, how things are at home, and so forth. It is not about being nosy or about getting into social or family dynamics. But it is about knowing that one employee is struggling with a sick child while another employee is planning a wedding and a third employee is not adjusting well because they work too far away from their family. Each of us has challenges, and a leader can lend an ear, show they care, and refer their employees to the Employee Assistance Program (EAP) where needed. However, more importantly, a leader must figure out ways to meet each team member where they are and work to build the necessary support to get them on a better path.

VIGNETTE 5.4

Jay, a dedicated employee, was more recently void of expression, started showing up late to work, did not participate in team meetings as he used to, and left as soon as his shift ended. Over several weeks, his performance declined, and his supervisor noticed when the latest monthly quality performance reports indicated Jay had several complaints lodged against him from patients and team members. Jay's supervisor decided it was time for a discussion. Jay confessed that things at home had not been good. His mother recently passed away, and his wife wanted a divorce. His world had turned upside down in a matter of a few weeks. Jay's supervisor recommended Jay call the EAP and told him that no matter what is happening in his personal life, the work must not suffer. Jay apologized but left the office feeling unheard and unsatisfied. He felt his supervisor only cared about the organization but did not care about him as a person.

C. Fostering Teamwork

As interpersonal relationships start to strengthen, teamwork can flourish. Teamwork is defined as a process where a group of people works collaboratively to achieve a common goal. This means that everyone on the team understands their role and responsibilities and relies on each other to achieve the goal. A fully functioning team has the same priorities, does not duplicate efforts, and aligns with an organization's overall direction. Sometimes there are teams of people assembled that each has different goals. This setup's net result is the misalignment and causes teamwork to either break down or never occur. In general, when a leader reviews a misaligned team's results, they are often surprised at the lack of accomplishment and cause a flurry of work to happen in short order. We recommend the leader resist causing panic instead of focusing on why the work did not progress the way it should. Leaders must begin by asking, "How can I lead differently to get a better result?"

A final thought on teamwork is when dealing with problems between two team members. It is inherent that staff would rather talk to their leader independently on a project or address an ongoing problem with another staff member rather than work on building relationships with one another. Leaders need to push back against this approach because the leader will become the relationship line and communication channel between two workers. As soon as the leader turns their attention away, the two pick up with their issues where they left off. Thus, the best leaders work to get staff members to talk and building rapport with one another.

VIGNETTE 5.5

Phil ran an outpatient agency that provided housing solutions to patients with severe mental illnesses. He worked hard to convert properties in town to make this happen. He was very collaborative in his approach. Many of his clients needed services at higher levels of care. He made himself readily accessible to the clinical teams in the partial and inpatient programs. He worked hard to build bridges and relationships. Conversely, when an inpatient team needed group homes for one of their homeless clients, he did not leave any stone unturned to help these teams secure housing for their patients. The hospital clinical teams had a great deal of trust in him that he had worked hard to build over time. It helped his non-profit organization flourish. He always kept in mind that we all live in an interdependent world.

D. Giving Appropriate and Timely Feedback

Feedback is an essential element to make progress with performance improvement.

VIGNETTE 5.6

Theresa, a project manager, had a team member who was not pulling their weight. The rest of the team started to complain. Therefore, she decided to work with that team member to get them on the path to success. However, even after several counseling sessions, there were no appreciable changes. She could not figure out how to motivate her team member and decided to pursue disciplinary action and place him on a performance improvement plan.

However, feedback is not merely a one-sided discussion from the leader to the team member. The goal of feedback is to ensure that two-way communication occurs to get the most from the employee and help the employee develop and grow in the process. A useful framework for exchanging feedback for the leader is to use active listening and Socratic questioning skills.

Much of what is described in motivational interviewing is centered on these two constructs (Miller & Rollnick, 2012).[5] A leader must meet people and acknowledge them for where they are. This first step helps to reduce the initial defensiveness people feel when facing a need to change. A simple method within motivational interviewing is to repeat back to the team member what you heard to acknowledge their feedback. Many leaders fail in this regard because they are more interested in making their point and can be very directive in their communications. They can often counter what people are saying rather than genuinely listening to the feedback, making meaning of it, and respond in a way that shows support.

Next, a leader must ask Socratic questions to seek understanding rather than provide judgment or answers. The idea is to unleash the inherent potential and creativity of each employee. Employees on the front line have a keen idea of the challenges faced in the course of work. They are also in the best vantage point to develop creative countermeasures to deal with these challenges. A good leader communicates the vision but then uses Socratic questions to help elicit the best ideas to deal with current challenges and, by doing so, communicates trust and a belief in the capabilities of the employee. Over time, this creates a strong and more capable workforce as it leads to the employee internalizing the problem-solving and improvement mindset.

VIGNETTE 5.7

Abdul was a very thoughtful leader. He invested in relationships with his team members. He cared about their growth and well-being. One thing his supervisees remarked on was the detailed and thorough performance appraisals that he conducted. First, nothing there was a surprise. He wrote detailed comments highlighting the strengths and contributions of his team members. Every one of his team members felt he paid careful attention to their work. He was committed to safety and quality, and he never compromised whenever those were concerned. Abdul challenged his team members to continuously learn and grow and checked in monthly to see how his team members worked toward their mutually agreed-upon goals. He had an uncanny ability to match the team member's strengths with a need in the organization. He would ensure that they gave their best. He would check periodically to see that they were satisfied with the assignment and help them resolve systemic barriers. Many felt that they owed a considerable portion of their success to his guidance and encouragement. His retirement drew a packed auditorium, and all the tributes to him were glowing. He left behind an incredible legacy.

Not all feedback is positive and can lead to problems with trust, relationships, and teamwork. Therefore, an additional element is to sandwich any negative comments between a positive beginning and a positive end. Many consultants and outside agencies employ this approach when working with a hospital. However, the same holds for any leader. The goal is to ensure the message is heard without the receiver feeling threatened. A threatened worker moves into a mental space of fear, which breeds mistrust. Likewise, a leader who gains feedback from staff negatively may not receive it well and may cause a rupture in the relationship. Any critique must be constructive to allow the receiver to internalize the message.

When it comes to feedback, using the foundational concepts of motivational interviewing and leading with heart are the basic building blocks for any improvement process to work well over time. It does not matter which improvement approach an organization utilizes. Lean, Six Sigma, Quality Circles, PDCA, and Kaizen all have pluses and minuses. Instead, what matters is to determine what will work to drive the right level of communication and collaboration throughout the process.

We have shared the A3 approach earlier in this book to give the reader a simple universal tool to ensure the communication process occurs during performance improvement activities. The A3 process ensures communication upfront when developing the 'why' for the project. Communication continues within the review of customer and stakeholder requirements and investigates the root cause of the problem and developing solutions to try. When a project is complete, communicating the results to the team and recognizing staff as a leader helps close the feedback loop and enhance trust. In some cases, lessons learned are vital to the feedback process because it allows a team to understand what went well and what did not to correct any mistakes and continue to make sustained improvement.

A leader must also learn to become a coach when providing feedback. The best approach to feedback is to ensure it occurs in real-time instead of a delayed response, it is clear instead of ambiguous feedback, and it is positive and constructive rather than negative. A great feedback tool for leaders is the use of coaching Kata (Rother, 2009).[6] Toyota utilizes the following five questions based on the PDCA cycle for improvement:

 i. What is the target condition?
 ii. What is the actual condition now?
 iii. What obstacles do you think are preventing you from reaching the target condition? Which one are you addressing now?
 iv. What is your next step? What do you expect?
 v. When can we go and see what we have learned from taking that step?

We can slightly alter and use these same five questions as a way to coach individual employees weekly; we get a coaching check-in regimen weekly that looks something like this:

 i. What are your goals?
 ii. What did you accomplish this past week?
 iii. Were there any obstacles or barriers preventing you from making adequate progress on your priorities?
 iv. What is your next step?
 v. When can we review what you have learned from taking the next step?

Some employees may not prefer a weekly check-in approach and select monthly meetings. However, there is a certain rigor that weekly check-ins provide to any team member or team's relative progress. The best teams discuss progress daily with a visual board in the work area that provides a focal point for workers to align toward a common goal. Daily evaluations of progress surface problems close to when they occur and are easily recalled. In contrast, the weekly review can delve deeper into these problems and probe root causes. The weekly reviews also help the leader understand systemic barriers in the organization and help each of their direct reports develop better improvement capabilities. This feedback regimen helps to reinforce the previously mentioned constructs of trust, interpersonal relationships, and teams. There is a need to focus on both the value an employee provides and their associated strengths to ensure that individual feedback stays positive.

II. High-Performing Leadership

The foundational context of trust, strong interpersonal relationships, teamwork, and regular feedback provides an excellent environment for high-performing leadership to thrive. Spot improvements, small-scale projects, suggestion systems, root-cause analysis meetings, and brainstorming sessions can provide a great wealth of ideas. These improvement ideas can only take hold if the cultural context is conducive. Leadership attributes can hinder improvement, or they can facilitate improvement. Optimum leadership is a vital prerequisite to the development of high-performing organizations.

Leaders are considered motivators-in-chief. They are at the helm of an organization, and all accomplishments and failures fall back on the leader's shoulders. Therefore, the stress of being successful can sometimes turn a culture from positive to negative. A leader sets the cultural tone for an organization. To understand this point well, let us first examine some examples of toxic cultures that lead to low-performing environments.

A. Toxic Cultures

We describe three common kinds of toxic cultures that exist in the workplace.

1. An Aggressive or Hostile Culture

The culture is one of aggressiveness where the leader preys on individual team member weaknesses or leads with aggressiveness and hostility, thus causing defensive postures that limit interaction and team formation. When working in this environment, a team member either feels lost and maintains peace and status quo or becomes equally aggressive by mirroring the leader's behavior (identifying with the aggressor). Within a noticeably short amount of time, team members who were once vocal become silent. Improvement stops, and team members start getting disengaged. Aggressiveness causes a defensive posture for some team members who are afraid to speak up. They do not feel the psychological safety needed to speak freely for an honest dialogue, or they do not have the confidence that their viewpoint will be heard fairly and given the time and attention required. They end up worrying more about their survival than about the productivity and effectiveness of the organization.

2. An Analysis-Paralysis Culture

The culture is one of heavy contemplation where endless discussions yield little action, thus causing disinterested team members. When there are multiple committees with endless discussions about important organizational topics that seem to go nowhere, there is a problem with organizational growth and momentum. The hierarchical structures, lack of alignment, and limited project management experience can be highly detrimental to the innovative yet fragile ideas needed for redesign and culture change. While some leaders may be afraid of making the wrong decision, the improvement process drags on endlessly, causing great staff dissatisfaction. It's better to conduct a small scoped test or pilot experiment to positively and proactively advance the team discussion to determine the validity of an option when making a decision. Otherwise, the team will quickly lose focus. Sometimes it may need a reexamination of values if two opposing values clash, causing a stalemate or a state of analysis-paralysis.

3. The Fire-Fighting Culture

The culture is one where there always seems to be a fire to fight, and it always somehow begins on Monday when the leader returns to the office. Leaders do not like to fail, and they especially don't like it when there is a surprise failure. A surprising failure might be a missed financial target, a quality measure that did not meet expectations, a disgruntled team member calling out the organization on social media, or even a less than flattering article in the press. All of these and more are failures that can consume a leader's time. Often, when a leader is consumed with these daily or weekly happenings, the team responds to the fire as good foot soldiers do in the process of getting through another week. However, this leads an organization to implement change to make change rather than take the time to ensure improvement is warranted.

Whether one of these or other toxic or problematic cultures exists in the workplace, leadership has a vital role. Many leaders are simply unaware that they cause such cultures to form, but in just about every organization, they exist in one form or another or have some features of each. The more important point here is each one of these cultures opposes organizational improvement. They limit focus on innovation and growth. There is also limited time for developing oneself if the mind is always focused on dealing with the whims, inefficiencies, or reactivity of the leader. Thus, a leader must learn how to properly motivate their team and incorporate a 'leadership management system' that supports improvement.

Another clue to a leader that something might be amiss or problematic is to ask honest questions about safety, quality, delivery, morale, and cost. Usually, all frank discussions of these problems, when examined, deeply point to long-standing systemic flaws that need to be surfaced and worked up if any movement is to be seen. Otherwise, an organization can get into a repetitive and reactive 'fire-fighting' cycle that is incredibly wasteful and burns up precious resources. Clues to problems in culture could be recurrent safety and quality issues, very high turnover, poor financial performance, or very low customer satisfaction. For an organization to succeed in each of these outcomes, good leadership is critical. On the positive side, working toward building a high-performing culture can be a great team-building tool for the entire organization.

B. High-Performing Leadership: The Case of High-Reliability Organizations

Today, many high-performing health organizations utilize performance improvement methods such as Lean and Six Sigma to stay viable, to achieve better outcomes, to gain a competitive advantage, and to aim for 'High-reliability' as introduced in Section one.

High-reliability is not a specific methodology. It is a way of thinking about the challenges of safety and quality in highly complex environments. Healthcare and quality leaders have been studying industries outside of healthcare such as commercial air travel and nuclear power to understand how they achieve and sustain very high safety levels. These industries are highly complex, carry very high risks, and yet can avoid serious failures and accidents for prolonged periods. They are called high-reliability organizations (HROs). Working on patient safety can motivate clinicians who are interested in good outcomes as it appeals to their sense of professionalism. Weick and Sutcliffe describe how HROs stay safe by creating an environment of "collective mindfulness" (Weick & Sutcliffe, 2007) and "situational awareness."[7]

Leaders of such organizations strive for these five characteristics. The five features described in the context of HROs are as follows:

1. Preoccupation with Failure

When issues occur outside a specified standard, a leader in an HRO will consider the symptoms of a larger system problem. A leader would challenge the staff to proactively think of how the system could breakdown or fail in the future. If that were to happen, how would they act?

It would be commonplace in a highly reliable organization to ask questions such as: Are supply levels adequate? Is there enough staff to support the needs of patients? Why does the wrong medication get into the hands of the wrong patient? Teams can expect that they will make errors and continually adjust the process to prevent errors in the future. In healthcare, mock codes and simulation methods are methods to learn about potential failure modes.

If leaders do not see accidents or errors happening, they should be careful not to become complacent. For instance, if leaders hear no problems or barriers reported in their walk rounds consistently, they wonder if the staff on the front line were looking hard enough. They should encourage their direct reports to probe more carefully and analyze special-cause variations and near-misses to understand potential failure modes.

2. Reluctance to Simplify

Healthcare is very complex. Thus, when faced with a problem, the best leaders will ask the team to go to the place where the problem occurred, bring the team together and drive toward understanding root causation. Once the root system issue is identified, then and only then can action be put into place to fix the problem. Otherwise, a leader risks utilizing a 'whack-a-mole' approach to the 'crisis-of-the-day.' Low-reliability organizations often respond to regulatory audits with simplistic solutions, such as heaping one administrative burden after another on their workforce to shape the behaviors of team members.

On the contrary, a leader in an HRO would resist the temptation to come up with a simplistic explanation or solution. Multiple factors can cause threats to safety, and the staff has to try to distinguish the symptom from the deep-rooted systemic cause. A fish-bone diagram or even a process map could illustrate how complex a process or operation can be. Systems can fail in new ways, and HROs have to use all their team members' diverse experiences to improve their processes continually.

3. Sensitivity to Operations

An HRO must be situationally aware and sensitive to normal operations. This allows several team members to sound an alarm when there is an unexpected variation. For example, if a physician writes an order for an unusually high medication dosage, the pharmacist and the nurse act as reliability controls to prevent such an order from ever reaching the patient. Many organizations discuss safety on a daily basis as a way to sound such alarms in faulty processes. A good leader has to be courageous enough to let problems surface so that the current process can be replaced by a better-optimized process or system.

A leader in an HRO encourages everyone to think how his or her role impacts the whole system. Sensitivity to operations may mean more than just paying attention to vital signs, medication effects or discharge plans. It may also mean paying attention to contextual issues that can impact the delivery of patient care. For example, paying attention to working conditions, degree of turnover or burnout, or even thinking about factors such as staff engagement. These factors are just a few that can impact patient outcomes.

4. Commitment to Resilience

Teams must expect that they will make mistakes. "The hallmark of an HRO is not that it is error-free but that errors don't disable it" (Weick & Sutcliffe, 2007).[7] They ensure that small errors do not balloon into significant problems that reach the patient. They work on the continuous examination of their latent failures and keep on working to bolster their defenses. Team members in an HRO learn from their mistakes and move forward. There is also resiliency built into the daily routines and working relationships with the team. Part of the resiliency also comes from preventing uneven workloads or overburden on team members. It involves investing in the learning and growth of all team members.

It is very similar to what is necessary for the 'human system' to develop resilience — enough sleep, a balanced diet, adequate exercise, and stress management. Similarly, organizational resilience requires adequate pacing of improvement to allow for some creative tension, sufficient resources to meet the challenge, a learning environment with a robust feedback loop, and a just culture that provides universal accountability and safety.

5. Deference to Expertise

HROs lean on those with the expertise to help solve problems. Problem-solving is pushed to lower levels in the organization and the front line as much as possible as they are nearest to the work that is being done. This approach is not about formal authority, seniority, rank, or hierarchy but about the authority that comes from the knowledge, experience, and competencies of staff relevant to the issue and built over time. This is what makes them most qualified to tackle problems. Here too, a leader needs to establish an environment of psychological safety where the person at the lowest level in an organization, a patient, or a family member can call out a safety or quality problem.

Establishing such an environment can be a formidable challenge for leaders because many leaders are promoted to their positions due to being good clinicians and problem solvers. However, an HRO will engage the front line in finding and fixing the problem. This method is extremely important for the larger group to adopt changes to the process and sustain new practices over a more extended period. Here again, a robust lean daily management system allows for front-line innovation, the strategic pillars provide the needed alignment. The coaching provided by the leadership team provides an environment to play catch-ball. The ideas come from everywhere, and leaders help remove systemic barriers and motivate the team members to move the organization toward the desired vision. Through a respectful and iterative daily dialogue, fledgling ideas lead to seeds of improvement. A nurturing environment and a just culture provide the right soil and nourishment for such seeds to blossom into a vibrant and dynamic organization.

As shown from the principles of an HRO, the need for a constant pursuit of perfection will require attention on multiple fronts. It will require an ongoing situational awareness or collective mindfulness, a need for an entire organization to function as one system, working on potential failure modes, reducing variation, and improving continuously. Such work is the essence of how to create high-reliability environments in healthcare.

III. Leadership and Motivation

Influencing team members to make such changes is often an arduous task. In the field of mental health, an excellent method for motivating individuals to change comes from the clinical treatment of patients suffering from addictions. Psychologists William Miller and Stephen Rollnick developed motivational interviewing to motivate their patients to internalize and become self-efficacious at creating change. It helps patients become ready, willing, and able to change. It helps them attain clarity, focus, and direction to advance from their baseline condition to an improved state of mental health. Open-ended questions help to invite the patient to discuss what matters to them; affirmations help ensure a clinician stays optimistic about what patients share and encourages them to share more. Clinicians validate and encourage change statements. If they encounter resistance or witness a desire to maintain the status quo, they move to validate the patient till the resistance subsides. Reflective listening ensures that a clinician repeats back what we heard in the form of a statement to encourage continuous dialogue. Summarizing helps a clinician focus the conversation on moving the patient toward change. The spirit of motivational interviewing is complementary to the DiClemente and Prochaska 'stages of change model' in Figure 5.3 (Prochaska & DiClemente, 2005).[8]

The stages of change are essential to understand because there is a need to meet a patient where they are. Some may not consider a change to their current behavior (pre-contemplation). In contrast, others may know they need to change but just don't want to (contemplation) as they are ambivalent and unwilling to commit to imminent change. Some others may know they need to change and get ready by asking questions (preparation). Once the clinician understands the starting point, the motivational interviewing process can help lead a patient toward action where the change occurs and maintenance where sustaining the change over a long period is needed.

While motivational interviewing was designed for patients in a clinical setting, an improvement leader can deploy the same concepts. Understanding where team members are in their willingness to change, their ability to make a change, and their readiness to take action goes a long way in figuring out how to approach workplace problems. We added an arrow into the diagram originally rendered by Prochaska and DiClemente to signify that once a team is on the path of improving, there is a continuous nature to improvement work. The best method for sustaining improvement is using the last improvement as the minimum acceptable level or stepping stone and working as a team to improve further.

Motivational interviewing has been used to address ambivalence and engagement of employees and leaders. These skills can help one become a transformational leader who can respond effectively to ambivalence and discord and lead through individual and group resistance (Wilcox et al., 2017).[9]

Throughout this leadership section, the reader will note that we have not emphasized a specific improvement tool or model as the main driving force. We have simply provided some contributing

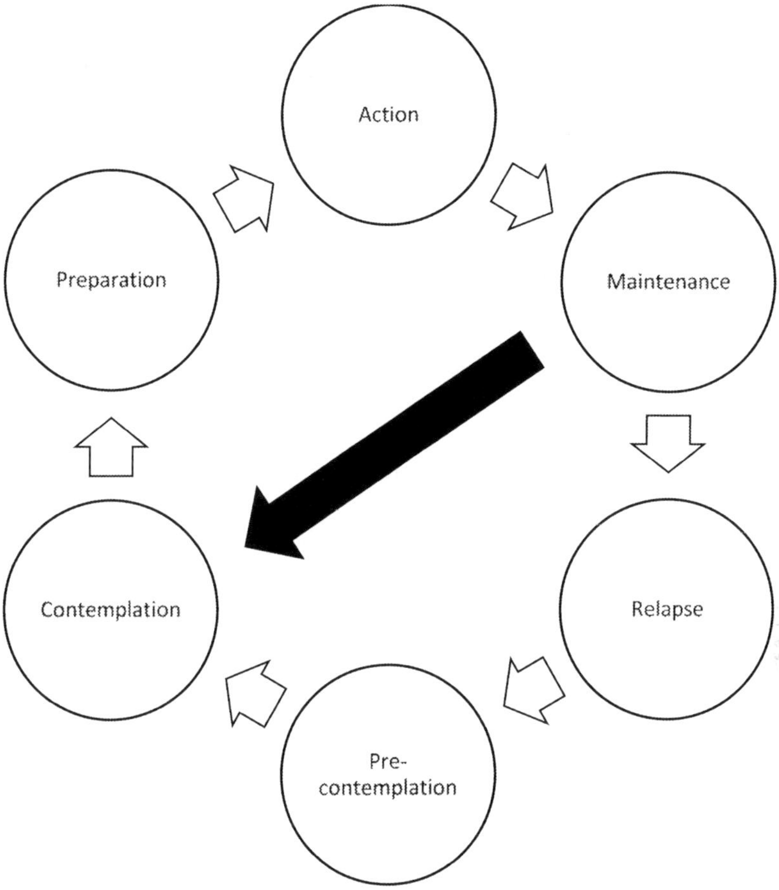

Figure 5.3 Stages of change. (Adapted from Prochaska & DiClemente 2005.)

cultural factors why some organizations proceed very well down the improvement path while others seem to struggle. Sometimes, there is also a tendency to hop from one tool to the next, hoping the next tool will be the answer. Unfortunately, the tool does not drive improvement success. Leaders do.

People often ask what approach to performance improvement works best, PDCA, Six Sigma, Lean, Kaizen, Quality Circles, and so forth. The answer is the same, 'use the tool or set of tools that work to get a team to the solution most efficiently and effectively. Sometimes that is Lean. In other times, where multiple variables play into the solutions, a Six-Sigma approach may work best. It does not matter what type of problem the team faces nor what method is used. Good leadership will be a crucial predictor of success.'

Leadership is the core driving force within our model of organizational change. Deming believed that transformation occurs when we make a conscious decision to adopt a change mentality. He wrote, "Adopt the new philosophy. We are in a new economic age. Western management must awaken to the challenge, must learn their responsibilities, and take on leadership for change." (Deming, 2018).[2] Thus, the foundation for change starts with leadership building a culture through deliberate action.

IV. Getting Started

Individuals get started locally in their span of control and slowly build influence within the organization. Keep in mind that Rome was not built in a day, and neither will a culture of improvement.

The basic approach for starting improvement follows the PDCA framework.

i. *Pick a starting point*: Find a simple starting point that a small team can find manageable and completed within a few days.
ii. *Get your team engaged*: Use this starting point to get you and your team actively focused and aligned on the one most important improvement activity.
iii. *Plan the improvement*:– Seek an experienced facilitator or coach if available to help plan the improvement activity. Determine the appropriate baseline measure.
iv. *Make it visual*: Post the baseline measure in central places to generate more discussion and awareness.
v. *Go and see*: Observe the current state as a team to gain an aligned understanding.
vi. *Use action planning*: Document the waste found and improvements that are needed throughout the process. Action planning adds discipline and accountability to act.
vii. *Standardize*: Document the new process, train all employees to the new standard, and learn from it.
viii. *Determine best practice*: As best practices emerge, determine where these best practices can be applied and adopt or adapt to them.
ix. *Recognize the team's efforts*: As cycles of improvement are completed or best practices are adopted, celebrate with the team to provide positive reinforcement.

As an organization gets comfortable with the process, the simplicity of picking a starting point leads to the complexity of asking 'what's next.' We highlight that the same approach of completing a single project can be utilized to implement an improvement system within your organization. Such a pervasive continuous improvement culture requires the buy-in and support of leadership at an organization's helm.

V. A Long-Term Investment

Creating an improvement system and creating a culture that fosters the mastery of these competencies across an organization to solve systemic challenges is a *long-term endeavor*. It may require the help of improvement experts. It requires a lot of upfront work with a payoff that might take a long time to materialize. Developing a workforce with such capabilities is vital to any organization's success today.

Creating a culture of improvement requires the articulation of a long-term vision from a leader. A palette of *ideas* isn't enough. It also requires *willingness* and an *execution* skill-set to create such a culture. Creating such a culture requires an investment of time, energy, effort, and people's support at the top.

It also requires leaders to surface problems, provide psychological safety, articulate such a long-term vision, and have the courage and humility to solve systemic-barriers even if it may mean some short-term losses. A leader could share power and co-design such a culture with others in an authentic relationship (Hilton & Anderson, 2018).[10] Such culture-building work also cannot be delegated by the leader to a department or quality resource. Everyone has to feel that the leader is doing this with them, and the leader has to model the behavior he or she wants everyone to emulate. Otherwise, one will see limited results.

VI. An Uphill Task

In its early stages, such a developing culture is a very *fragile endeavor* – especially when it is being contemplated or planned or being just initiated. A leader will have to weather a lot of initial questions, doubts, skepticism, and pessimism which can come from various corners of an institution. It takes an unwavering commitment and constancy of purpose (Deming, 2018).[2]

Once underway, a budding improvement culture will surely encounter resistance from all corners and will have to be protected and shielded by forces that want to preserve the status quo, but also by competing needs and ever-changing foci of attention in a modern-day organization. A leader might have to work hard to create and guard the impulse to learn and improve which is budding in some corners of the organization and find ways to support the early adopters. It can be hard to stay focused on one's long-term vision of performance improvement and keep the momentum going. To create such a proactive culture, the leader will have to counter the apathy in the workforce about the 'flavor of the month' syndrome. A consistent improvement kata discipline can help keeps the message fresh and meaningful.

This is especially challenging when such capability development has to be inserted into an already overfull plate of activities. In addition to increasing pressures of providing services, the need to engage in education and research, the leader will have to stress the need for and provide resources for improvement activities. In addition to the two legs of education and research, improvement has to become the '*third-leg*' of a stable organizational structure. It may also need an unwavering focus on eliminating wasteful activities – documentation, meetings, unclear or wavering philosophies, constant shifts in operational goals to release vital time, energy, and resources for improvement. All that waste otherwise saps vital energy from employees in an organization.

It is common for staff in a large organization to have already had multiple exposures to 'quality improvement' efforts, either in the context of improving quality or safety or customer service. They have been exposed to and were expected to participate in efforts to assure quality such as participating in audits, surveys, and performance improvement plans. They may have been also exposed to various metrics and maybe even to pay-for-performance bonuses or penalties.

Many interventions that have probably been introduced to them that were meant to assure quality *antithetically can impede improvement* efforts. One cannot assume that because an organization passes a regulatory survey, those providers learn about improving quality. Ironically, sometimes just the opposite happens. Many healthcare workers become savvy at hiding problems when a surveyor walks through their doors, or an inordinate amount of effort goes into documenting an incredible amount of detail in a chart, which as we said earlier is a flawed assumption, and it is not a measure of good quality. Retrospective audits are very labor-intensive, expensive, ways of assuring quality. There are reports too of providers gaming pay-for-performance systems, either by selecting easier patients or by altering data to make metrics look favorable.

Usually, directives to comply lead to passive participation and fatigue if the staff is already stressed by doing their work while *putting out multiple fires*. Healthcare workers also become *adept at creating workarounds* in the service of getting the patient's needs met in the moment. Thus the leadership acumen described in this chapter is essential for long-term improvement success.

While this chapter helps to provide a framework for longer-term leadership thinking when it comes to improvement, the best approach a leader can take is to just get started. Reading this book cover to cover will surely make the reader feel that the process of improvement is complex. However, the principles that govern improvement are rather simple to understand. The complexities come from the size and structure of organizations, existing internal and external pressures, and resource constraints. The best initial step is to get started.

Today, there are hundreds of resources to guide you along the way in the form of books, websites, organizations, and consultants that are available as guides along such a journey of improvement. Never has the need in healthcare been greater and now more than ever, there is a wealth of resources available to help you along in this journey.

The only thing that is needed is your willingness and commitment to question the status quo and do better. More than anything, you and your patients deserve the pursuit of the quadruple aim. If it was your loved one going to a mental health clinic or hospital, you would not expect any less from a mental health practitioner – to respect you and the desire to continuously improve.

References

1. Ezez. 2020. "MUDA, MURA, MURI". *Lean Enterprise Institute.* https://www.lean.org/lexicon/muda-mura-muri. Accessed August 15, 2020.
2. Deming, W. E. 2018. *Out of the Crisis.* MIT Press, Cambridge, MA.
3. Ezez. 2004. "Intimidation: Practitioners Speak Up About This Unresolved Problem (Part I)". *Institute for Safe Medication Practices.* https://www.ismp.org/resources/intimidation-practitioners-speak-about-unresolved-problem-part-i. Accessed August 23, 2020.
4. Lopez-Trigo, P., Khanfar, N. M., Alameddine, S., & Harrington, C. 2015. Banning Tobacco Sales at the Retail Pharmacy: Natural Evolution of Drug Store as Responsible Health Provider or Effective Marketing Strategy? *Health Marketing Quarterly* 32 (4), 382–393.
5. Miller, W. R. & Rollnick, S. 2012. *Motivational Interviewing: Helping People Change.* Guilford Press, New York, NY.
6. Rother. M. 2009. *Toyota Kata: Managing People for Improvement, Adaptiveness, and Superior Results.* McGraw Hill Professional, New York, NY. p. 18. ISBN 978-0-07-163985-9.
7. Weick, K. E. & Sutcliffe K. M. 2007. *Managing the Unexpected – Assuring High Performance in an Age of Complexity.* Jossey-Bass, San Francisco, CA.
8. Prochaska, James O. & DiClemente, Carlo C. 2005. "The Transtheoretical Approach". In: Norcross, John C. & Goldfried, Marvin R. (Eds.). *Handbook of Psychotherapy Integration.* Oxford Series in Clinical Psychology (2nd ed.). Oxford University Press, Oxford; New York, NY.
9. Wilcox, J., et al. 2017. *Motivational Interviewing For Leadership MI-LEAD.* Gray Beach Publishing, Roseburg, OR.
10. Hilton, K. & Anderson, A. 2018. *IHI Psychology of Change Framework to Advance and Sustain Improvement.* Institute for Healthcare Improvement, Boston, MA.

Afterword

Congratulations! Having read this book, you are now armed with a vision and roadmap for improving the delivery of care. I applaud my colleagues, Sunil Khushalani, MD, and Antonio DePaolo, PhD, for presenting a passionate and systematic exposition on implementing change within your own organization. In the words of Lao Tzu, "The journey of a thousand miles begins with one step."

As the President and CEO of Sheppard Pratt, the largest private, nonprofit provider of mental health, substance use, developmental disability, special education, and social services in the nation, I can attest to the importance of performance improvement. It is important for our patients who deserve access to high-quality, reliable, and effective care. It is important to providers and all members of the care team who yearn for the ability to bring forth meaningful change to improve care outcomes while eliminating non-value-added steps in their daily work. Given that so many in our country lack access to mental healthcare, failure to optimize our delivery care model is inexcusable. We must remember that the end users for new innovations are real people who face enormous health challenges. There is a moral and social responsibility to deliver better care and find solutions for the people we serve.

I. The Role of Culture

Throughout my career, I have led hundreds of performance improvement processes and know that the key to the success of any project is the central role of organizational culture. Regardless of the best team, performance improvement will not occur in a sustainable manner without the ability to understand readiness for change, the ability to navigate barriers to implementation, a keen understanding of change management – and – this is key, the involvement of the right executive champion.

A highly skilled performance improvement team will never achieve optimal outcomes unless their efforts are paired with an engaged project team of local stakeholders and a key leader to ensure that the necessary focus, time, and resources are provided to achieve meaningful results. That being said, I can also attest that the most recalcitrant, deeply entrenched individuals and teams who don't want to accept change can also become your strongest and loudest supporters when they experience the benefits of performance improvement. So, before you jump to action, make sure that you understand the culture and have the key support and resources necessary to keep progress moving forward.

II. Creating Change, Continually

There are essential elements that help create an organization that embraces change. First, it begins with a vision. You can't reach the finish line if the team doesn't understand the desired end state or if they don't share a common understanding of what they are working toward. To do so, work to create that shared vision of success. If you are a leader, be sure that your communications advocate for and convey the incredible transformative power of continuous process improvement.

Like the person who can't visualize the final product of a home renovation project, expect that you will have team members who won't understand how to get from here to the future state. For those individuals, it is helpful to set measurable goals and break down the project into smaller steps where you can regularly assess progress. If you are missing the mark, be honest with each other to ensure accountability and be sure to make adjustments as you go.

Second, understand the motivation for change. Beyond the vision, why is <u>this</u> improvement project important? Of the hundreds of projects that we could take on, what makes this one the most pressing one facing us today? If we accomplish the intended improvement, what will it mean for our patients, for our team members, and for all stakeholders? Keep the 'why' central to improvement efforts. When change becomes hard, the 'why' will carry the day.

This leads to the third element, in which employees are the fuel of the engines of transformative power. Their expertise, harnessed by a strategic vision, drives the sustainability of any changes you implement. Empower your people to have a substantial voice in the improvement process. Allow those most knowledgeable about the work to drive change forward. I fundamentally believe that the best solutions will come from those who are closest to the work. The role of the leader is to remove organizational barriers, provide the appropriate resources, and invest in the success of the team. The engagement and empowerment of frontline staff will directly correlate to your ability to drive outcomes through continual process improvement.

Finally, be careful not to fall into the trap that ensnares many organizations: they successfully create new initiatives, only to find that once the focus shifts to new projects, the gains from 'completed initiatives' revert back to the status quo. Your plan for sustaining process improvement is just as important, if not more, than the plan that helped you achieve it.

III. Measuring Change

For those who believe it is unattainable for behavioral healthcare to implement a culture that applies continuous process improvement to its delivery of care, I ask you to look at what Sheppard Pratt does every day. Through patient-reported outcome measures and objective rating scales, mental and behavioral health can apply the same rigor to the investigation of care delivery and outcomes as any healthcare organization. In fact, when we consider the impact of our field and the quantifiable ways we contribute to broader population health, it is imperative that we adopt objective measurement as a core ingredient in any performance improvement project. While these metrics are often used to prove the success of a program to executive leaders, the ultimate goal should be to use the metrics to improve the quality of the care we provide to our communities.

Unfortunately, there are many barriers that threaten to impede our progress toward that goal. These challenges include a burdensome and antiquated regulatory environment, imperiled fiscal viability of our programs, inefficiencies and the hassle of using electronic medical records, and the emotional toll of caring for a population with complex health needs. Addressing these challenges is important; however, they should not deter the imperative to improve outcomes and achieve clinical transformation.

IV. Clinical Transformation

So, what does 'clinical transformation' look like? Again, we need to visualize the finish line in order to understand where process improvement is leading us. The Institute for Healthcare Improvement (IHI) defines the 'Triple Aim,' focusing on patients, as improving the health of populations, enhancing the experience of care for individuals, and reducing the per capita cost of healthcare. To drive performance improvement, it is helpful to consider the 'Quadruple Aim' that many healthcare organizations have adopted. Namely, fostering higher healthcare workforce satisfaction. This standard implies an ongoing effort of *continually striving* towards better outcomes, care, costs, and workforce satisfaction. So, perhaps I knowingly led you astray with my finish line metaphor. In actuality, the finish line of one performance improvement is actually the start line for the next project. In other words, as soon as we think that we have reached the finish line, it moves. There is always room for growth, improvement, and for achieving the 'Quadruple Aim.'

V. Improving Care Now

The time is now for continuous performance improvement as we see the impact of mental health in America. For nearly a decade, we have been in the midst of two raging mental health crises: the suicide epidemic takes more than 48,000 lives each year, and the skyrocketing rates of opioid overdoses have climbed to more than 80,000 deaths annually. Additionally, experts estimate 200,000 US deaths from COVID-related mental health conditions, overdoses, and suicides within the next year. These alarming numbers underscore the urgency of having access to high-quality services. Further, continuous improvement not only helps our patients; it helps you. Engaging in performance improvement leads to a feeling of empowerment: you can create and measure change. Ultimately, when you create a culture of change, you can impact the health of entire populations.

My sincere thanks to Sunil and Antonio for this practical, evidence-based, and innovative text. I wish all who read it much success in transforming care. And I look forward to hearing of your successes as we all move forward together.

Be well, Harsh K. Trivedi, MD, MBA
President and CEO, Sheppard Pratt
Baltimore, MD

Index

Note: *Italicized* page numbers refer to figures.

A

ABMS, *see* American Board of Medical Specialties
ACA, *see* Affordable Care Act
Access to care, 5, 20, 49
    AOT or conditional release, 11
    boarding in emergency room, 12–13
    de-institutionalization movement, 10
    homelessness, 13
    impact on society, 9–11
    inadequate access, 10
    lack of access, 9–10
    mental illness in jails, 13–14
    patient-to-staff ratio, 11
    State of the Mental Health Report in America 2019, 9–10
Accreditation Council for Graduate Medical Education (ACGME), 87
ACEs, *see* Adverse Childhood Experiences study
ACGME, *see* Accreditation Council for Graduate Medical Education
ACT, *see* Assertive Community Treatment
Action plans, 130–131, *131*
Addiction, 11, 12, 21, 28, 37, 129, 152
Adverse Childhood Experiences (ACEs) study, 8–9
Affordable Care Act (ACA), 29
Agency for Healthcare Research and Quality (AHRQ), 12
Aggression, 12, 15–16, 25, 50, 53, 59, 68, 101, 104, 148
AHRQ, *see* Agency for Healthcare Research and Quality
Alcohol use disorder, 7, 9, 17
American Board of Medical Specialties (ABMS), 87
American Psychiatric Association (APA), 5
Any mental illness (AMI), 1
AOT, *see* Assisted outpatient treatment
APA, *see* American Psychiatric Association
Appreciation for system, 76; *see also* System of profound knowledge
A3 problem-solving tool, 97–98, *98*, *132*
Assertive community treatment (ACT), 10, 11
Assisted outpatient treatment (AOT), 10, 11
Autism spectrum disorder, 12

B

Behavioral and psychological symptoms of dementia (BPSD), 18, 88
Bipolar depression, 7
BPSD, *see* Behavioral and psychological symptoms of dementia
Brainstorming, 125–128, 130, 148
Burnout
    definition, 24
    medical students, 26
    in nurses, environmental characteristics, 25
    physician, 24
    predictors of, 26
    risk for, 25

C

Carnegie Foundation, 70
CAS, *see* Complex adaptive system
Case management, 5, 10
Cause-effect diagram, 122–123, *123*
CBT, *see* Cognitive behavior therapy
Centers for Medicare and Medicaid Services (CMS), 19
Change management
    external actors, 129
    organizational perspective, 130
    resistance factors, 129–130
Change measurement, 158–159
Clinical transformation, 159
CMHA, *see* Community Mental Health Act
CMHCs, *see* Community Mental Health Centers
CMS, *see* Centers for Medicare and Medicaid Services
Cognitive behavior therapy (CBT), 12
Community Mental Health Act (CMHA), 10
Community Mental Health Centers (CMHCs), 19
Complex adaptive system (CAS), 6
Conditional release, 11
Continuum of care, value and, 52–53
Control waste, 59
Cost/waste, 22–23
COVID-19 crisis, 129
    isolation, 103

US deaths, 159
video-conferencing telehealth application, 106
Culture
    improvement, 155–156
    and leadership, *see* Leader/leadership
    role of, 157
    toxic, *see* Toxic cultures
Customer satisfaction survey, 30

D

DALYs, *see* Disability-adjusted life years
Data, visual representation of
    bar charts (column charts), 117, *118*
    histogram, 119, *120*
    Pareto chart, 118–119, *119*, 121, *121*
    pie chart, 117, *118*
    run charts, 78, 117–118, *119*
    scatter charts, 119–120, *120*
DBT, *see* Dialectical behavior therapy
Delivery of care (fragmentation of care), 20
    care coordination, failures in, 22
    continuity, types, 21
    coordination or communication, 21
    issues, 22
    psychiatrist and non-physician therapist, 21
    readmissions, 22
    reimbursement or payment model, 21
Dementia, 7, 18, 28, 37, 99
Deming's cycle, *see* Plan-Do-Check-Act cycle
Depression, 3, 17, 28–29, 73, 85, 119, 129
    bipolar, 7
    lifestyle factors, 8
    medical costs, 8
    unipolar depression, 7
    use of ketamine, 19
Dialectical behavior therapy (DBT), 12
Disability-adjusted life years (DALYs), 7
Dreyfus Model of Knowledge Development, 87

E

EAP, *see* Employee Assistance Program
ECT, *see* Electroconvulsive therapy
Edison, Thomas, 127
Einstein, Albert, 126
Electroconvulsive therapy (ECT), 19
Electronic medical record (EMR), 20, 21, 38, 46, 55, 57, 61, 65–66, 94, 96, 126
    adoption of, 46
    in inpatient and outpatient settings, 30–32
    job demands, 24–25
Emergency Medical Treatment and Labor Act (EMTALA), 15
Emergency room (ER), 9, 14–15, 21, 32, 47–48, 60, 76, 101
    boarding in, 11, 12–13
    depression, 19

Employee Assistance Program (EAP), 9, 144
EMR, *see* Electronic medical record
ER, *see* Emergency room
Experiential learning
    improvement as contact sport, 85
    new experience, 84
    newly acquired skill, 85
    reflect on experience, 84
    sense-making concepts and mental models, 84–85
    standardization or reduction of waste, 85

F

Family, value and, 47–48
    families or caretakers, 48
    Families or caretakers, secondary customer role, 48
    guardianship, primary customer role, 48
    parent or caregiver, 48
Feedback
    A3 process, 147
    check-in regimen, 147–148
    goal of, 146
    motivational interviewing, 146, 147
    negative comments, 147
5-Why analysis, 123, *124*, 124–125

G

Gaussian (normal) curve, *115*
Goal alignment waste, 59
Goal setting, 79, 122, 142
Government, value and, 52

H

Health Care Financing Administration (HCFA), 19
Health care workforce improvement
    adverse effects of medications, 68
    checklists or standards in health care, 69
    continuous improvement, 66, 68
    development of improver, *see* Improver, development of
    emergency medications, 67–68
    first-order problem-solving, 67
    health care settings, 68
    highly reliable organizations, 69–70
    Lean and Six Sigma, 35
    managers and leaders, role of, 68
    missing medications, 66–67
    operational failures, 66, 68
    performance improvement skills, 87–89
    second-order problem-solving, 67
    spot and repair wasteful processes, 66
    Toyota Production System, 70
    TQM, 35
    workaround culture, 66

High-performing leadership; *see also* Leader/leadership
  case of high-reliability organizations, 149–152
  getting started, 154
  improvement culture, 155–156
  leadership and motivation, 152–153
  long-term investment, 154–155
  stages of change, *153*
  toxic cultures, 148–149
High-reliability organizations (HROs)
  commitment to resilience, 151
  deference to expertise, 151–152
  Lean and Six Sigma, 149
  preoccupation with failure, 150
  reluctance to simplify, 150
  sensitivity to operations, 150–151
Homelessness, 10, 11, 13, 14, 22, 61, 69
Hospitalizations, 10, 11, 21–22, 97
HROs, *see* high–reliability organizations

I

Improvement methods for mental health organizations, *see* Plan-Do-Check-Act cycle
Improver, development of; *see also* Health care workforce improvement
  awareness development, 72–74
  best practices, 72–73
  developmental steps, *71*, 71–72
  experiential learning, 84–85
  Habits of an Improver, 85–86
  improvement capability cycle, *72*
  improvement mindset, 74, 86
  improvement skills, applying and practicing, 84–85
  medical education, 70
  performance improvement knowledge, *see* System of profound knowledge
  TWI training, 71
Incarceration, 10–11, 14
Information waste, 59
Inpatient
  beds, 10, 12, 15
  care, 52–53
  psychiatric unit, 5–6, 15, 25, 47, 55, 99, 107
  setting, 48, 52, 53
  stay, 28, 48, 55
  suicides, 16
Institute of Healthcare Improvement (IHI), 36, 159
Institute of Medicine (IOM), 15
Interpersonal and communication skills, 87
Interpersonal relationships
  appreciating staff, 142–143
  changes, 143
  leader-team member relationship, 141, *142*
  person's abilities, 144
  understanding employees, 144
IOM, *see* Institute of Medicine
IPO diagram, 104–105, *105*

K

Knowledge, theory of; *see also* System of profound knowledge
  evidence of improvement, 80
  learning and development, 80
  measurement and proper communication of ideas, 80
  PDSA cycle, *see* Plan-Do-Check-Act cycle
  setting goals for improvement, 79–80
  standard work document, 80

L

Leader/leadership
  accountability, 140–141
  consistency, 140
  and culture
    feedback, 145–148
    foundational interdependent behaviors, *138*
    teamwork, 145
    trust, 139–141
  definition, 138
  discipline, 141
  high-performing, *see* High-performing leadership
  interpersonal relationships, 141–144
  and motivation, 152–153
  primary role, 137
Lean and Six Sigma, 35

M

Measurement
  continuous data, 114
  discrete data, 114
  Gaussian (normal) curve, 114–115, *115*
  for improvement, 114–116, *115*
  tips, 116–117
  variation, 116
Medical Health Systems Act, 10
Medical knowledge, 87
Medical professional
  active way of learning, 85
  performance improvement skills, 87–89
  redesigning systems, 26
Medicare Access and CHIP Reauthorization Act (MACRA), 29
Medicare Modernization Act of 2003 (MMA), 19
Medicare or Medicaid programs, 10, 22, 52
Medicare Partial Hospitalization program, 19
Mental health practitioner, 2, 5, 36–38, 156
Mental Health Study Act, 10
Mental illness
  any, 1
  burden of, 7–8
  in jails, 13–14
  serious, 1, 14
Merit-based Incentive Payment System (MIPS), 29

MIPS, *see* Merit-based Incentive Payment System
Model for Improvement, 35
Motivation
    for change, 158
    intrinsic or extrinsic, 81–82
    stages of change model, 152, *153*
Motivational interviewing, 146–147, 152

N

National Institute of Mental Health (NIMH), 1, 7, 10
National Patient Safety Foundation (NPSF), 36
Nightingale, Florence, 34
    Coxcombs, *34*
NIMH, *see* National Institute of Mental Health
Non-value-added (NVA) work, 54, *54*, 110
NPSF, *see* National Patient Safety Foundation
NVA, *see* Non-value-added work

O

Omnibus Budget Reconciliation Act of 1987 (OBRA-87), 18
Organizational value, 48–49
    concept of True North metrics, 50–51
    engagement model in health care, 50, 51
    factors of, 49
    house of value, *49*
    pillars of safety, 50
    quadruple aim, 51
    quality and delivery, 50
    segmentation of, *49*
Outpatient
    care, 11
    commitment, 10–11
    provider, 4
    settings, 30
    treatment, 10–11, 53
Overproduction, 55

P

Partial hospitalization program, 21, 58
Partial Hospitalization Services, 19
Patient care, 4, 11, 20, 24, 26, 31, 52–53, 66, 70, 87–88, 151
Patient injury rate, *see* Project Y
Payer, value and, 52
PBLI, *see* Practice-based learning and improvement
PDCA or PDSA cycle, *see* Plan-Do-Check-Act cycle
Performance improvement
    access to care, 9–14
    Adverse Childhood Experiences study, 8–9
    behavioral interventions, 9
    biomedical and psychotherapeutic approaches, 37
    care's financial implications, 2
    clinicians or administrators experience, 6
    collaborative or integrated mental health care, 9
    competent practitioners, 37
    complex adaptive system, 6
    consumer movement, 32–34
    cost/waste, 22–23
    de-institutionalization or managed care, 37
    delivery of care, 20–22
    diagnosis, 37
    evidence-based care, 4, 6
    genuine, responsive mental health system, 5
    health care structure and processes, 3–4
    health care workers experience, 4
    improvement efforts in medicine, 34–36
    improving care, 159
    knowledge of improvement science, 5
    mental health practitioner, 2, 37
    mental health system of care, 1–4
    mental illness, burden of, 7–8
    morale/workforce challenges, 23–26
    patient experiences, 3–6
    post-industrial care, 28–30
    Quadruple Aim, 28
    quality, 16–20
    Quality Chasm report, 27–28
    redesigning mental health care, 36–38
    reliable health care provider, availability of, 1–2
    rising health care costs, 4
    safety, 14–16
    technology, 30–32
    well-designed learning organizations, 6
Performance improvement skills
    habits of an improver, 85–86
    medical professional, 87–89
Plan-Do-Check-Act (PDCA or PDSA) cycle, 75, 79, 93, *94*
    Act, 132
        A3 process, *132*
        cascade plan, 134, *135*
        monitor and response plan, 134, *135*
        standard work, *133*, 133–134
    A3 problem-solving tool, 97–98, *98*
    Check, 131–132
    continual improvement, 93–95
    Do, 125
        action plans, 130–131
        brainstorming, 125–126
        change management, 128–130
        pilot studies, 128
        try-storming, 127–128
    for improvement, 147
    improvement vs. research, 97
    innovative thinking, 96–97
    iterative nature of improvement, 94, *95*
    Kata, 135–136
    Plan, 98
        business case, 99–101, *100*
        cause-effect diagram, 122–123, *123*

goal setting, 122
measure, 104–105, *105*
measurement for improvement, 114–116, *115*
measurement tips, 116–117
observation, 105–106
process map, 106–108, *107*, *108*
project management, 103–104
project title, 98–99
Project Y, 101
root cause analysis, 122
scope, 102–103
spaghetti diagrams, 111–114, *112*, *113*, *114*
sub-process map, 108–111, *109*
time and motion study, 111
visual representation of data, 117–121
5-Why's, 124–125
quality, focus on, 93
scope of change *vs.* resistance, 94, *95*
standard work, 96–97
starting improvement, 154
Practice-based learning and improvement (PBLI), 87
components of, 87
mirror metaphor, 88
Problem-solving, 151; *see also* Plan-Do-Check-Act cycle
A3 problem-solving tool, 97–98, *98*
first-order, 67, 86, 124
goal setting, 122
or improvement efforts, 36
second-order, 67, 68, 70, 124
Process mapping
business process or workflow, 106–107
definition, 77
example, 107, *107*
hand hygiene requirements, 107–108
steps of, 107
with storm clouds, 108, *108*
tips, 108
Professionalism, 53, 87, 150
Project Y, 101, 102, 104, 122
Provider, value and, 51–52
Psychology, 75
caregiver's response, 83–84
communication, 84
documentation, 81
fear, 81, 82
Just Culture, 83
leadership, 83
motivation, intrinsic or extrinsic, 81–82
unsafe conditions and human errors, 83
Psychotherapy, 10, 12, 21, 50

Q

Quadruple Aim, 28–29, 51, 156, 159
Quality
improvement efforts in medicine, 34–36
misuse, 19–20

overuse, 18–19
Quality Chasm report, 27–28
Quality of Health Care in America, 17
RAND Corporation, 16–17
underuse, 17–18

R

RAND Corporation, 16, 23
RCA, *see* Root cause analysis
Recovery Audit Contractor (RAC) program, 19
Root cause analysis (RCA), 89, 96, 122, 125, 130, 148

S

Safety, 14–15
aggression, 15–16
medical errors, 15
mental health system's complexity, 15
Swiss cheese model of system failure, 15, *16*
Safety, Quality, Delivery, Cost, and Morale (SQDCM), 99
SBP, *see* Systems-based practice
Schizophrenia, 7, 11, 17, 22, 28, 85
Scoping, project
customer requirements, 103
expensive projects, 102
high technology, 103
scope creep, 102
stakeholder feedback, 103
teaming process, 103
timing, 102
Serious mental illness (SMI), 1, 14
SMART (goals), 122
Spaghetti diagrams
after improvement, 112–113, *113*
before improvement, 112, *112*
result of improved organization, *113*, 113–114, *114*
staff and patients' movement, 111–112
Standard work
benefits, 133
definition, 133
example, *133*
misconceptions in health care, 134
Sub-process map
improved process, 110, *111*
improved process map, *111*
swim-lane process map, 108–109, *109*, *110*
types of work, 110
valuable or wasteful, patient's perspective, 110, *110*
Substance Abuse and Mental Health Services Administration (SAMHSA), 10
Substance abuse treatment, 10
Suicides, 2–3, 8, 14, 16, 22, 115, 159
Swiss cheese model of system failure, 15, *16*
System of profound knowledge, 74–75, *75*, 80
appreciation for system, 76–77

knowledge variation, *see* Variation
psychology, 81–84
theory of knowledge, 79–80
Systems-based practice (SBP), 87
    components of, 88
    metaphor of village, 89

T

Task waste, 59
Teamwork, 138, 145, 147, 148
Telemedicine, 35, 38, 57
Toxic cultures
    aggressive or hostile culture, 148
    analysis-paralysis culture, 148–149
    fire-fighting culture, 149
Training
    competence and capability, 87
    leadership and manager, 25
    metaphor of village, SBP, 89
    mirror metaphor, PBLI, 88
    residency training, 11, 17, 23
Training Within Industry (TWI) program, 71
Triple Aim, 28, 89, 159
True North metrics, concept of, 50–51
Try-storming, 127–128
TWI, *see* Training Within Industry program

V

VA, *see* Value-added work
Value
    and continuum of care, 52–53
    definition, 45–46
    equation, 46
    and family, 47–48
    and government, 52
    house of value, *49*
    and organization, 48–51
    and patient, 46–47
    and payer, 52
    and provider, 51–52
    stages of change, 46–47, *47*
    value added, value enabled, and waste, 53–55
Value-added (VA) work, 53, *54*, 110
Value-enabling (VE) work, 53–54, *54*, 110
Variation
    common cause variation (chance-cause variation), 78–79
    special cause variation (assignable-cause variation), 78
    statistical thinking, 77
    use of data, 77
VE, *see* Value-enabling work

W

Waste
    constraint management, 60–61
    cost of, 62
    forms of
        defects, 56
        extra processing, 57–58
        inventory, 58
        motion, 57
        non-utilized talent, 58–59
        overproduction, 55
        transportation, 57
        waiting, 56
    in psychiatry, 61
    between treatment waste, 62
    within treatment waste, 61
    types of
        control waste, 59
        goal alignment waste, 59
        information waste, 59
        task waste, 59
        workaround waste, 59
    waste walks, 59–60
WHO, *see* World Health Organization
Workarounds, 86, 155
    definition of, 66
    use of, 15
    waste, 59, 122
Workforce; *see also* Health care workforce improvement
    burnout, 24–26
    challenges, 23–26
    EMR, 24–25
    leadership and culture, *see* Leader/leadership
    level of autonomy, 25
    medical professionals, 26
    mission statement, 140
    workplace fear, 139
    Workplace Intimidation Survey, 139
World Health Organization (WHO), 7, 24, 33

Printed in the United States
by Baker & Taylor Publisher Services